THE BEDFORD BIBLIOGRAPHY FOR TEACHERS OF BASIC WRITING

Fourth Edition

Chitralekha Duttagupta
Utah Valley University

Robert J. Miller
The Community College of Baltimore County

for The Conference on Basic Writing

Bedford/St. Martin's   Boston ◆ New York

For Bedford/St. Martin's

Vice President, Editorial, Macmillan Higher Education Humanities: Edwin Hill
Editorial Director for English and Music: Karen S. Henry
Publisher for Composition and Business and Technical Writing: Leasa Burton
Executive Editor: Karita dos Santos
Developmental Editor: Alicia Young
Assistant Production Editor: Lidia MacDonald-Carr
Production Manager: Joe Ford
Marketing Manager: Emily Rowin
Project Management: Books By Design, Inc.
Director of Rights and Permissions: Hilary Newman
Senior Art Director: Anna Palchik
Cover Design: William Boardman
Composition: Achorn International, Inc.
Printing and Binding: RR Donnelley and Sons

0   9   8   7   6   5
f   e   d   c   b   a

For information, write: Bedford/St. Martin's, 75 Arlington Street, Boston, MA 02116 (617-399-4000)

ISBN 978-1-4576-8894-2

For all our basic writing students and their teachers, whose dedication to the profession makes this bibliography possible.

—C. D.

To my mentors, Peter Adams, Greg Glau, and Jean Zukowski-Faust. They taught me to be more than I am. And, of course, family, friends, and the professor.

—R. J. M.

Preface

This fourth edition of the *Bibliography* celebrates the past editorial contributions of Linda Adler-Kassner, Gregory Glau, and Chitralekha Duttagupta, and welcomes a new coeditor: Robert J. Miller of Community College of Baltimore County.

The idea for the first edition of this bibliography began with Patricia Bizzell, Bruce Herzberg, and Nedra Reynolds's valuable work in *The Bedford Bibliography for Teachers of Writing*. In 2000, as cochairs of the Conference on Basic Writing (CBW), Greg and Linda asked themselves why there wasn't a similarly useful resource for teachers of basic writing. They talked about this at some length among themselves and with members of the CBW and decided we should have our own basic writing bibliography. And in 2002, thanks to numerous CBW volunteers and Bedford/St. Martin's, the first edition of *The Bedford Bibliography for Teachers of Basic Writing* was published.

In 2005, the CBW celebrated its twenty-fifth anniversary as an organization. To mark this milestone, Greg and Linda undertook the second edition of the *Bibliography*, turning their focus from defining what basic writing is and who basic writers are to tracing how the field has developed and what its future may hold. To that end, they included Karen S. Uehling's "The Conference on Basic Writing, 1980–2005," a history of the organization honored with the second edition of the *Bibliography*. Additionally, the work annotated in that volume gathered the key discursive threads of the various and sometimes disparate narratives that have contributed to the field of basic writing.

At pivotal moments in the last fifteen years, the field's quest for a history and a cohesive narrative has been particularly visible. The debate over the legacy of Mina Shaughnessy and other basic writing pioneers is one such moment (Gunner, Lu, and Ritter). Another is the debate over mainstreaming (Adams, Bartholomae, Gleason, Greenberg, and Rodby and Fox). Yet another debate concerns the purpose of basic writing classes (Adams, Collins, Greenberg, Gilyard, and Shor). The 2010 third edition of the *Bibliography* addressed the field's most compelling issues: questions about what basic writing is, who basic writers are, how teachers should work with students in basic writing courses, and what the future of basic writing holds.

Within the pages of this fourth edition, Chitralekha and Robert continue to catalog the discussions that have shaped and continue to shape the field of basic writing. A recent and noticeable example is the growing number of second-language learners and students with special needs in our basic writing classes. Emphasis has also been placed on the discussions surrounding accelerated learning programs and developmental education at community colleges.

By compiling the work developed for and by basic writing teacher-researchers, we hope that the fourth edition of this *Bibliography* will continue to be a useful resource for anyone interested in the field of basic writing and a document, an artifact, that contributes to educators' understanding of the field of basic writing—its past, present, and future.

The conscientious efforts of the 60 teachers who annotated more than 400 entries made this edition of *The Bedford Bibliography for Teachers of Basic Writing* possible. We list their names here as contributing editors and hope that one day we can thank each one of them personally for contributing in this significant way to the ongoing conversations in our field:

Amanda Athon, Bowling Green State University

Nicholaus Angelo Baca, Bowling Green State University

Kim Ballard, Western Michigan University

Gita Das Bender, Seton Hall University

Barbara Bird, Taylor University

Jeremy Branstad, North Shore Community College

Kaitlin A. Briggs, University of Southern Maine

Jody A. Briones, Texas A&M University–Kingsville

Angela Clark-Oates, Arizona State University

Kim M. Davis, Oakland Community College

Shelley DeBlasis, New Mexico State University

Margot DeSalvo, Kingsborough Community College, CUNY

Arlene Dewey, The Illinois Institute of Art–Tinley Park

Patricia DiMond, University of South Dakota

Jenica Draney, College of Western Idaho

Cheryl Hofstetter Duffy, Fort Hays State University

Gael Fonken, St. Cloud State University

Sarah B. Franco, University of New Hampshire

Scott Gage, Colorado State University–Pueblo

Matt Gomes, Michigan State University

David F. Green, Howard University

Fiona Harris-Ramsby, University of Utah

Thomas Henry, Utah Valley University

Jana Herbert, College of Western Idaho

Michael D. Hill, Henry Ford Community College

Joyce Inman, University of Southern Mississippi

Karen Johnson, Shippensburg University of Pennsylvania

Elaine M. Jolayemi, Glendale Community College

Lisa Jones, Fort Hays State University

Aimee Krall-Lanoue, Concordia University Chicago

Lisa Litterio, Bridgewater State University

Dawn Lombardi, University of Akron

Michael T. MacDonald, University of Michigan–Dearborn

Natalie Malin, Texas Woman's University

Kelly Concannon Mannise, Nova Southeastern University

Aimee C. Mapes, University of Arizona

Craig A. Meyer, Texas A&M University–Kingsville

Abigail L. Montgomery, Blue Ridge Community College

Marco Fernando Navarro, Rensselaer Polytechnic Institute

Meagan Newberry, College of Western Idaho

Beatrice Mendez Newman, University of Texas–Pan American

Liana Odrcic, University of Wisconsin–Milwaukee

Wendy Olson, Washington State University Vancouver

Heather Ostman, SUNY–Westchester Community College

Amy Edwards Patterson, Moraine Park Technical College

Gwendolynne Rei, North Carolina State University

Lynn Reid, Fairleigh Dickinson University

Michael Rifenburg, University of North Georgia

Abraham Romney, Michigan Technological University

Iris Ruiz, University of California–Merced

Nina Salmon, Lynchburg College

Crystal Sands, Excelsior College

Bradley Smith, Governors State University

Marjorie Stewart, Art Institute of Pittsburgh

Meghan A. Sweeney, University of Nevada, Reno

Josh Tucker, Chattanooga State Community College

Jennie L. Vaughn, University of Alabama

Sara Webb-Sunderhaus, Indiana University–Purdue University Fort Wayne

Abby Wolford, College of Western Idaho

Erin Workman, Florida State University

We owe special thanks to Karen S. Uehling, former Conference on Basic Writing cochair, for kindly allowing us to include her revised and updated history of the CBW, as well as to the Center for Research on Developmental Education and Urban Literacy (now part of the New College of Education and Human Development at the University of Minnesota) for its permission to reprint this adapted history. At Bedford/St. Martin's, we wish to thank Karen Henry, Alicia Young, Elise Kaiser, and Lidia MacDonald-Carr, who have been wonderful to work with on this project.

Contents

Introduction

Teachers of basic writing know that much is at stake when they talk about students, classes, or programs. In this climate of restructuring, budget cuts, standardized testing, state-mandated assessments, and performance-based definitions of literacy, no conversation about writing—especially basic writing—is ever neutral or conducted in a vacuum. With each conversation, teachers and students alike become increasingly engaged in a larger debate about language and literacy and contribute to the narratives that continue to shape the field of basic writing.

This fourth edition of the *Bibliography* continues to serve as a resource for those participating in conversations about basic writing and students in basic writing classes. But this edition of the *Bibliography* is also an artifact, a body of scholarship that provides the basic writing community with an opportunity to reflect on its history and the narratives about basic writing that have emerged over the past decades. By exploring basic writing's past and present, we hope to better understand the questions and issues that will shape the field in the years to come.

In every era, campaigns have been waged to exclude from the academy those values, ideologies, and abilities that are perceived to be threatening by those in power. Matthew Arnold led a movement to preserve the humanities in nineteenth-century England, Cambridge University intellectuals created a literary canon in the early 1900s, and teachers and parents raised concerns about "why Johnny can't write" in American schools in the 1960s. Indeed, such campaigns often have sought a "return" to an idealized, mythical time when all citizens knew the same things and shared the same values, ideologies, abilities, and, presumably, culture.

However, none of these campaigns has ever been or could ever be wholly successful because the mythical past never existed. Individuals and groups understand education differently, and some will fight what Michel de Certeau called a "war of position" within (and sometimes against) the seemingly staggering opposition of the dominant authority. The Conference on Basic Writing (CBW), which celebrated its silver anniversary in 2005, is one such group fighting for position, and the research produced by basic writing researchers chronicled in this bibliography attests to the positioning that has taken place in the midst of, and sometimes in response to, discussions and debates about basic writing and literacy.

For those looking for a citation, a resource, or an article, the third edition of this volume is certainly enormously useful, but it is also useful as a collective summary of the conversations about basic writing that have taken place and the narratives that have been constructed over the last thirty years. In addition, Karen S. Uehling's "The Conference on Basic Writing, 1980–2005" provides historical context to these conversations and narratives, tracing how the CBW has grown and adapted to changes in the field. In this sense, the fourth edition of the *Bibliography* captures the threads that these conversations have followed, and perhaps it can give basic writing teachers insight into the field's next thirty years.

While compiling these four editions of *The Bedford Bibliography for Teachers of Basic Writing*, we reflected frequently on some of the field's most compelling issues: questions about what basic writing is, who basic writers are, how teachers should work with students in basic writing courses, and what the future of basic writing holds.

Who Are Basic Writers?

Beginning with Mina Shaughnessy's *Errors and Expectations* [126], basic writing researchers have sought to answer several questions about basic writers: Do students who are labeled as basic writers share characteristics or qualities? Do scores on placement measures indicate whether students are prepared for college writing? Along with Shaughnessy's foundational text, many of the other articles and books included in the *Bibliography* address these questions as well.

Like *Errors and Expectations*, some works seek to define the characteristics associated with basic writers. More recently, however, some authors of early works have reconsidered these definitions, even questioning whether they are harmful to students. Peter Adams's article "Basic Writing Reconsidered" [345], for example, explores whether the *basic writer* label becomes a controlling feature in students' work. Thomas Hilgers's "Basic Writing Curricula and Good Assessment Practices" [355] echoes this sentiment, arguing that students often are defined as basic writers because of the work that they do on problematic assessment measures. Laura Gray-Rosendale's "Back to the Future: Contextuality and the Construction of the Basic Writer's Identity in JBW, 1999–2005" [74] continues the tradition of examining who basic writers are by how we in the field construct their identities.

Other works—like "Remediation as Social Construct: Perspectives from an Analysis of Classroom Discourse" (Hull et al. [82]), "Defining Basic Writing in Context" (Troyka [45]), "Redefining the Legacy of Mina Shaughnessy: A Critique of the Politics of Linguistic Innocence" (Lu [107]), and "Literacies and Deficits Revisited" (Scott [113])—suggest that definitions of basic writers often stem from deficit models that ultimately marginalize students' literacies in the face of academic discourse.

What Do (Students Called) Basic Writers Do?

Researchers who focus on what basic writers do generally are trying to define who basic writers are, and the research included in this bibliography addresses this line of inquiry in several ways. Early cognitivist basic writing researchers investigated the writing processes of basic writers. This orientation can be located in early studies like *Errors and Expectations* (Shaughnessy [126]), for example, and in works like "A Look at Basic Writers in the Process of

Composing" (Perl [147]). It is also reflected in some later pieces, like "Using a 'Write-Speak-Write' Approach for Basic Writers" (de Beaugrande and Olson [133]), that examine the effectiveness of particular approaches to basic writing.

In the late 1970s and early 1980s, some researchers shifted their focus away from the writing process and began considering the relationships between students' discourse communities and the academic discourse community, as it was then conceptualized. Studies like "Inventing the University" (Bartholomae [2]) examined students' texts rather than students' processes to identify the ways in which students diverged from the discourse conventions of academic writing.

In works based on ethnographic methodologies, like "'This Wooden Shack Place': The Logic of an Unconventional Reading" (Hull and Rose [136]) and *Writing in an Alien World* (Mutnick [86]), researchers delve into students' culture by spending time with and listening to students placed in basic writing classes. A few articles also incorporate the voices of the students whose work serves as the subject of the research.

What Is Basic Writing?

Researchers who have sought to understand who basic writers are and what they do have also tried to form a definition of basic writing that different audiences can accept—and their efforts have grown more urgent as basic writing students, courses, and programs face increasing challenges from inside and outside the academy. The works included in this bibliography represent several perspectives on basic writing. Some works are ambivalent and argue that the institution of basic writing is unjust but serves an important function for the university and its students. Works like *Lives on the Boundary* (Rose [124]), which incorporates portraits of both somnambulant and lively basic writing classes, and "The Tidy House: Basic Writing in the American Curriculum" (Bartholomae [3]), which argues that basic writing classes are important but exist in part to segregate students and employ writing teachers, reflect this position.

Other works, most notably "Our Apartheid: Writing Instruction and Inequality" (Shor [41]), argue that the institution of basic writing should be dismantled because it perpetuates the unequal class system that currently exists in American culture. A number of articles, like "A Response to Ira Shor's 'Our Apartheid'" (Collins [8]; and Greenberg [15]), counter this position, arguing that basic writing courses benefit students and the academy alike by ensuring the inclusion of a broader range of students.

How Can Basic Writing Teachers Help Students Work on Writing?

The question of how teachers can help basic writers work on writing has long dominated basic writing research, and teacher-researchers have examined specific approaches and strategies for teaching basic writing. For instance, a number of articles discuss successful strategies for working on aspects of the writing process with basic writers. Pieces as diverse as "Rethinking the 'Sociality' of Error: Teaching Editing as Negotiation" (Horner [165]) and "The Connection between Reading Aloud and Stylistic Improvement for Basic Writing Students" (Moran [176]) cover revision. *Grammar and the Teaching of Writing* (Noguchi [218]), "The Effect of Error Correction on Learners' Ability to Write Correctly" (Truscott [219]), "When Is a Verb? Using Functional Grammar to Teach Writing" (Fearn and Farnan [208]), and "Explaining Grammatical Concepts" (Harris and Rowan [211]) center on editing, style, and grammar.

Other researchers have looked at additional aspects of writing, such as reading and texts, that are crucial for basic writing classes and students. Works like "Reading and Writing: Making the Connection for Basic Writers" (Deming [102]), "Critical Literacy and Basic Writing Textbooks: Teaching toward a More Just Literacy" (Bruch and Reynolds [99]), "Writing to Learn: The Nickel and Dimed Project" (Bernstein and Johnson [169]), "BWe 2007: Practice, Professional Development, and Favorite Books" (Bernstein [116]), and "Are You Using? Textbook Dependency and Breaking the Cycle" (Jones [172]) explore issues related to the use of textbooks and other texts in the basic writing classroom.

In addition to examining these specific strategies for practice in basic writing classes, researchers have also investigated how best to work with student populations, particularly second- and foreign-language students. This fourth edition of the *Bibliography* includes a greatly expanded section on special student populations. Books like *Second Language Writing Research: Perspectives on the Process of Knowledge Construction* (Matsuda and Silva [327]), and *Teaching ESL Composition: Purpose, Process, and Practice* (Ferris and Hedgcock [297]) include essays that address questions of practice and power as they relate to second-language writing classes.

A number of scholars feel that basic writing classroom strategies are problematic and have challenged some of the research focusing on these strategies. "Warning: Basic Writers at Risk—The Case of Javier" (Reagan [273]) and *Basic Writing as a Political Act: Public Conversations about Writing and Literacy* (Adler-Kassner and Harrington [1]) challenge existing approaches to basic writing instruction. The view that some of these approaches help students to learn the discourse conventions of the academy—but not to understand or challenge them—resonates in these works.

What Alternative Models Have Been Used in Basic Writing Programs?

One outgrowth of the debate over the function of and possible approaches to basic writing courses is that some researchers have examined questions related to program design. The articles on that subject in this bibliography share some common characteristics: they explain the rationale for an "alternative" approach to basic writing programs, describe the model used and the work done in the programs, and describe the effects of the alternative design. "The Accelerated Learning Program: Throwing Open the Gates" (Adams et al. [181]) summarizes some of these models; "*Stretch* at 10" (Glau [380]) provides ten years of data on the pioneering Stretch Program at Arizona State University; and "From the Margins to the Mainstream: Reconceiving Remediation" (Soliday [401]) focuses on a mainstreaming project at the City College of New York. "What's It Worth and What's It For? Revisions to Basic Writing Revisited" (Rodby [395]) discusses the institutional challenges created when the noncredit basic writing course at California State University, Chico, was dismantled and replaced with a curriculum that mainstreamed students and supported them in their work. Similarly, "Basic Writing in One California Community College" (Fitzgerald [377]) describes how Chabot College integrated transitional strategies throughout its curriculum.

What Is the Current State of Basic Writing?

As basic writing has been established as a subfield of composition, some researchers have analyzed how basic writing scholarship has shaped the discipline. Some of their works—like "Conflict and Struggle: The Enemies or Preconditions of Basic Writing?" (Lu [269]) and "Basic Writing and the Issue of Correctness, or, What to Do with 'Mixed' Forms of Academic Discourse" (Bizzell [5])—have explored the ways that powerful ideas have shaped teaching and research in the field. Other works, like "Iconic Discourse: The Troubling Legacy of Mina Shaughnessy" (Gunner [17]), question the ways in which research has constructed teachers and students and how those constructions affect the basic writing classroom. Still others, like "Writing on the Margins: The Concept of Literacy in Higher Education" (Bartholomae [67]), analyze how work in the field has defined basic writers and basic writing.

In addition to examining how the discipline has constructed a narrative of its own development, researchers have also looked at how the scholarship has shaped approaches to teaching and research. *Rethinking Basic Writing* (Gray-Rosendale [77]), for instance, suggests that fixating on defining who basic writers are has come at the expense of studying what basic writers can do. "Discoursing Basic Writing" (Horner [18]) argues that basic writing's historical association with Marxian philosophies has been neglected, marginalizing questions of the social, cultural, and institutional "realities" faced by basic writing instructors and their students.

What Is the Best Case for Basic Writing, and Who Should Make It?

If—as some researchers and theorists argue—basic writing teachers have not always made the best case for basic writing and basic writers, as is argued in some of the analyses of basic writing research described earlier, what should that case be, and how should we make it? Increasingly, basic writing teachers and students have realized that they must voice their own positions on basic writing in public venues.

Work like "Going around in Circles: Methodological Issues in Basic Writing Research" (DeGenaro and White [10]) approaches this issue, arguing that basic writing researchers frequently miss opportunities to produce a "convincing generalization" that might present a united front among basic writing teacher-researchers in discussions of writers and writing.

How Are Writing, Language, and Culture Interrelated?

All of the previous questions asked in this introduction are linked to this larger one, which suffuses many of the pieces annotated in this bibliography. Some of the works here also directly address issues of language and culture.

For instance, "Assessing Our Assessments: A Collective Questioning of What Students Need—and Get" (Bruna et al. [352]) discusses students' desire to master standard English as a key to accessing power in the broader culture. "Basic Writing, Cost Effectiveness, and Ideology" (Gilyard [11]) argues that basic writing is double-edged: the term *basic writing* is problematic, but the courses in basic writing ensure university access for students who would not have been accepted without them.

At the same time, however, research in basic writing must consider students' cultural and ideological contexts and not examine writing divorced from those contexts. Articles like "Basic Writing and the Process Paradigm" (Collins [132]) use this approach.

A number of the works included in this bibliography also study specific aspects of the larger question of social context. "Group Work and Autonomy: Empowering the Working-Class Student" (Hidalgo [235]) focuses on issues of class. "Those Crazy Gates and How They Swing: Tracking the System That Tracks African-American Students" (Agnew and McLaughlin [258]) focuses on race. "Giving Voice to Women in the Basic Writing and Language Minority Classroom" (Cochran [261]) focuses on gender.

All these questions have contributed to the history and development of basic writing as a subfield of composition and continue to shape it as it emerges as a distinct discipline. The research represented here reflects the work that the editors and contributors find important. We hope that the fourth edition of this bibliography will continue to serve as a useful resource for those interested in the field of basic writing.

Where Do We Go from Here?

It is the best of times and the worst of times. Basic writing and developmental studies in general are under attack from a number of states. Budgets are being cut, and programs are being either cut or mandated. At the same time, basic writing faculty, as discussed earlier, are coming up with alternative models that are increasing student success (however it is measured). We need to respond with new models of teaching basic writing and adapt those that are working to the needs and cultures of our own campuses. As composition instructors, we need to make data our friend in order to justify the alternative models. It is also up to us to make sure these models are debated outside our own campuses.

As numbers of adjunct faculty grow, we need to respond with data that ensures our survival as well as allows for faculty development to assist full-time and adjunct faculty members alike. We need to respond on the faculty, department, and school levels to make our concerns heard. Finally, we need to remember that we hold the hopes, dreams, and aspirations of our students in our hands. It is up to us to make sure that they are not let down.

The Conference on Basic Writing

The Conference on Basic Writing (CBW) is a special-interest group of the Conference on College Composition and Communication. Over the thirty-five years since it was founded, the CBW has developed into a vibrant community of teachers and scholars. For this fourth edition of the *Bibliography*, we wanted to provide as much of the historical record as possible, so we have again included Karen Uehling's thoughtful retrospective on our group.

The Conference on Basic Writing, 1980–2005 [by Karen Uehling][1]

In 2005, the Conference on Basic Writing celebrated its silver anniversary as an organization. As we celebrated our first quarter century, we took the time to look back at the critical issues and defining moments of the past and forward to the future.

Twenty-Five Years of Community

The Conference on Basic Writing is an inclusive organization composed of a spectrum of basic writing faculty—those new to the field as well as tenured professors who serve as writing administrators on their campuses. CBW members teach at diverse institutions: community colleges, private rural colleges, research universities, and urban state universities from all regions of the country. Jeanne Gunner, CBW chair from 1995 to 1997, describes the variety of people within CBW and the organization's democratic nature:

> They may be interested because they have taught BW [basic writing] classes for years and have made BW the center of their professional lives, or because they are about to begin to teach them and are seeking information and support from experienced BW teachers. They may be famous researchers we all read and whose ideas inform our classes, or graduate students who will be the next generation of famous names. They may be BW instructors with ideas . . . to share on pedagogic and curricular innovations, or those who defend traditional approaches. They may teach graduate students or freshmen, at community colleges or research institutions. What they have in common are professional and personal concerns related to the field of basic writing ("From the Chair" 1–2).

Perhaps the key motive for developing a professional basic writing organization over the years has been the genuine concern that basic writing instructors feel for their students and their desire to work collaboratively with

---

[1] Adapted with permission from the author.

8

them. Students are placed into classes labeled "basic writing" by a variety of measures and have varying degrees of control over this placement. At one pole of the placement spectrum are institutions that place students (without consultation) based on their performances on standardized tests like the COMPASS test of grammar or the ACT or SAT, which claim to measure students' reading comprehension and acuity with logic and vocabulary. At the other pole are institutions that use directed self-placement, a strategy originally developed at Grand Valley State University (Royer and Gilles, "Basic Writing and Directed Self-Placement" and *Directed Self-Placement*). Here, students receive information about writing and reading on the campus, details about the writing courses offered, and a list of questions about their own writing and reading practices. Students then choose the courses they feel are best for them. In the middle of the placement spectrum are institutions that use other placement methods, from timed writing exams to portfolio placement systems, although the number of institutions using portfolio placement is dwindling due to cost.

The students who take basic writing courses, for whatever reason, are especially vulnerable within higher education because they are often the first to be excluded or considered for exclusion when budget cuts or demands for "excellence" are issued (Fox, *Defending Access* and "Standards and Access"; McNenny, "Writing Instruction" 1–6; Rose 5–8). Sometimes basic writing students are viewed as misusing taxpayers' money to pay for a "second chance" at education when those tax dollars could be better spent on students who are already doing well.

However they are placed, students in basic writing classes represent a diverse and shifting population—first-generation college students, people of color or speakers of more than one language or dialect, refugees or immigrants, reentry students (such as displaced homemakers, older learners who are retraining, or former members of the military), people who experienced erratic or interrupted high school educations or who dropped out of high school and later earned a general equivalency diploma, people with learning or other disabilities, very young parents, and people who work long hours. Sometimes characterized as "at risk" or "underprepared," some basic writing students have experienced especially difficult lives. Some have waited many years, craving an education, and are grateful for any help and instruction. Others of traditional age are equally committed because they want to escape their parents' lives of monotonous, low-paying jobs and make the most of their sports or other scholarships. Some are traditional-age college students who have had less than positive experiences with writing and reading. Others took the basic writing placement tests on days when their attention was focused on other matters. Whatever their situations, they contribute to the rich diversity within our educational institutions.

Perhaps because basic writing students are sometimes viewed as marginal within the university, the faculty appointed to teach these students are often underpaid and overworked. Sometimes instructors serve as adjunct faculty at several institutions simultaneously, are paid by the course, and are not given medical or other benefits. This faculty is given the complex job of teaching writing to students who desperately need to write well to survive in college and attain their goals. Although some basic writing professionals hold tenure-track positions, such appointments are not the norm.

Despite these obstacles, basic writing instructors need to promote best practices in writing instruction. Their students need to write and read full-length essays about appealing and relevant topics rather than engage in skill-and-drill exercises, which overburdened instructors might view as an efficient approach to teaching. By working together, basic writing instructors and students can effectively advocate for informed basic writing classes at their institutions. The Conference on Basic Writing was born to facilitate this process—that is, to advocate best practices for basic writing instruction (including placement and assessment), to provide a scholarly community for instructors of basic writing, and to promote the critical importance of college literacy.

From CBWS to CBW: Early History and Original Goals

At the 1980 Conference on College Composition and Communication (CCCC), Charles Guilford posted a sheet on the message board of the Washington Hilton inviting people to participate in a professional organization for basic writing teachers. Interested educators filled four sheets. With advice and support from Lynn Quitman Troyka, the Conference on Basic Writing Skills (CBWS) began to take shape as a special-interest group of CCCC (Guilford and Uehling 4). The new organization's first flyer outlined its advocacy role—a role that continued throughout Charles Guilford's term as chair (from 1980 to 1983) and continues to be an important one for today's Conference on Basic Writing: "Our purpose is to respond to the needs of this rapidly growing professional field. For too long, teachers and scholars across the country have worked in relative isolation, with far too little opportunity for professional growth and recognition. CBWS will be working to provide those opportunities" (Guilford).

In its early days, CBWS focused on developing a network of basic writing professionals and providing its members with professional resources. The organization conducted annual surveys of members' needs, formed committees to work on different issues, initiated a special-interest group at CCCC, and recruited members. According to Guilford and Uehling, "In a short time, the group grew to over 175 members from almost every state and Canada" (4).

The Beginnings: Overcoming Isolation and Creating a Community, 1980–1986

CBWS came into existence to help basic writing instructors overcome the sense of isolation they sometimes experienced and to foster professionalism in the emerging field of basic writing; in the early years, issues of self-definition, community building, and teaching practices dominated the organization. One venue for the fledgling basic writing community was the special-interest group (SIG) meetings. The first CBWS SIG meeting was held at the CCCC in Dallas in March 1981. At the 1982 SIG in San Francisco, Charles Guilford initiated a thematic focus for the meetings, a format that was maintained until the mid-1990s.

In 1982, the first attempt to establish a professional print dialogue to support a basic writing community was through the *Conference on Basic Writing Skills Newsletter*. That issue contained the first part of an interview that Karen Thomas (Uehling), CBWS chair from 1983 to 1986, conducted with Sondra Perl, recipient of the National Council of Teachers of English Promising Researcher Award in 1979 for her study of basic writers. The newsletter was created on an electric typewriter and laid out by hand using press-on lettering. Issued sporadically, the newsletter often made it into mailboxes just days before the annual CCCC meeting. Eight issues were published from 1981 to 1986.

Definition as a Field: The National Basic Writing Conferences

In 1985, Sallyanne Fitzgerald, later CBW cochair from 1997 to 1999, placed an announcement about the first National Basic Writing Conference in the *Conference on Basic Writing Skills Newsletter*. This event, which was held in September 1985 at the University of Missouri–St. Louis, was described as "a one-day Basic Writing Conference, cosponsored by NCTE [the National Council of Teachers of English]." Fitzgerald organized and chaired the first three of these conferences, developing them "out of my own frustration in the early 80s with professional conferences like NCTE, CCCC, and NADE [National Association of Developmental Educators], where only a few sessions could be devoted to basic writing" ("Basic Writing Conference" 1).

The keynote speakers at these conferences — Andrea Lunsford, Lynn Quitman Troyka, and Glynda Hull — were on the cutting edge of basic writing research. Like CBWS's early efforts to establish itself as an organization, the early National Basic Writing Conferences dealt with addressing definitions (of *basic writing* and a *basic writing conference*) and practical matters (such as creating a community and researching teaching).

Emergence as the Conference on Basic Writing, 1988–1992

By 1987, CBWS was in a state of institutional limbo, and early chairs were concerned that the organization might fall apart. However, in 1988, CBWS was reborn and renamed as the Conference on Basic Writing under the guidance of Peter Dow Adams and Carolyn Kirkpatrick, who served as chair and associate chair, respectively, from 1988 to 1991. The decision to drop the word *skills* from the organization's name was influenced by the 1986 publication of David Bartholomae and Anthony Petrosky's groundbreaking *Facts, Artifacts, and Counterfacts*, which made a persuasive case for full-length discourse in beginning writing instruction, immersion reading, and the teaching of basic writing as a rich, seminar-type course.[2] Indeed, the first issue of the revived newsletter contained an enthusiastic review by Adams of *Facts, Artifacts, and Counterfacts* ("Review").

Bartholomae and Petrosky's influence is also apparent in the 1988 CBW reorganizational special-interest group meeting. This particularly memorable SIG, held in St. Louis, is described by Suellyn Duffey, who served as CBW chair from 1992 to 1994:

> We had come from all over North America and from different types of schools: a community college in New Orleans, a Big Ten public university, Chicago and St. Louis, Nevada and Kentucky. . . . Nicholas Coles, Marilyn DeMario, and Mariolina Salvatori, contributing authors to David Bartholomae and Anthony Petrosky's *Facts, Artifacts, and Counterfacts*, and all teachers of the basic reading and writing course described in the book, were behind the table at the front of the room. . . . The time was right for renewing the Conference on Basic Writing. (4)

Adams and Kirkpatrick capitalized on this spirit of camaraderie to continue developing the organization. In an appeal for volunteer members for the Executive Committee in 1991, Adams and Kirkpatrick wrote: "Keep in mind that most CBW members (including the officers) don't know each other except through this organization; it's here that we are meeting new friends in the profession" ("From the Chairs" 2). By spring 1989, membership had grown to 325 members, and bylaws had been proposed (Adams and Kirkpatrick, "The State of CBW" 2). From 1988 to 1992, chairs Adams and Kirkpatrick (and later Duffey) edited the *Conference on Basic Writing Newsletter* and published nine issues.[3] Responding to the interests of CBW's membership, the editors made articles, book reviews, and columns permanent features of this more "scholarly" newsletter.

Along with the increasing visibility of basic writing scholarship, CBW's revival contributed to a renewed sense of community among basic writing professionals. The revitalized commitment to basic writing was evident in special-interest group meetings at the Conference on College Composition and Communication as well. In 1989, the SIG in Seattle featured presentations by the contributing editors of *A Sourcebook for Basic Writing Teachers*: Theresa Enos, David Bartholomae, Andrea Lunsford, and Lynn Quitman Troyka. At the Chicago CCCC in 1990, CBW sponsored a panel titled "Black Students, Standard English, and Basic Writing" that drew more than 180 attendees (Adams and Kirkpatrick, "SIG Scoreboard" 2). Panelists included Miriam Chaplin, Eugene Hammond, Lisa Delpit, and Geneva Smitherman, respondent. An increased sense of professionalism in the organization was also reflected in the SIG. At the 1991 meeting in Boston, *Journal of*

[2] Although the founders of CBW believed strongly in working with whole texts and were never especially skill-and-drill oriented, they felt it was appropriate to drop *skills* from the organization's name because of the word's negative connotations.
[3] The newsletter continued publication, sometimes intermittently, until 1998. Twenty-two issues were published. Editors and contributors for the 1993 to 1998 issues included Suellyn Duffey, Jeanne Gunner, Kay Puttock, Gerri McNenny, and Sallyanne Fitzgerald. In 1995, CBW entered the electronic age with the development of the CBW e-mail list and Web site. In 1999, the newsletter became *Basic Writing e-Journal* at http://bwe.ccny.cuny.edu/. Both the newsletter and *BWe* are indexed through CompPile at http://comppile.org.

Basic Writing editors Bill Bernhardt and Peter Miller presented the biannual Shaughnessy Writing Award for the best *JBW* article to Kathleen Dixon for her essay "Intellectual Development and the Place of Narrative in 'Basic' and Freshman Composition."

The Fourth National Basic Writing Conference: Mainstreaming and Marginalization, 1992

The Fourth National Basic Writing Conference, held in College Park, Maryland, in 1992, was a turning point for the organization and for basic writing teacher-researchers. The Conference on Basic Writing organized this conference, which grew from one to three days. Carolyn Kirkpatrick stepped down as associate chair of CBW to cochair the National Basic Writing Conference with Eugene Hammond, CBW member and earlier board member. Titled "Critical Issues in Basic Writing: 1992," the conference marked the emergence of two critical issues that have continued to stimulate discussions in the field: (1) should basic writing students be placed in separate courses or be mainstreamed into freshman composition courses, and (2) how do we keep from marginalizing basic writing students?

At the Maryland conference, discussions of these questions emerged in presentations about defining and assessing literacy, the politics of error, the place of grammar, connections between basic writing and English as a second language, the design of basic writing programs, and adaptations of Bartholomae and Petrosky's *Facts, Artifacts, and Counterfacts* approach (Uehling, "Report"). One notable example was David Bartholomae's keynote address, "The Tidy House: Basic Writing in the American Curriculum," in which he argued that students entering the curriculum should not be negatively labeled by being placed in a basic writing class and should instead be mainstreamed. At the 1992 conference (and in the subsequent special issue of the *Journal of Basic Writing* published in spring 1993),[4] issues that had long been at the core of CBW—how to work with students in basic writing classes and who was doing that work—converged with new questions related to instruction, most notably whether the enterprise of basic writing was the most just and ethical way to work with students or whether alternatives should be sought. These issues moved to the forefront of discussions within the organization and the field.

A Foundational Shift: Grappling with Mainstreaming, Mid- to Late 1990s

The mid- to late 1990s were marked by vigorous debates on mainstreaming, which were initiated at the 1992 conference. These arguments raged in

---

4 See Bartholomae; Adams, "Basic Writing Reconsidered"; Berger; Fox, "Standards and Access"; Greenberg, "The Politics of Basic Writing"; Gunner, "The Status of Basic Writing Teachers"; Jones; and Scott. In addition, a particularly interesting conference panel called "Rereading Shaughnessy" focused on Mina Shaughnessy; two of these presentations were also published in the Fall 1993 issue of *JBW* (Gay; Laurence).

meetings and in the halls at the Conference on College Composition and Communication. The 1995 special-interest group in Washington, D.C., was a defining moment for the Conference on Basic Writing. As Gunner recalls, "The politics of mainstreaming proved a uniting topic, even as different points of view made for intense exchanges" ("From the Chair" 2). The importance of continuing these conversations and keeping in touch generally led to some new initiatives, including the creation of the CBW e-mail list and Web site in 1995 and the proposal for a pre-CCCC all-day workshop in lieu of a national conference. Participants in the 1996 workshop, called "Exploring the Boundaries of Basic Writing," at CCCC in Milwaukee heard, among others, presentations by Tom Fox, Judith Rodby, Charles Schuster, and Ira Shor, in which each challenged the advantages and disadvantages of mainstreaming as it was perceived at that time. Shor's remarks were later developed in "Our Apartheid," published in the *Journal of Basic Writing* in 1997. In response, Karen Greenberg and Terence Collins published separate, vigorous rebuttals.

In 1996, in reaction to this debate, Gerri McNenny, CBW cochair from 1997 to 1999, proposed that CBW support a collection of essays on basic writing and mainstreaming. CBW distributed a flyer soliciting manuscripts, and McNenny, with the assistance of Fitzgerald, saw the volume through to publication as *Mainstreaming Basic Writers: Politics and Pedagogies of Access*.

Subsequent workshops continued to address questions related to mainstreaming and marginalization,[5] but presenters also began to focus more on innovative classroom strategies designed to help students challenge definitions of literacy and status in the classroom. The annual pre-CCCC one-day workshop has developed into one of the highlights of the CCCC for basic writing professionals. Bill Lalicker, 2002 to 2005 cochair, remarks that workshops need to be both "theory-stimulating and practice-energizing in ways that make a difference in BW classrooms all year" because workshops must "serve people at community colleges, regional schools, all kinds of universities" (e-mail). Tom Reynolds, 2002 to 2005 cochair, also comments on those varied local situations: "The workshop, and the SIG group always remind me of how conditions in one state, one city, one school, differ so greatly from another" (e-mail).

The 1995 special-interest group meeting in Washington, D.C., also led to the formation of the CBW-L, the Conference on Basic Writing e-mail list, which provides a forum for online exchanges about mainstreaming and other issues relevant to the work of basic writing instructors and students in basic writing classes. "An ongoing discussion of the theory and practice of basic writing," the CBW-L allows subscribers to engage in professional conversations that are fast, frequent, and far ranging. The CBW Web site was also a response to the 1995 special-interest group discussions on mainstreaming and the resulting need for greater communication. Like the e-mail list, the special-

---

[5] The 1997 CBW workshop, for example, was titled "Race, Class, and Culture in the Basic Writing Classroom," and the presentations from this workshop, as well as pieces by the cochairs, were published in a special issue of the *Journal of Basic Writing* (see Gunner and McNenny; Maher; Royster and Taylor; Shor; Soliday and Gleason; Tate, McMillan, and Woodworth; and Villanueva).

interest group meetings, and the preconference workshops, the Web site is another way that basic writing teacher-researchers can build community and access resources useful for their work. The site contains links to information on CBW membership, the CBW e-mail list, online resources, basic writing programs, a reading list, the *Journal of Basic Writing*, the CBW archive, and the CBW Award for Innovation.[6] The Web site also has a link to *Basic Writing e-Journal*, a free, peer-reviewed online journal that began publication in summer 1999 and is designed to expand conversations about basic writing.

CBW Defines the Field of Basic Writing with Its Bibliography, 1999–2005

The years 1999 to 2005 again brought new direction to the Conference on Basic Writing as it faced state budget cuts, "outsourcing" of basic writing, and high-stakes testing. In response to these challenges, CBW continued to make the work of basic writing teacher-researchers more public and to advocate for teachers and students in basic writing classes.

Perhaps CBW's most notable achievement to date is the publication of four editions of *The Bedford Bibliography for Teachers of Basic Writing*. The first two editions were edited by Linda Adler-Kassner and Gregory R. Glau, CBW cochairs from 1999 to 2002; the third edition was edited by Gregory R. Glau and Chitralekha Duttagupta; this fourth edition is edited by Duttagupta and Robert J. Miller. The *Bibliography* abstracts books, articles, and periodicals; more than sixty teachers from around the country annotated more than four hundred entries for this fourth edition. As Mike Rose notes, "In the academy . . . your life [is] the record of all you [have] to say about the particular booklists you [have] made your own" (70). The same can be said of CBW as an organization and the field of basic writing: our life is the record of all we have to say about the particular booklists we have made our own. The fees the editors would normally receive from the *Bibliography* are used to fund the CBW Fellowship, which supports travel to the annual Conference on Basic Writing workshop and to the Conference on College Composition and Communication meeting. CBW Fellowship applications are judged on their benefit to the instructor's professional interests, their benefit to students, and the applicant's clear dissemination plan.

An important aspect of the CBW community has always been an emphasis on informal collegiality. This tradition continues, especially at conferences, with a primary focus on the special-interest group meeting as a place to gather. Glau observes, "I've been especially pleased at the special-interest group meetings over the past couple of years—more and more people (we often are overflowing our room!) with lots of good ideas and suggestions and comments" (e-mail).

Honoring those who have made contributions to the field and celebrating their successes have sometimes been features of SIG meetings. This idea was revived in 2004 with the institution of the annual CBW Award for

---

[6] The CBW Web site can be accessed at http://bwe.ccny.cuny.edu/.

Innovation. According to the CBW Web site, this award "recognizes writing programs for innovations that improve educational processes for basic writers through creative approaches" (Glau, *Conference on Basic Writing*). The winning schools are presented with a plaque and invited to give a brief presentation about their innovative program to SIG members. Lalicker identifies the CBW Award for Innovation and the CBW Fellowship as "the newest high points and those with the most transformative potential for the future" (e-mail).

CBW-L, the Conference on Basic Writing online discussion list, continues as an electronic forum. Topics of discussion include reading in the basic writing classroom, basic writing and learning disabilities, and teaching the process of writing.

Over the last thirty-five years, the Conference on Basic Writing has established a professional community that is interested equally in practice and theory. Lalicker characterizes the equal focus on research and teaching as an "exemplary dialectic" and adds that "the emphasis on both of these values is something that attracted me to the organization. . . . The invitation to newcomers operates productively to bring new ideas and practical energy to counter the natural institutionalization of theory" (e-mail). The CBW community was developed through a network created by the early newsletters, its online successors CBW-L and *BWe*, the Web site, books, the early national conferences and current annual workshops, and the continuing special-interest group meetings. Through informal conversations, information sharing, formal presentations, debates, and scholarship—in person, in print, and in electronic media—the organization has developed into a thriving community of diverse educators who work together to create a rich, professional practice.

The Next Thirty-Five Years, 2015 and Beyond

As the Conference on Basic Writing looks forward to its next thirty-five years, the students will always be there. But how can basic writing educators meet their needs? Some issues we may need to address include reduced funding for education, high-stakes testing, widely varying local conditions, working conditions for basic writing faculty, the community college voice, and global literacy.

As state budgets tighten, we may need to work to reduce or eliminate extra fees for basic writing instruction, particularly because basic writing students often are the ones who can least afford them. Another challenge is motivation: basic writing is often a noncredit course, and our students are frequently controlled by mandated tests for initial placement or for prerequisites for higher-level classes, which essentially lock them out of a serious education.

One response to these external demands is to link them back to our local situations and particular students. Reynolds conveys the importance of local conditions and programmatic assessment: "The CBW group has been valuable to me, as a program administrator and a scholar, for its constant attention to the differences among BW programs. . . . If there's a unifying factor in these discussions, it seems to be that everyone is under pressure to show results, usually through state-mandated testing of one sort or another. A high point of my time as cochair has been to see people sharing knowledge of these pressures and, in so doing, making it a national concern" (e-mail). Reynolds identifies program accountability as "one of the major issues facing the field": "Although we are getting better at documenting what it means for an individual writer to advance one's writing 'skills' through our classes, a more difficult challenge is to show that an approach, identifiably 'BW,' can be applied and measured (quantitatively) to show progress" (e-mail).

McNenny agrees: "As cautionary tales, the dismantling of various basic writing programs signals a need for a more public, proactive role for writing program administrators and instructors, to present a convincing and comprehensive picture of the gains that students achieve through writing programs, and the intellectual work involved for both students and faculty" ("Writing Instruction" 5). Lalicker suggests that we create a picture of ourselves based on broadly defined goals "in terms not just of discrete student 'skills' but in terms of students' inclusion in the academy and students' power in the larger culture. . . . We need to define program goals and outcomes in ways that are congruent with real student needs (as students see them, not just as we dictate them)," and we need to argue for "ways of assessment that can recognize these qualitative outcomes" (e-mail).

Perhaps as another response to external mandates, the Conference on Basic Writing might become a clearinghouse for information on high-stakes assessment, state mandates, local conditions, and programmatic assessments. The CBW Web site offers a venue for posting this information. There has already been some excellent work done in this area by CBW members such as Terence Collins ("Basic Writing Programs") and Gregory Glau (*Arizona State University's Stretch Program*).

We also must address the conditions under which basic writing faculty work. Reynolds notes how "BW classes are still handed off as 'last resort' teaching assignments. . . . Most BW courses are not part of a formal BW program but rather some other 'remedial' effort at colleges" (e-mail). Lalicker mentions how "too many outstanding BW teachers [are] . . . seen as piece-workers, contingent faculty in the pink-collar ghetto" (e-mail). Reynolds suggests that a challenge for CBW is "to improve working conditions and make the job of teaching BW an attractive one," perhaps by "seeing the job as a wider project, one that embraces literacy issues more generally" (e-mail). Lalicker agrees: "In too many of our institutional relationships, BW is seen as a separate room, a kind of subacademic support center" instead of "an academic field" that draws "creatively on the knowledge bases" of several subdisciplines: "mainstream composition, reading and literacy, ESL, and advanced rhetoric" (e-mail).

A related working-condition issue is employment contracts for adjunct faculty teachers. No one can survive on wages that are paid by the course and do not include benefits. "Freeway flyers" who are worried about paying their utility bills, buying food for their children, finding a parking space, and making it to class at the next institution cannot be expected to make a serious commitment to students and teaching. Improving working conditions is part of what Lalicker calls "the continuing struggle to encourage the several levels of academia (the department, the institution, the national professional establishment) to see BW instructors as serious professional practitioners" (e-mail). Being taken seriously means being funded and offering "well-theorized and practical programs," and as Lalicker concludes, "only those with a first-class institutional voice proportionate to their educational role can influence budgets, program goals, syllabi, and teaching methods. . . . Politics are pedagogy" (e-mail).

In some states that follow a business model, basic writing instruction has been "downsized" and "outsourced," moved from four- or six-year colleges to community colleges or from colleges to private providers. Another challenge for the future of the Conference on Basic Writing is to allow more space within the community for community college and private provider voices. Although three of CBW's chairs have been from community colleges (Adams, Kirkpatrick, and Fitzgerald), community college teacher representation in CBW has not been broad. In the first volume of this bibliography, only nine of the 119 contributors were from community colleges (although some contributors were working in the community college arm of four- or six-year institutions). McNenny notes that "much of the mainstreaming debate has indeed excluded the voices of two-year college decision makers" (Preface vi). Fitzgerald adds, "Where do our community college students and faculty fit in the discussion? . . . Why do my colleagues in the Conference on Basic Writing have to be reminded that basic writing is a universal term that can be applied to many contexts, not just the universities where they teach?" ("The Context Determines Our Choice" 222).

Within the organization, the Conference on Basic Writing must also continue to include instructors from many types of institutions, from two-year colleges to PhD-granting institutions. We serve every basic writing student. Conversations between teacher-researchers and researcher-teachers across geographic boundaries, between private and public environments, across open admissions and selective admissions lines, and among differing levels of academic institutions strengthen our practice.

Another challenge is global literacy and online teaching. As Reynolds notes, "We will have to start to address more global literacy issues. Our students are already in competition with students overseas now for employment, and literacy issues here are literacy issues there. Education offered through accredited online colleges has started to include lower-division courses, including composition. I expect that we need to start thinking more carefully about how to bring our theoretical and practical concerns to current global literacy practices" (e-mail).

In his final column as the chair of the Conference on Basic Writing, Adams articulated the importance of CBW's work:

> The teaching of basic writing is important—as important as anything being done in higher education. Often we are the last chance at college-level education for students who have plenty of ability but who have not been served well previously or who have not taken advantage of the opportunities offered. . . . Further, we are one of the few areas in the academy where differences between students are reduced rather than exaggerated. . . .

Because the teaching of basic writing is so important, the work of this organization is similarly important. . . . CBW's most important role is to insure CCCC continues to provide a place where teachers of basic writing feel that their needs are being addressed and to insure that the considerable intelligence of the combined membership of CCCC continues to address the thorny problems involved in teaching basic writers. ("From the Chairs" 2–3)

As Charles Guilford, founder of the Conference on Basic Writing, said before he retired in 2004, "There are many, many students who continue to need quality teaching." The future of those students rests in the hands of those teachers and scholars who are committed to students and serious about providing them with access to quality education.

Works Cited[7]

Adams, Peter. "Basic Writing Reconsidered." *Journal of Basic Writing* 12.1 (1993): 22–36. Print.

————. "From the Chairs: From the Old Chair." *CBW Newsletter* 11.2 (1992): 2–3. Print.

————. "Review of *Facts, Artifacts, and Counterfacts*." *CBW Newsletter* 7.1 (1988): 1–3. Print.

Adams, Peter, and Carolyn Kirkpatrick. "From the Chairs." *CBW Newsletter* 10.2 (1991): 2. Print.

————. "From the Chairs: SIG Scoreboard." *CBW Newsletter* 9.2 (1990): 2. Print.

————. "From the Chairs: The State of CBW." *CBW Newsletter* 8.2 (1989): 2. Print.

Bartholomae, David. "The Tidy House: Basic Writing in the American Curriculum." *Journal of Basic Writing* 12.1 (1993): 4–21. Print.

Bartholomae, David, and Anthony Petrosky. *Facts, Artifacts, and Counterfacts: Theory and Method for a Reading and Writing Course*. Portsmouth: Heinemann, 1986. Print.

Berger, Mary Jo. "Funding and Support of Basic Writing Programs: Why Don't We Have Any?" *Journal of Basic Writing* 12.1 (1993): 81–89. Print.

Collins, Terence G. "Basic Writing Programs and Access Allies: Finding and Maintaining Your Support Network." *CBW Newsletter* 13.3 (1998): 1–6. Print.

————. "A Response to Ira Shor's 'Our Apartheid: Writing Instruction and Inequality.'" *Journal of Basic Writing* 16.2 (1997): 95–100. Print.

Dixon, Kathleen G. "Intellectual Development and the Place of Narrative in 'Basic' and Freshman Composition." *Journal of Basic Writing* 8.1 (1989): 3–20. Print.

Duffey, Suellyn. "A Drama: The Tinkling of Glasses, the Sound of a New CBW." *CBW Newsletter* 8.1 (1988): 4. Print.

English Department at Arizona State University. n.d., Web. 16 Feb. 2004.

---

[7] The CBW Web site, the *CBW Newsletter*, and issues of *Basic Writing e-Journal* can now be accessed at http://bwe.ccny.cuny.edu/. Other resources for teaching basic writing can be found on the CBW blog at http://cbwblog.wordpress.com/.

Enos, Theresa, ed. *A Sourcebook for Basic Writing Teachers.* New York: Random, 1987. Print.

Fitzgerald, Sallyanne. "Basic Writing Conference Scheduled for St. Louis in September." *CBW Newsletter* 8.2 (1989): 1–3. Print.

———. "The Context Determines Our Choice: Curriculum, Students, and Faculty." *Mainstreaming Basic Writers: Politics and Pedagogies of Access.* Ed. Gerri McNenny. Mahwah: Erlbaum, 2001. 215–23. Print.

Fox, Tom. *Defending Access: A Critique of Standards in Higher Education.* Portsmouth: Boynton, 1999. Print.

———. "Standards and Access." *Journal of Basic Writing* 12.1 (1993): 37–45. Print.

Gay, Pamela. "Rereading Shaughnessy from a Postcolonial Perspective." *Journal of Basic Writing* 12.2 (1993): 29–40. Print.

Glau, Gregory R. Home page. Conference on Basic Writing (CBW). 23 Jan. 2004. Web. 10 Aug. 2009.

———. Message to the author. 16 Apr. 2001. E-mail.

Greenberg, Karen L. "The Politics of Basic Writing." *Journal of Basic Writing* 12.1 (1993): 64–71. Print.

———. "A Response to Ira Shor's 'Our Apartheid: Writing Instruction and Inequality.'" *Journal of Basic Writing* 16.2 (1997): 90–94. Print.

Guilford, Charles. *Introducing CBWS.* 1980. Print.

Guilford, Charles, and Karen Uehling. "A Word from the Founders of CBW." *CBW Newsletter* 7.1 (1988): 4. Print.

Gunner, Jeanne. "From the Chair." *CBW Newsletter* (1996): 1–2. Print.

———. "The Status of Basic Writing Teachers: Do We Need a 'Maryland Resolution'?" *Journal of Basic Writing* 12.1 (1993): 57–63. Print.

Gunner, Jeanne, and Gerri McNenny. "Retrospection as Prologue." *Journal of Basic Writing* 16.1 (1997): 3–12. Print.

Jones, William. "Basic Writing: Pushing against Racism." *Journal of Basic Writing* 12.1 (1993): 72–80. Print.

Lalicker, William. Message to the author. 11 Feb. 2004. E-mail.

Laurence, Patricia. "The Vanishing Site of Mina Shaughnessy's *Errors and Expectations.*" *Journal of Basic Writing* 12.2 (1993): 18–28. Print.

Maher, Jane. "Writing the Life of Mina P. Shaughnessy." *Journal of Basic Writing* 16.1 (1997): 51–63. Print.

McNenny, Gerri, ed. *Mainstreaming Basic Writers: Politics and Pedagogies of Access.* Mahwah: Erlbaum, 2001. Print.

———, ed. "Preface." *Mainstreaming Basic Writers: Politics and Pedagogies of Access.* Ed. Gerri McNenny. Mahwah: Erlbaum, 2001. xi–xvii. Print.

———, ed. "Writing Instruction and the Post-Remedial University: Setting the Scene for the Mainstreaming Debate in Basic Writing." *Mainstreaming Basic Writers: Politics and Pedagogies of Access.* Ed. Gerri McNenny. Mahwah: Erlbaum, 2001. 1–15. Print.

Reynolds, Tom. Message to the author. 5 Feb. 2004. E-mail.

Rose, Mike. *Lives on the Boundary: The Struggles and Achievements of America's Underprepared.* New York: Free, 1989. Print.

Royer, Daniel J., and Roger Gilles. "Basic Writing and Directed Self-Placement." *Basic Writing e-Journal* 2.2 (2000): n. pag. Web. 10 Aug. 2009.

————, eds. *Directed Self-Placement: Principles and Practices*. Cresskill: Hampton, 2003. Print.

Royster, Jacqueline Jones, and Rebecca Greenberg Taylor. "Constructing Teacher Identity in the Basic Writing Classroom." *Journal of Basic Writing* 16.1 (1997): 27–50. Print.

Scott, Jerrie Cobb. "Literacies and Deficits Revisited." *Journal of Basic Writing* 12.1 (1993): 46–56. Print.

Shor, Ira. "Our Apartheid: Writing Instruction and Inequality." *Journal of Basic Writing* 16.1 (1997): 91–104. Print.

Soliday, Mary, and Barbara Gleason. "From Remediation to Enrichment: Evaluating a Mainstreaming Project." *Journal of Basic Writing* 16.1 (1997): 64–78. Print.

Tate, Gary, John McMillan, and Elizabeth Woodworth. "Class Talk." *Journal of Basic Writing* 16.1 (1997): 13–26. Print.

Uehling, Karen S. "The Conference on Basic Writing: 1980–2001." *Histories of Developmental Education*. Ed. Britt Lundell Dana and Jeanne L. Higbee. Minneapolis: Center for Research on Developmental Education and Urban Literacy, 2002. 47–57. Print.

————. "Report on the Fourth National Basic Writing Conference." *CBW Newsletter* 12.1 Winter (1993): 1–4. Print.

Villanueva, Victor. "Theory in the Basic Writing Classroom? A Practice." *Journal of Basic Writing* 16.1 (1997): 79–90. Print.

History and Theory: Basic Writing and Basic Writers

Basic Writing: Definitions and Conversations

1   Adler-Kassner, Linda, and Susanmarie Harrington. *Basic Writing as a Political Act: Public Conversations about Writing and Literacy*. Cresskill: Hampton, 2002. Print.

Basic writing instruction often perpetuates an autonomous model of literacy that separates writing and reading from the contexts in which they are situated. This model fails to help students familiarize themselves with the culture of the "academic community." To make this case, the authors analyzed basic writing research, interviewed basic writing students, and studied the portrayal of "remedial" writing in mainstream media. The authors find that basic writers and basic writing are portrayed as violating a narrative in which mastering autonomous literacy strategies is a key element. Basic writing programs are portrayed as successful when they place students within the narrative. The authors suggest new curricular strategies for basic writing classes and new terms for conversations about basic writing, arguing that these will help writers and others to develop connections between writing and culture and will make basic writing a political act.

2   Bartholomae, David. "Inventing the University." *When a Writer Can't Write: Studies in Writer's Block and Other Composing-Process Problems*. Ed. Mike Rose. New York: Guilford, 1985. 134–65. Print.

Basic writing students should be immersed in academic discourse so that they can begin to appropriate it for their own ends. Bartholomae contends that basic writing studies should not center simply on error. Instead, we must better understand how basic writers' lack of understanding about constructions of authority and the rules of academic discourse put them at a disadvantage in an arena that values such knowledge. As a result, Bartholomae argues that the basic writer "has to invent the university by assembling and mimicking its language" (135), often long before the skills of writing in an academic setting are learned. Drawing from scholars such as Linda Flower, John Hayes, and Patricia Bizzell, Bartholomae supports his own conclusions while investigating potential reasons for the choices made in student discourse.

3   Bartholomae, David. "The Tidy House: Basic Writing in the American Curriculum." *Journal of Basic Writing* 12.1 (1993): 4–21. Print.

Borrowing from historian Carolyn Steedman, Bartholomae argues that basic writing courses segregate students and replicate social divisions. "In the name of sympathy and empowerment," he writes, "we have once again produced the 'other' who is the incomplete version of ourselves, confirming existing patterns of power and authority, reproducing the hierarchies we had meant to question and overthrow . . . in the 1970s" (18). He also argues that these classes are ultimately necessary because they provide an entry point for students. However, Bartholomae offers several curricular possibilities for basic writing classes in which students are segregated: looking for students' abilities to provide unusual texts as a placement mechanism, eliminating tracking, and creating classes that become "contact zones" in which writers examine and engage differences between one another and the academy. Echoing Mary Louise Pratt, Bartholomae proposes a "curricular program designed not to hide differences . . . but to highlight them, to make them not only the subject of the writing curriculum but the source of its goals and values (at least one of the versions of writing one can learn at the university)" (13).

4   Bernstein, Susan Naomi. "Social Justice Initiative for Basic Writing." *Basic Writing e-Journal* 7.1 (2008): n. pag. Web. 21 May 2014.

Bernstein discusses the continued marginal status of basic writing students, teachers, and courses. She argues that basic writing should not be defined as "remedial," but as educational enrichment, and that basic writing students should be seen as authentic members of their colleges and universities. She also proposes a formal resolution for the Conference on Basic Writing to argue for improved funding for basic writing programs; to remove any "remedial" label and to conceptualize basic writing classes as college level; to educate students about and to provide adequate resources for basic writing students as well as for better articulation with K–12 teachers and administrators; and to link basic writing to social justice concerns for historically disenfranchised communities.

5   Bizzell, Patricia. "Basic Writing and the Issue of Correctness, or, What to Do with 'Mixed' Forms of Academic Discourse." *Journal of Basic Writing* 19.1 (2000): 4–12. Print.

By reflecting on how hybrid, or mixed, discourses have appeared in academic work and how these discourses might affect basic writing pedagogy, Bizzell seeks to extend and refine arguments raised in her earlier article, "Hybrid Academic Discourses." In this follow-up article, she argues that the increased use of mixed forms means that students no longer need initiation into traditional academic discourse but may need time and assistance to try out various forms combining the academic and nonacademic. Bizzell acknowledges two main points that were not emphasized clearly enough in her earlier article. First, because of cultural fusion in the United States, students come to college with "already mixed linguistic and discursive resources" (9). Second, these mixed, comfortable forms are "being used by everyone," as "they allow their practitioners to do intellectual work in ways they could not if confined to traditional academic discourse" (10).

6   Bizzell, Patricia. "Cognition, Convention, and Certainty: What We Need to Know about Writing." *PRE/TEXT* 3.3 (1982): 213–43. Print.

Compositionists form two theoretical camps: those who are outer-directed, thereby focused on the social processes that influence language learning and thinking, and those who are inner-directed, hence interested in universal writing processes and individual capacities. As inner-directed theorists, Linda Flower and John Hayes support a linear, cognitive model of writing that separates thought, or "planning," from writing, or "translating," yet Flower and Hayes fail to account for individual knowledge and contextual influences. Outer-directed theorists remain skeptical of all models that claim an understanding of inner processes. Accordingly, outer-directed theorists stress the role of community, ethics, politics, and social interaction in the development of thinking and language. A synthesis of theories from both camps will offer a fuller understanding of writing.

7   Bloom, Lynn Z. "A Name with a View." *Journal of Basic Writing* 14.1 (1995): 7–14. Print.

Bloom focuses on the issue of renaming the *Journal of Basic Writing* in view of its changing perspective and content. Naming and renaming are significant actions because of the connotations and expectations related to a name. When the journal began publishing in 1974, its goal was to change the connotation of *remedial*, which suggests deficiency, to a more positive descriptor, *basic*. The topics covered over the next ten years focused mainly on methods of teaching basic writers, but even in the first years, some articles dealt with issues that applied to other composition students. After the 1980s, articles routinely covered a greater range of topics and writing populations. Bloom thinks that the diversity covered currently in the journal suggests a revision of the name to better situate basic writing studies in the field of composition today and to attract more diverse contributors. Over time, *basic writer* has taken on the connotations that *remedial writer* had in the past.

8   Collins, Terence G. "A Response to Ira Shor's 'Our Apartheid: Writing Instruction and Inequality.'" *Journal of Basic Writing* 16.2 (1997): 95–100. Print.

Collins contends that Ira Shor is "emphatically wrong" (95) in his assertions about basic writing. Shor presents an "artificially homogenized landscape" (95) of basic writing when, in fact, institutions of higher education deal with the needs of these underprepared writers in diverse ways, some successful and authentic, some not. Furthermore, Shor was in error when he stated that the University of Minnesota General College's basic writing program was a "cash cow" (95) for the university, paying part-time instructors to teach full-tuition students. Rather, General College's basic writing program operates with four full-time, tenured or tenure-track faculty who are among the best paid in the college. The program has an excellent track record as an integral part of the "eventual success" (97) of General College students. With his "mis-statements" (96) about General College's basic writing program and his correlation of basic writing with "cynical apartheid" (99) agendas on the part of institutions of higher education, Shor paints basic writing instruction as destructive and exploitative and misses the opportunity to discuss the pedagogy in more realistic terms.

See: Ira Shor, "Our Apartheid: Writing Instruction and Inequality" [41].

See: Karen L. Greenberg, "A Response to Ira Shor's 'Our Apartheid'" [15].

9   DeGenaro, William. "Why Basic Writing Professionals on Regional Campuses Need to Know Their Histories." *Open Words: Access and English Studies* 1.1 (2006): 54–68. Print.

Much basic writing scholarship is framed within a "literacy-as-generative model," which often focuses on the development of the individual rather than the historical and material conditions that shape literacy education at a given moment and location. In response to what he identifies as an apolitical and ahistorical realm of basic writing (57), DeGenaro calls for a comprehensive history of basic writing situated within local histories and institutional narratives. Works such as Ira Shor's "Our Apartheid: Writing Instruction and Inequality" (1997) and, more recently, Mary Soliday's *The Politics of Remediation: Institutional and Student Needs in Higher Education* (2002) model the political possibilities that historical methodologies can uncover, and it is through Soliday that DeGenaro transitions from the larger historical terrain into his own situated history at a regional campus designing and implementing a new basic writing course.

See: Ira Shor, "Our Apartheid: Writing Instruction and Inequality" [41].

See: Mary Soliday, *The Politics of Remediation: Institutional and Student Needs in Higher Education* [114].

10   DeGenaro, William, and Edward M. White. "Going around in Circles: Methodological Issues in Basic Writing Research." *Journal of Basic Writing* 19.1 (2000): 22–35. Print.

The field of basic writing studies has not reached professional consensus on such fundamental issues as the mainstreaming of developmental writers and the "universal requirement." While most writers in the field work to democratize educational practices, few share similar research methodologies or even agree about what counts as valid evidence. A critical perspective on methodology reveals the ways in which some texts blend philosophical, practitioner, and historical work but does not allow other voices or perspectives into the scholarly conversation. As a result of this lack of dialectic, researchers frequently reiterate basic positions and overlook opposing claims instead of debating and testing findings to produce convincing generalizations. At a time when those in charge of basic writing programs frequently need to present a unified front to outside groups, such as administrators and policy makers, more methodological awareness could help them to build consensus and establish common ideological goals.

11   Gilyard, Keith. "Basic Writing, Cost Effectiveness, and Ideology." *Journal of Basic Writing* 19.1 (2000): 36–42. Print.

Looking back on the history of basic writing at the City University of New York and his own experiences as a student, teacher, and scholar, Gilyard asserts that the future of basic writing should involve critiquing "cost effectiveness" arguments in favor of basic writing and framing arguments for students' abilities to voice and gain facility with language. He also challenges the easy use of the term *basic writing* for its inherent racism, sexism, and classism, while recognizing that it has institutional and personal value for many students and teachers. For Gilyard, basic writing scholarship that ignores students' own social, political, and cultural ideologies often results in privileged pedagogies that center on the formal considerations of students' writing alone. Citing the critical nature of scholarly work like Deborah Mutnick's, Gilyard favors basic writing scholarship that involves continued careful critique of its ideological, political, cultural, and social practices and interests.

12   Gleason, Barbara. "Reasoning the Need: Graduate Education and Basic Writing." *Journal of Basic Writing* 25.2 (2006): 49–75. Print.

In this essay, which appeared in the twenty-fifth anniversary edition of the *Journal of Basic Writing*, Gleason uses her 2005 speech from the Conference on College Composition and Communication as a jumping-off point for discussing the future of basic writing. She carefully examines just how well today's graduate students schooled in rhetoric, composition, and English studies are being prepared to actually teach the growing numbers of nontraditional basic writing students appearing in community colleges and adult literacy programs. Gleason looks closely at various graduate courses in basic writing theory and practice taught across the country from 2000 to 2005, lists key scholarly texts recommended to graduate students interested in basic writing research, charts important theoretical and practical developments in the discipline (such as the publication of the *Bedford Bibliography*), and discusses the Two-Year College Association's commitment to better serving basic writing students. In the end, Gleason creates a compelling argument for why we must create more and better graduate courses that prepare future teachers to teach basic writers.

13   Greenberg, Karen L. "The Politics of Basic Writing." *Journal of Basic Writing* 12.1 (1993): 64–71. Print.

Greenberg responds to David Bartholomae's contention at the Fourth Annual Conference on Basic Writing that basic writing programs generally do more harm than good to students. She points out that many writing instructors fall into the trap that Bartholomae describes. Refusing to include themselves in the design and implementation of assessment procedures in basic writing, these writing teachers relinquish responsibility for their program to administrators, legislators, and others who know little about basic writing. Greenberg then draws on her own experiences at the City University of New York. She shares some of the political challenges basic writing programs face and discusses strategies for meeting those challenges. She also suggests ways to improve basic writing instruction and assessment that will empower basic writing students. Greenberg notes that if basic writing courses are eliminated, our colleges and universities will once again become bastions of elitism.

See: David Bartholomae, "The Tidy House: Basic Writing in the American Curriculum" [3].

14 Greenberg, Karen L. "Research on Basic Writers: Theoretical and Methodological Issues." *A Sourcebook for Basic Writing Teachers.* Ed. Theresa Enos. New York: Random, 1987. 187–207. Print.

Greenberg addresses the importance of research methods and priorities in basic writing. After summarizing Janet Emig's formative research in composition, Greenberg recommends that the best research on writing and writers will have "an explicit, comprehensive theoretical foundation based on past and current research in applied linguistics, in cognitive-developmental psychology, in discourse analysis, and in literary theory" (191). Greenberg then describes more than a dozen such studies of basic writers and writing, concluding that they depict developing writers as struggling with writing tasks, rules, and errors due to three interrelated problems: "(1) distorted notions about writing and the composing process, (2) intense writing apprehension in certain contexts, and (3) a tendency to block while writing specific academic tasks" (202). These findings, Greenberg contends, have implications for teaching and for future research in basic writing.

15 Greenberg, Karen L. "A Response to Ira Shor's 'Our Apartheid: Writing Instruction and Inequality.'" *Journal of Basic Writing* 16.2 (1997): 90–94. Print.

Greenberg offers a strong counterpoint to Shor's [41] contention that basic writing courses should be eliminated in favor of courses based on cultural ideologies and empowerment. Basic writing courses are not "grammar graveyards" or "ghettos" (91) populated only by "Blacks" and "children of poor and working families" (90). They are safe places for a diverse population of underprepared college writers who can use these opportunities for individualized attention to better achieve their own potential in higher education. Greenberg accuses Shor of being an outsider to basic writing issues, of making decontextualized overgeneralizations about basic writing programs, and of treating basic writers stereotypically. Greenberg counters by depicting an effective basic writing classroom that is fully integrated into the English course sequence, displays progressive teaching strategies (such as workshopping, collaboration, and writing process), and provides a safe environment for students to develop necessary writing and critical thinking abilities. Greenberg argues that Shor's approach would lead to the exclusion of underprepared students and support "reactionary" efforts to restrict such students' access to higher education (94).

See: Ira Shor, "Our Apartheid: Writing Instruction and Inequality" [41].

See: Terence G. Collins, "A Response to Ira Shor's 'Our Apartheid'" [8].

16   Gunner, Jeanne. "Afterthoughts on Motive." *Journal of Basic Writing* 16.1 (1997): 3–6. Print.

Gunner examines the professional and personal motives behind her creation of the 1997 workshop "Race, Class, and Culture in the Basic Writing Classroom." The Conference on College Composition and Communication workshop was sponsored by the Conference on Basic Writing and was a forum for the discussion of professional issues like mainstreaming and analysis of class, identity, and cultural awareness in the basic writing classroom. The invited speakers, including Victor Villanueva, Gary Tate, Jacqueline Jones Royster, and Ira Shor, offered both professional and institutional gravitas to the workshop and to the topic's importance in the profession. Gunner's personal motives emerged from her realization that basic writing concerns were not addressed as an independent field but took place "in other professional arenas" (4). Responding to a paper presented by Charles Schuster in that session, Gunner recognized the need to bridge basic writing and "mainstream" composition. Gunner also admits to being motivated by a "concern for status" (5), in that she identified with and raged against the outsider status, loss of agency, and powerlessness that basic writers experience.

17   Gunner, Jeanne. "Iconic Discourse: The Troubling Legacy of Mina Shaughnessy." *Journal of Basic Writing* 17.2 (1998): 25–42. Print.

Gunner outlines the debate between scholars and teachers of basic writing, identifying two primary types of discourse. Iconic discourse relies on the legacy of Mina Shaughnessy and her work as an iconic teacher-figure. Critical discourse challenges basic writing conventions. Researchers like Min-Zhan Lu and Ira Shor question Shaughnessy's work and other accepted practices in the field and threaten to diminish the iconic status of Shaughnessy. Gunner maintains that these conflicting discourses can explain the attention and widespread resistance to such critiques of Shaughnessy.

18   Horner, Bruce. "Discoursing Basic Writing." *College Composition and Communication* 47.2 (1996): 199–222. Print.

In this alternative history of basic writing, Horner reads a number of texts that are often neglected in basic writing scholarship (including City University of New York memos and internal documents and Mina Shaughnessy's unpublished or lesser-known writings) as well as well-known texts (including *Errors and Expectations* [126] and the *Journal of Basic Writing*). He argues that these texts were critical in basic writing's formation as a discourse during the 1970s. Through close readings informed by Marxist and poststructuralist theory, Horner criticizes the ways in which this discourse has marginalized the concrete material, political, institutional, and sociohistorical realities facing basic writing teachers and students. Horner also investigates this discourse's convergence with an ongoing public discourse on education that problematically denies the academy's involvement in material, political, social, and historical worlds. Finally, Horner calls for more histories of basic writing that recover and expose the material, historical, and political contexts of basic writing, teaching, and theorizing.

19   Horner, Bruce. "Relocating Basic Writing." *Journal of Basic Writing* 30.2 (2011): 5–23. Print.

Based on his presentation for the Council on Basic Writing, Horner's article situates basic writing as an area of pedagogy and research fundamental to composition. Rather than merely applying knowledge from other domains, basic writing constitutes a long tradition of actively producing knowledge about writing. He suggests that strides made by basic writing represent struggles that must be won repeatedly in the face of cultural and institutional pressures. Though these gains may seem like mere repetitions, they are different in that they are located in different times, around differently motivated individuals. Increasingly, through its association with learners of other languages, basic writing challenges the monolingual nature of composition and the conflation of English with writing. Basic writing students are not merely writing and revising *in* English, Horner argues, but are actively writing and revising the English language itself. In these ways, scholars, teachers, and students of basic writing are engaged in understanding such crucial questions as what it means to write, while continuing to challenge dominant notions of languages as discrete spheres of activity.

20   Horner, Bruce, and Min-Zhan Lu. *Representing the "Other": Basic Writers and the Teaching of Basic Writing.* Urbana: National Council of Teachers of English, 1999. Print.

In its descriptive representation of student needs and problems, the "new" discourse of basic writing that emerged during the 1960s and 1970s positioned basic writing outside the social, political, and historical contexts of its production and reception. Rather than trace what might be considered a canon of basic writing texts, the eight cultural materialist readings that Horner and Lu present in this book analyze the discourse of basic writing as a discourse of renegotiation shaped and reshaped by the context of its production and reception.

21   Hunter, Paul. "'Waiting for Aristotle': A Moment in the History of the Basic Writing Movement." *College English* 54.8 (1992): 914–27. Print.

Hunter provides a rhetorical analysis of "Toward a Literate Democracy," the 1980 *Journal of Basic Writing* issue published in memory of Mina Shaughnessy. Hunter applies the characteristics of the *epitaphios logos* (funeral oration) to the essays gathered in this memorial volume: the *enkomion* (praise), *parainesis* (lament), and *paramythia* (consolation). At the same time, he describes the political purpose of the funeral oration in Athenian society and raises questions concerning the political dimension of the current addresses. Noting that none of the five speakers included from the First Shaughnessy Memorial Conference had any experience teaching basic writing, Hunter considers the focus of each of the speakers' addresses and attempts to assess Shaughnessy as outside the historical context in which she worked, which served to "enshrine [her] within the tribe of a conservative academic elite" (925).

22   Laurence, Patricia, et al. "Symposium on Basic Writing, Conflict and Struggle, and the Legacy of Mina Shaughnessy." *College English* 55.8 (1993): 879–903. Print.

These six presentations explore and critique the foundations and philosophies of basic writing. Four of the contributors to this symposium are responding to critiques by Min-Zhan Lu and Paul Hunter in the December 1992 issue of *College English* of the work of basic writing pioneers Kenneth Bruffee, Thomas Farrell, and, especially, Mina Shaughnessy. Lu had argued for a pedagogy of conflict to help basic writers reposition themselves, and both Lu and Hunter had pointed to the influence of these pioneers and their followers as the conservative element resisting such pedagogy. Patricia Laurence and Barbara Gleason present the case for historicizing the discussion—for evaluating both the philosophy of the pioneers and the criticism of Lu and Hunter from the contexts in which each worked or works. Peter Rondinone, a former open-admission student at the City University of New York and now a college English professor, takes Lu to task for missing the point about conflict in the lives of many basic writing students, while Thomas Farrell includes personal experiences with Shaughnessy. The symposium concludes with responses by both Hunter and Lu, with Lu's being the more in-depth response to each of the preceding critiques.

23   Lerner, Neal. "Rejecting the Remedial Brand: The Rise and Fall of the Dartmouth Writing Clinic." *College Composition and Communication* 59.1 (2007): 13–35. Print.

Lerner argues that many universities, both public and private, are under increasing pressure to supplement shrinking government funding by securing private donations. To encourage alumni contributions, schools have to attract the highest achieving students, which they do by increasing their selectiveness and by adopting brands such as *flagship*, *excellence*, and *signature*. Lerner says, however, that adopting brands of excellence necessitates driving out or covering over any "remedial" brand of educational access, such as those that dominated the twentieth century. Lerner reads the history of Dartmouth's writing clinic in the context of the disappearance of remedial brands. He argues that Dartmouth's brand was re-envisioned in the 1950s to highlight the excellence of its students, and with the new brand, it was accepted that Dartmouth should expect the most of its students. The Dartmouth writing clinic, however, was branded from its inception in 1930 as "remedial," a place where students who needed extra help could go or to which they could be remanded. Ultimately, Dartmouth's institutional brand was in competition with the "remedial" brand of the writing clinic, which led to the eventual dismantling of the clinic as unhelpful and unnecessary. Lerner ends by calling for writing programs to present themselves in rhetorically savvy ways in order to avoid the fate of the Dartmouth writing clinic and to be afforded the opportunity to continue to serve the needs of developing writers.

24 Lu, Min-Zhan, and Bruce Horner. "Expectations, Interpretations and Contributions of Basic Writing." *Journal of Basic Writing* 19.1 (2000): 43–52. Print.

In its history of student-centered research and its commitment to students who have been traditionally marginalized and devalued by higher education, basic writing has been at the forefront of diversity and student-centered learning. Because students in basic writing exist in the borderlands between discourse communities, they are, presumably, the diverse students that the university's promotional materials seem to pursue. Thus, Lu and Horner suggest that basic writers can teach faculty about the challenges diverse students face and the kinds of pedagogies that work for them. The authors also argue that basic writing must recognize and draw on basic writers' political agency, as students and faculty together fight against the nationwide assaults on basic writing programs.

25 Maher, Jane. "Writing the Life of Mina P. Shaughnessy." *Journal of Basic Writing* 16.1 (1997): 51–63. Print.

In this article, Maher introduces her biography, *Mina P. Shaughnessy: Her Life and Work*. Maher describes how her own education, ideals, and career have intersected with that of her subject. Similar working-class backgrounds, attendance (Maher) and teaching (Shaughnessy) at City University of New York colleges, and careers devoted to the education of basic writing students bring biographer and subject together. Maher tells the story of the biographical process—her interest in and respect for Shaughnessy's work, the initial impulse to write the story of Shaughnessy's life, the quest for information, and the difficulties of telling a life story. Readers are introduced to Mina Shaughnessy's life and, in its unfolding, discover what motivated her to advocate for open admissions and what made it possible for her to write the landmark work *Errors and Expectations* [126]. The overview of Shaughnessy's life from her family history to her death provides a mini-biography, while Maher's personal perspectives show the relationship of biographer to subject.

26 McBeth, Mark. "Arrested Development: Revising Remediation at John Jay College of Criminal Justice." *Journal of Basic Writing* 25.2 (2006): 76–93. Print.

Since the open-admissions era of Mina Shaughnessy, "remedial courses" have shaped the identity of the City University of New York (CUNY); these sub-freshman courses have been revised depending on institutional missions, curricular initiatives, university policies, and political climates. Mark McBeth briefly reviews the history of remediation at

CUNY and then describes an intensive developmental writing course implemented at John Jay College of Criminal Justice, explaining its strategies, rationales, successes, and remaining challenges. By synthesizing the perspectives of Lev Vygotsky and Mary Louise Pratt, this article demonstrates how this basic writing course combined these theories to offer students "a contact zone of proximal development." While responding to the constraints of a university policy where a gatekeeping exam (over)determines students' educational possibilities, this course curriculum resists teaching *to* the test and, instead, strives to teach *with* it. While helping students to fulfill a mandatory, high-stakes requirement, this instructional approach offers students the exposure to composition and critical thinking that productively launches their college careers.

27   McNenny, Gerri, ed. *Mainstreaming Basic Writers: Politics and Pedagogies of Access.* Mahwah: Erlbaum, 2001. Print.

This collection of essays presents many of the positions taken in response to recent challenges posed to basic writing instruction on four-year college campuses. At the same time, it offers alternative configurations for writing instruction that attempt to do justice to both students' needs and administrative constraints. Contributors include Edward M. White, Ira Shor, Mary Soliday, Trudy Smoke, Barbara Gleason, Terence G. Collins, Kim Lynch, Eleanor Agnew, Margaret McLaughlin, Marti Singer, Rosemary Winslow, Monica Mische, Mark Wiley, Gerri McNenny, and Sallyanne Fitzgerald.

28   Mutnick, Deborah. "On the Academic Margins: Basic Writing Pedagogy." *A Guide to Composition Pedagogies.* Ed. Gary Tate, Amy Rupiper, and Kurt Schick. New York: Oxford UP, 2001. 183–202. Print.

Mutnick outlines a detailed history of basic writing, beginning in the late 1960s with Mina Shaughnessy. She argues that Shaughnessy's major contributions were her ability to shift the focus of research from the students to the "teachers, administrators, and society" (185) and her understanding that the logical errors produced by students held the key to their attempts to arrive at conventional forms. Mutnick's history moves on to other theories of error that followed those of Shaughnessy and then to a discussion of process and cognitive theories and rhetorical theories. Mutnick also warns that we must prepare ourselves to counter political decisions now being made in higher education.

29   Pavesich, Matthew. "Reflecting on the Liberal Reflex: Rhetoric and the Politics of Acknowledgment in Basic Writing." *Journal of Basic Writing* 30.2 (2011): 84–109. Print.

The debate in the 1990s over the role of "liberalism" in basic writing programs cemented the views of both supporters and detractors. In an overview of the scholarship regarding liberalism in basic writing, Pavesich claims that neither side of the basic writing debate manages to escape the liberal hegemony present in higher education. The pervasiveness of liberalism creates and recreates itself reflectively: manifesting itself in, for example, basic writing models (stretch, studio, and enrichment) that do not address the inherent exclusionary and assimilationist liberalism of the academy. In order to politically reenvision basic writing, Pavesich offers a rhetorical teaching practice influenced by Patchen Markell's *politics of acknowledgment* and Chantal Mouffe's *agonistic pluralism* as the means of addressing, responding to, and resisting liberalism in the academy. Citing his experiences with Roosevelt University's basic writing program, Pavesich describes the challenges of re-envisioning basic writing within an institutional context. Nonetheless, Pavesich endorses acknowledgment as a classroom and an institutional practice capable of "generating productive forms of pressure on traditional liberal practices" (103).

30   Quint, Janet C., et al. "Bringing Developmental Education to Scale: Lessons from the Developmental Education Initiative." *MDRC*. MDRC, Jan. 2013. Web. 21 Sept. 2014.

With required developmental classes posing roadblocks for students and decreasing retention rates, fifteen colleges participating in Achieving the Dream were selected to pilot a small-scale program intended to increase support for students' early academic success. Funded by the Developmental Education Initiative (DEI), the program implemented forty-six focal strategies categorized into four types emphasizing various objectives: instructional strategies, support strategies, policy changes, and strategies directed toward high school students. In this, the second and final report, the authors indicate that participation in focal strategies more than doubled over the course of the study, Fall 2009–Fall 2011. While the majority of outcomes during this period indicated no change, positive change was associated with an estimated one-third of the strategies, and negative results were associated with a minimal percentage. The authors stress that causal effects are inconclusive given several uncontrollable factors; still, the authors credit the DEI for offering the support needed to develop and create interventions for students in developmental classes, and, in so doing, paving the way for further conversations regarding student success.

31   Ray, Brian. "A New World: Redefining the Legacy of Min-Zhan Lu." *Journal of Basic Writing* 27.2 (2008): 106–27. Print.

In this article Ray discusses exchanges between a number of scholars during the 1990s centering on Min-Zhan Lu's controversial essay "Conflict and Struggle: The Enemies or Preconditions of Basic Writing?" In some ways, "Conflict and Struggle" blazed a trail for later work in "hybrid" or "mixed" forms of academic writing while at the same time igniting debate over Mina Shaughnessy's legacy. Rather than take sides, Ray considers what perspectives and considerations were left out of this years-long standoff and attempts to reconcile this issue in basic writing theory through relevant but less discussed work in linguistics. The concept of linguistic charity, an area of growing interest in composition studies, offers a particularly refreshing new direction for discussion regarding the ambiguous and often controversial role of Standard English in our pedagogies.

See: Min-Zhan Lu, "Conflict and Struggle: The Enemies or Preconditions of Basic Writing?" [269].

32   Ribble, Marcia. "Redefining Basic Writing: An Image Shift from Error to Rhizome." *Basic Writing e-Journal* 3.1 (2001): n. pag. Web. 21 May 2014.

Ribble advocates a shift in our thinking about basic writing and writers: from error as the defining characteristic to the metaphor of a rhizome as a connected, ecological system. Ribble shows the way a student's paper simultaneously exhibits good writing, creativity in expressing ideas and feelings, and multiple errors in spelling, punctuation, and grammar. Drawing on Gilles Deleuze and Felix Guattari, Ribble discusses four rhizomic principles: connectivity relates to our desire to communicate with others; heterogeneity represents linguistic variety; multiplicity represents the complexity of writing and writers; and a signifying rupture addresses the fragmentation that change creates. Errors therefore are a necessary part of the lifelong process of learning and writing. The rhizome metaphor is especially relevant to technological communication: "only a metaphor as complex as the rhizome can handle the multi-tasking our students are born into" (par. 33). We would do well, Ribble suggests, to rethink our conceptions of basic writing in similar ways.

33   Ritter, Kelly. "Before Mina Shaughnessy: Basic Writing at Yale, 1920–1960." *College Composition and Communication* 60.1 (2008): 12–45. Print.

Ritter's article is an insightful piece using archival materials to point out and describe the "Awkward Squad" at Yale. It includes a historical perspective of basic composition courses. She compares and contrasts the use of basic studies in composition as a means to hold standards high, to include the elite at Ivy League schools, and to exclude others. During that time a course to remediate basic writers was not officially on the course list. It had a derogatory name, and being a part of this so-called unprepared group of students had a negative connotation. As Ritter brings the reader up to date with the changes in the academic world, in the makeup of college students and their preparation for the higher education experience, she argues for "a re-definition of *basic* in composition studies" (12). She cites many references and statistics to give readers insight into this topic.

34   Rose, Mike. "The Language of Exclusion: Writing Instruction at the University." *College English* 47.4 (1985): 341–59. Print.

Rose argues that "institutional language about writing instruction in American higher education" effectively "keeps writing instruction at the periphery of the curriculum" (341). This language and its attendant metaphors are based on behaviorist models and misunderstandings about writing and do not take students' abilities and needs into account.

Rose discusses in detail the effects of behaviorism and quantification on thinking about writing: they emphasize correctness, mechanistic para-digms, and pseudoscientific reasoning rather than the social context of error. Defining writing as a "skill" rather than as a means of inquiry has political and educational implications. The terminology associated with remediation originated in law and medicine, and its application to writing instruction is critiqued in the context of this medical metaphor. The language of literacy and illiteracy is inadequate to represent the realities of basic writing instruction. Also, according to the "myth of transience" (355), the problems associated with basic writing and writ-ers could be cured and thereby eliminated if certain criteria could be met. Remediation as a metaphor must be abandoned. Rose concludes that "wide-ranging change will occur only if the academy redefines writing for itself, changes the terms of the argument, [and] sees instruc-tion in writing as one of its central concerns" (359).

35   Rose, Mike. *Possible Lives: The Promise of Public Education in America.* New York: Penguin, 1995. Print.

With this study, Rose seeks to inspire more careful critique of schools because "our national discussion about public schools is despairing and dismissive, and it is shutting down our civic imagination" (1). Rose observed classrooms across the country, concluding that good class-rooms are safe classrooms where teachers respect students and manage to share authority with them. Teaching like this involves the interplay of multiple "knowledges," some of which are brought to the classroom by teachers, and some by students. Even in the "at-risk" environments Rose describes, there is great possibility for public education to con-struct active and critical citizens, but only if schools recognize the "pos-sible lives" that fill the halls each day.

36   Royster, Jacqueline Jones, and Rebecca Greenberg Taylor. "Construct-ing Teacher Identity in the Basic Writing Classroom." *Journal of Basic Writing* 16.1 (1997): 27–50. Print.

Royster and Taylor challenge us to examine the place of teachers in the classroom, calling for a shift in the gaze that has been turned—nearly throughout the whole of basic writing scholarship—toward students. How are teachers, they ask, located in the basic writing classroom? This reading is decidedly against the grain of basic writing scholarship, for Royster and Taylor interrogate teacher identity and its absence as a focus of research in basic writing. They remark that they had "become impatient with the discussion of identity, most especially in basic writ-ing classrooms, as the *students'* problem, rather than also as the *teacher's* problem" (28). Their call for additional research on teacher identity as an informing element of classrooms speaks to the tendency in composi-tion studies at large to deny the power of teacher authority. The essay stands as a call for new and vigorous inquiry into the location of teach-ers in the college writing classroom, the ways students see teachers, and the implications of those constructs for the basic writing classroom.

37   Rutschow, Elizabeth Zachry, and Emily Schneider. "Unlocking the
      Gate: What We Know about Improving Developmental Education."
      MDRC, MDRC. June 2011. Web. 21 Sept. 2014.

      This report, published by nonprofit and nonpartisan MDRC and
      funded by the National Center for Postsecondary Research (NCPR)
      and the Carnegie Corporation of New York, reviews recent research
      studies about efforts to improve success rates in developmental educa-
      tion programs, specifically highlighting quantitative studies that com-
      pare innovative approaches with the traditional model of sequenced
      courses. The authors argue the following interventions show the most
      potential for increased student success: revising placement processes
      so that some students may avoid developmental courses altogether; re-
      designing curriculums for modularized or compressed courses that may
      accelerate students' progress; contextualizing basic skills into occu-
      pational or college-level courses; and enhancing academic support ser-
      vices, specifically tutoring and advising. The authors emphasize that
      the studies on these interventions demonstrate minor improvements in
      developmental student success. Thus, the authors call for more research
      on both the effects of current reforms and other possible approaches to
      developmental education such as curricular redesign directed at career-
      specific skills, technology-aided strategies, and skill alignment between
      high schools and colleges.

38   Salas, Spencer. "Roberta; or, the Ambiguities: Tough Love and High-
      Stakes Assessment at a Two-Year College in North Georgia." *Journal of
      Basic Writing* 27.2 (2008): 5–28. Print.

      This ethnographic narrative employs a neo-Vygotskian perspective
      (Holland et al.) to examine how, in the setting of a remedial English as
      a second language (ESL) program at a public two-year college in North
      Georgia, the subject position of an ESL basic writing instructor was me-
      diated by her understandings of and engagement with the multiple and
      interactive contexts of her professional activity. Despite a wide variety
      of tensions that complicated the instructor's understandings of who she
      was professionally, she was able to position herself in ways that allowed
      her to make sense of her professional choices. However, her construc-
      tion of gatekeeping as advocacy brought with it an emotional toll at
      the end of each semester when some students passed and some students
      failed—shaking the sense of her tough-love pedagogical stance. Rep-
      resentations of basic writing professionals are critiqued to argue for the
      need for more nuanced research for and with basic writing faculty in the
      activist college composition literature.

39   Shor, Ira. "Errors and Economics: Inequality Breeds Remediation." *Main-
      streaming Basic Writers: Politics and Pedagogies of Access*. Ed. Gerri Mc-
      Nenny. Mahwah: Erlbaum, 2001. 29–54. Print.

      Shor begins this essay with an analysis of the work of Mina Shaugh-
      nessy, Adrienne Rich, and Leonard Greenbaum, all teachers of writing
      at the City College of New York during the open-admissions period,

who believed that the emphasis on "correctness" in language instruction could "debase" (Shaughnessy) and disempower students. Shor then connects their positions to John Kenneth Galbraith's proposal that economics drives education policy. An analysis of the economic context of first-year writing instruction, according to Shor, can help explain its political contradictions, complaints, and choices, such as its focus on error and correctness. This focus, he argues, reflects the values of an elite culture and reproduces the inequalities necessary for that culture to remain elite. The kind of long-term instruction in the "correct" use of language embedded in K–16 writing instruction shapes students' and teachers' views of the world. To change those views, Shor proposes a critical writing curriculum that would replace the one currently in place and a democratic labor policy that would replace the exploitation of cheap labor in the staffing of courses.

See: Mina P. Shaughnessy, *Errors and Expectations: A Guide for the Teacher of Basic Writing* [126].

40   Shor, Ira. "Inequality (Still) Rules: Reply to Collins and Greenberg." *Journal of Basic Writing* 17.1 (1998): 104–8. Print.

This response to criticism by Karen Greenberg [15] and Terence Collins [8] repeats Shor's basic points from his original article: teachers of basic writing are an exploited labor force; claims for the success of basic writing programs are equivocal; minority and working-class students are overrepresented in basic writing classes; and most basic writing curricula perpetuate a pedagogy of disembodied language arts and impede a pedagogy of critical engagement with everyday life.

41   Shor, Ira. "Our Apartheid: Writing Instruction and Inequality." *Journal of Basic Writing* 16.1 (1997): 91–104. Print.

Shor argues that basic writing as a field is in a state of permanent crisis. While composition functions as a linguistic gatekeeper in the university, basic writing acts as a gate below the gate. As part of the undemocratic tracking system in mass education, basic writing successfully impedes the academic progress of nonelite students. In effect, Shor suggests that basic writing supports a top-down, business-oriented agenda that is designed to keep the status quo by moving nonelite students into vocational jobs and disciplined lives. As a basement course that is often taught by marginalized, overworked adjuncts, basic writing fosters depressed wages and few health benefits. Democratic education demands an end to educational apartheid through the dismantling of basic writing.

See: Terence G. Collins, "A Response to Ira Shor's 'Our Apartheid'" [8].

See: Karen L. Greenberg, "A Response to Ira Shor's 'Our Apartheid'" [15].

42   Stygall, Gail. "Unraveling at Both Ends: Anti-Undergraduate Education, Anti-Affirmative Action, and Basic Writing at Research Schools." *Journal of Basic Writing* 18.2 (1999): 4–22. Print.

Basic writing programs at West Coast research universities face a double bind: the privileging of research and graduate education in comparison to all lower-division undergraduate writing courses (especially basic writing courses) and the passing of anti–affirmative action ballot initiatives. The University of Washington is a case in point. The "unraveling" of its basic writing program is demonstrated through critical discourse analysis of three texts: the university's "master plan" for the next twenty years; a Seattle newspaper's take on the Educational Opportunity Program, which houses basic writing, and Initiative-2000, which bans "preferential" treatment in education; and the conclusions of the Washington 2000 Commission, a gubernatorial commission formed to determine the future of higher education in Washington.

43   Summerfield, Judith, et al. "The City University of New York and the Shaughnessy Legacy: Today's Scholars Talk Back." *Journal of Basic Writing* 26.2 (2007): 5–29. Print.

Based on a thirtieth-anniversary roundtable discussion on the Shaughnessy legacy for the CUNY system, this article offers short contributions on topics ranging from a neglected text, *Beat Not the Poor Desk*, that was a direct challenge to the Shaughnessy project in *Errors and Expectations*, to the continuing necessity for educators to consider their own "deficiencies" as often as they consider those of the students; from the links that unite doctoral ways of researching with meaningful teaching to the ways Shaughnessy's attentiveness to systematic kinds of errors has enriched second-language instruction. The focus is on Shaughnessy's legacy of understanding, of valuing students typically devalued by the academy, and of "access politics," or the ways students learn the language of the academy in order to gain entrance to the kinds of education previously denied them.

44   Trimmer, Joseph F. "Basic Skills, Basic Writing, Basic Research." *Journal of Basic Writing* 6.1 (1987): 3–9. Print.

Survey responses from nine hundred two- and four-year colleges and universities reveal that a majority have some form of basic writing program and that most are housed in English departments. Teaching assistants or part-time faculty teach the bulk of basic writing courses, with only a few receiving systematic teaching orientation. Building on Robert Connors's study of the remedial textbook market, Trimmer interviewed representatives from twenty publishing houses, who revealed that editors find the remedial textbook market "difficult and disheartening" (6) because schools are caught in political predicaments that force them to adopt workbooks or sentence-grammar texts. Editors have read extensively on basic writing research but have witnessed good textbook proposals become publishing disasters. Perhaps basic writing research has little impact because remedial English teachers are too overworked to read research, or perhaps the research simply is not known, not understood, or not believed because it challenges tradition.

45   Troyka, Lynn Quitman. "Defining Basic Writing in Context." *A Sourcebook for Basic Writing Teachers*. Ed. Theresa Enos. New York: Random, 1987. 2–15. Print.

Although *basic writing* is a much more positive term than the medical *remedial* and the condescending *developmental*, readers are cautioned not to generalize about what basic writers do or who they are. *Remedial, developmental,* and *basic* oversimplify the diverse students who are often labeled as *underprepared*. Troyka defines basic writing in historical relation to remedial writing and developmental writing as well as through a national survey of basic writing essays she completed to better shape future basic writing scholarship and teaching. She offers two crucial conclusions. First, basic writers are not simply writers; hence any definition of basic writing must take into account how "basic writers need to immerse themselves in language in all its forms" (13). Thus, teachers and researchers need to consider the centrality of reading to writing. Second, teachers must define basic writers in context, which means teachers must "describe with examples our student populations when we write about basic writers" (13). This important essay demonstrates why the diversity of our students and the context of their specific writing situations cannot be generalized through the term *basic writing*.

46   Troyka, Lynn Quitman. "How We Have Failed the Basic Writing Enterprise." *Journal of Basic Writing* 19.1 (2000): 113–23. Print.

Written as a letter to the editors of the *Journal of Basic Writing*, this essay contends that basic writing scholars and practitioners have failed the "BW enterprise" (114). First, basic writing scholarship and practice have not dealt effectively with public relations issues. Troyka contends that to be more successful, basic writing needs to be more visible and articulate within the popular media. Second, Troyka argues that basic writing has suffered from the lack of real assessment outcomes. Since scholars have tended to avoid longitudinal studies, there has been little tangible evidence for the validity of the efforts. Third, Troyka contends that in an effort to value students' voices and political, social, and cultural differences, we have simultaneously ignored the potential values of grammar instruction. She urges us to find new and innovative ways to teach grammar rather than ignore it. Finally, Troyka proffers that basic writing has limited the kinds of scholarly inquiries that are considered valuable, necessarily marginalizing certain kinds of research while privileging others. In closing, however, she suggests that successes can be found in basic writing teaching, an important site for theorizing. For Troyka, this is a location where she feels innovative work continues to be accomplished, a place that, if studied closely, might help us rectify other problems.

47   VanHaitsma, Pamela. "More Talk about 'Basic Writers': A Category of Rhetorical Value for Teachers." *Journal of Basic Writing* 29.1 (2010): 99–124. Print.

VanHaitsma analyzes the rhetorical value of "basic writer" as a category of instruction in American academia under the umbrella of Michael de Certeau's definitions of strategy and tactic. In accordance with de Certeau's work, *strategy* is categorized as the implementation of the learning structures, and *tactic* is used to describe exchanges enabling action outside the field of academia. VanHaitsma uses the case study of five writing instructors at an unnamed urban California public university, identifying the limitations of the strategic use of the term when referring to both the students and the programs, asserting that the use of "basic writer" affects the perception of the programs and the students alike. She concludes by arguing that compositionists can deploy the term *basic writer* tactically to obtain more resources for teaching basic writing classes and to articulate an understanding of writing pedagogy as a form of social justice.

48   Wiener, Harvey S. "The Attack on Basic Writing—and After." *Journal of Basic Writing* 17.1 (1998): 96–103. Print.

Basic writing is under attack on many fronts, and such attacks are at least partly caused by ineffective marketing. That is, too many people see basic writing as remedial without understanding what it is, what it is intended to do, or where it fits in the academy. Wiener suggests that such attacks on funding and the outsourcing of basic writing classes and students will go on but that we must continue to work to counter these attacks.

Basic Writers: The Past, the Present, and the Future

49   Greene, Nicole Pepinster, and Patricia J. McAlexander, eds. *Basic Writing in America: The History of Nine College Programs*. Cresskill: Hampton, 2008. Print.

Seeking to recover the tradition of basic writing within the United States as a complex and multifaceted movement, editors Greene and McAlexander collect historical narratives on basic writing programs from a variety of institutions and geographical locations. In telling their program histories, contributors draw from such primary sources as institutional correspondences, reports, syllabi, and course catalogs; at times, they also include information gathered from interviews with faculty and program directors, as well as their own personal experiences with the programs. In doing so, they share how these distinct basic writing programs emerged, adapted, and sometimes disappeared, responding to—and embedded within—local and institutional material conditions and policies, national conversations about the politics of remediation, and the growth of basic writing as a subdiscipline. Themes represented across chapters include the valuing and/or devaluing of basic writing within departments and institutions; basic writing's relationship with the civil rights movement and connection to social and economic equity; and the move from the cognitive to the social in basic writing theory and pedagogy.

50   Lamos, Steve. "Minority-Serving Institutions, Race-Conscious 'Dwelling,' and Possible Futures for Basic Writing at Predominantly White Institutions." *Journal of Basic Writing* 31.1 (2012): 4–35. Print.

In response to facilities of higher education eliminating basic writing programs, Lamos analyzes strategies to improve the future of basic writing. Elitist educational attitudes common at many predominantly white institutions have reduced basic writing programs, resulting in decreased support for students of diverse backgrounds. Lamos argues it is necessary for basic writing programs to change how they publicize their programs to benefit students and, more important, the culture of higher education. Successful instructional methods that promote race-conscious education at minority-serving institutions are explained in terms of how they could be adopted at predominantly white institutions. Influenced by theories of Nedra Reynolds and Derrick Bell, Lamos explains how basic writing needs to emphasize that programs are "race-conscious" and therefore indispensable to such institutions; this can be achieved by telling race-conscious stories, developing race-conscious writing pedagogies, developing race-conscious programs, and documenting the success and value of race-consciousness. Lamos emphasizes that despite current trends, the future of basic writing is hopeful: the field is in a good position to adjust its focus to better serve students and positively change the culture of higher education.

51   Otte, George, and Rebecca Williams Mlynarczyk. *Basic Writing*. West Lafayette: Parlor, 2010. Print.

In this text, Otte and Mlynarczyk offer a broad survey of the field of basic writing. The authors locate the origins in the 1960s and follow this history through the first decade of the twenty-first century. Each chapter follows an aspect of basic writing and how it has changed over the course of the last fifty years. The first chapter offers a historical overview and provides a sense of the landscape of postsecondary education, as well as its influence on basic writing as a course and as a discipline. The second chapter offers a sense of the scope of the field, concentrating on definitions of basic writing and disputes over its purpose. The third chapter describes dominant practices and pedagogies of basic writing classrooms, while the fourth chapter summarizes research agendas in the field throughout each of these decades. In the fifth and final chapter, Otte and Mlynarczyk address future directions and concerns for the field. This text is especially useful for understanding historical trajectories in basic writing scholarship and pedagogies.

52   Otte, George, and Rebecca Williams Mlynarczyk. "The Future of Basic Writing." *Journal of Basic Writing* 29.1 (2010): 5–32. Print.

In a comprehensive review of the state of basic writing since the 1990s, Otte and Mlynarczyk provide a clear trajectory of the challenges it has faced while also making tentative predictions about its role in education in the twenty-first century. The authors trace how in colleges and universities across the country economic pressures led to a gradual but inevitable erosion of remedial writing programs and related support services that had for decades served the needs of underprepared students. In response, basic writing scholars and educators developed and adopted alternative approaches, pedagogies, and practices that include stretch and intensive programs, studio workshops, service learning, and community programs that represent new and more effective models of basic writing instruction. While they avoid making definitive claims about the future of basic writing, the authors conclude by projecting a significant rise in the nontraditional student population that will both necessitate the continuation of basic writing and reinforce its value.

53   Ritter, Kelly. *Before Shaughnessy: Basic Writing at Yale and Harvard, 1920–1960.* Carbondale: Southern Illinois UP, 2009. Print.

By discussing coursework devoted to underprepared writers at Yale and Harvard pre–*Errors and Expectations*, Ritter challenges the assumption that the politics of access and remediation emerged in the post open-enrollment era. At Yale, the "Awkward Squad" was a remedial basic skills course with no official recognition by the university. The course enrolled students at a variety of levels, showing that basic writers are neither easily defined by skills nor specific to certain institutions. Harvard had a more structured and seemingly kinder approach, actively recruiting students for its English F course, designed to prepare students for the mainstream English A course. Ritter argues that students have long been placed into remediation and calls for studies of basic writing coursework to examine issues of access on a longer timeline. She reiterates the view that the term *basic* can marginalize students placed into these courses and suggests using terminology that unites all first-year composition coursework as introductory.

54   Stanley, Jane. *The Rhetoric of Remediation: Negotiating Entitlement and Access to Higher Education.* Pittsburgh: U of Pittsburgh P, 2010. Print.

Starting in 1869 when the University of California–Berkeley opened its doors, Stanley's chronicle examines how state and national politics, demographics, social change, and economics have driven the rhetoric of remediation. Throughout Berkeley's history, 10–20 percent of entering students have been "held" in Subject A, the remedial English program. Stanley asserts that the remedial student is a *construct*, enabling Berkeley to safeguard its preeminence while expanding access but resulting in a "disdainful embrace" of remedial students. Throughout the 140-year span of Stanley's narrative, Subject A students are variously labeled "deficient," "incompetent," "lazy," "feeble-minded," and "conditional." Stanley's compelling, sometimes riveting story integrates a surfeit of details, quotes, and data from institutional documents (such as minutes of program meetings). J. Edgar Hoover, Earl Warren, H. R. Haldeman, Richard Nixon, and Ronald Reagan play substantive roles in her narrative. Stanley concludes there has been "no place in time when students' writing did not cause disappointment and occasion the public expression of dismay." In the end, she wonders if Berkeley's story of remediation offers insights to compositionists everywhere.

Basic Writing in the National Context

55   Achieving the Dream and MDC. "New Strategies for Developmental Education: Building on and Achieving the Dream Foundation." *Knowledge Center: Achieving the Dream*, Achieving the Dream, Inc. 1 Mar. 2009. Web. 21 May 2014.

Written to provide a framework for the Developmental Education Initiative (DEI), this article focuses on the partnership that Achieving the Dream colleges and states have formed with the Bill and Melinda Gates Foundation and Lumina Foundation to support and accelerate the achievement of higher-education goals at the two-year college level. The document first outlines the challenges faced by community colleges with regards to student success as measured by retention and graduation rates and then discusses the potential impact of the strategic changes being implemented in colleges that participate in the initiative. Building on the work of Achieving the Dream institutions, in this new phase the partnership will continue to emphasize data-driven efforts to implement pedagogical and curricular reform that leads to effective teaching and learning practices and ultimately to higher student success rates. The project aims to assist colleges to move in four strategic directions that involve adoption of institutional policies that support student success, accelerated progress of students through developmental courses, intensive student support, and implementation of innovative teaching methods.

56   Bailey, Thomas, Shanna S. Jaggars, and Judith Scott Clayton. "Characterizing the Effectiveness of Developmental Education: A Response to Recent Criticism." *Community College Research Center*. Teachers College, Columbia University. Feb. 2013. Web. 21 May 2014.

In response to criticism, Bailey et al. clarify their argument in favor of developmental education reform. They state they support improving, not dismantling, developmental programs nationally. They counter three specific criticisms raised by opponents of their research. First, that they "unfairly expect that remediation should raise outcomes . . . above those of college-level students" (10). Bailey et al. state that because their studies focus on students with near-identical placement test scores, it's reasonable to expect additional class time to have positive effects. Second, that they overemphasize negative aspects of developmental education while deemphasizing the positive. Bailey et al. show that the negative and null effects of traditional developmental education outweigh the positive effects. Third, that the studies they cite apply only to students with cutoff scores proximal to those of non-developmental students. Bailey et al. argue their conclusions are valid for students with a range of placement test scores. The authors conclude by stating that they aim to support administrators, professors, and officials in identifying opportunities to reform and improve developmental education.

57   Bailey, Thomas, and Sung-Woo Cho. "Developmental Education in Community Colleges." *Community College Research Center*. Teachers College, Columbia University. Sept. 2010. Web. 21 May 2014.

Prepared for the White House Summit on Community Colleges, this brief provides an overview of US community college remedial education while acknowledging many dedicated professionals serve remedial students, especially in terms of how the effectiveness, ineffectiveness, and institutional costs of such education connect with the Obama administration's 2020 goal of boosting community college graduation numbers by five million. The brief offers data-based and systemic negatives of such education, reviews positive efforts in the field (Accelerated Learning Programs, Integrated Basic Education and Skills Training, and Learning Communities), and concludes that, ultimately, more success is needed to meet the 2020 goal.

58   Barragan, Melissa, Maria Scott Cormier, and the Scaling Innovation Team. "Enhancing Rigor in Developmental Education." *Inside Out* 1.4 (2013): 1–5. Web. 21 May 2014.

Because evidence suggests that a curricular and pedagogical focus on any set of isolated skills fails to help students succeed in college, the Scaling Innovation team examined the content in the courses following the developmental ones and altered the developmental course content from reteaching lower-level skills to requiring the same kind of difficult texts and critical thinking tasks as those in subsequent courses. When students took these redesigned developmental courses, they rose to the challenge with high levels of motivation since the rigor invited them to actively construct their own knowledge. The readings and assignments pushed students (using appropriate scaffolding) and led students to succeed in the developmental *and* in subsequent courses (according to preliminary data). What is just as significant as their successful completion is that the rigorous content and pedagogy led these students to improve in key learner dispositions such as having a growth mind-set, being more self-directed, and accepting struggle as part of learning.

59   Bernstein, Susan Naomi, ed. *Teaching Developmental Writing: Background Readings*. 4th ed. Boston: Bedford, 2013. Print.

Bernstein provides a collection of thirty-one readings on basic writing, its scholarship, its practice, and its theory. The four sections of the text explore "Perspectives from the Field," "Literacy and Literacies," "Engaging Difference," and "Collaboration, Assessment, and Change." Included in this collection are numerous essays about teacher and student perspectives on basic writing; the processes of writing and research; intersected (or rather intersections of) literacies (of reading, writing, and critical thinking); teaching and learning new literacies; approaches to learning academic English (particularly grammar and style); classical perspectives on multicultural teaching and learning; transforming pedagogies; learning differences; English language learners; writing centers; and issues of access, placement, assessment, and retention. Motivated by some well-situated political ethics, the first section of the text provides a counterargument to the trend of downsizing and outsourcing basic writing courses. The second section explores the complexities of teaching literacy in the twenty-first century. The third section offers a discussion of the agency of educators, exploring identity formation and multiculturalism with some useful readings on English language learning. The fourth and final section explores issues of the "permeable boundaries" of our classrooms, which discuss the work of writers, tutors, the writing center, and issues of collaboration, as well as issues of assessment and placement in basic writing programs.

60   Boylan, Hunter R., and Alexandros Goudas. "Knee-Jerk Reforms on Remediation." *Inside Higher Ed*, 19 June 2012: n. pag. Web. 21 May 2014.

Boylan and Goudas review recent research on the efficacy of remedial courses, beginning with a pair of studies that use a regression discontinuity design by Mattorell and McFarlin in 2007 and Calcagno and Long in 2008, and are not "generalizable to the entire range of remedial courses and students." Boylan and Goudas find this problematic because "these are the major studies used to justify that all remediation has failed. Although none of the authors of these studies make this claim. . . ." While work on the positive effects of remedial courses by Attewell, Lavin, Domina, and Levey in 2006 and Boatman and Long's 2010 study concluded that remediation has both negative and positive effects depending on subject area, neither of these appear in the "Bridge to Nowhere" report by the Complete College America, which influenced the Connecticut Legislature's decision to require that "remediation be limited to one semester in all its colleges and replaced by embedded support services in gateway courses."

61   Bridges to Opportunity Initiative. "Bridges to Opportunity for Underprepared Adults: A State Policy Guide for Community College Leaders." *Community College Research Center*. Teachers College, Columbia University. 2008. Web. 21 May 2014.

Developed from the Ford Foundation–funded Community College Bridges to Opportunity initiative, this guide, which includes case studies from Louisiana, Ohio, and Washington, provides strategies for community college leaders to impact policy and advocate for underprepared adults. The initiative provided grant funding to improve education and employment outcomes for educationally and economically disadvantaged adults. The guide notes specific challenges faced by underprepared adult students: poor alignment between adult basic skills programs and college-level programs, occupational programs and academic programs being isolated, limited counseling and support, difficulty securing financial aid, and poor coordination with outside workforce and human service agencies. The authors propose linking educational opportunity and economic development, using state data to inform improvements in policy and practice, creating career pathways to accelerate college and career success, and bridging the gap between remedial education and careers. Stakeholders are given guidelines for impacting state policy, with recommendations for governors and legislators, state agency heads and board members, college presidents, business and labor leaders, and community-based organization directors.

62   Lu, Adrienne. "States Reform College Remedial Education." *Stateline*, The Pew Charitable Trusts. 25 July 2013. Web. 21 May 2014.

Developmental education courses cost taxpayers and the government money, and this funding angers policymakers because relatively few remedial students graduate. Some argue high school transcripts, not entrance exams, should determine student placement. To help more students graduate, Indiana legislation now requires early (high school) identification and tutoring, Colorado and Florida insist colleges allow students to skip noncredit courses and provide them extra support, Texas is working on making these courses free, and Connecticut makes developmental courses credit bearing and allows students to enroll in such courses only once. Others suggest making remedial courses two semesters long. Critics worry such drastic measures will leave already disadvantaged students more underprepared and suggest instructors be trained to be more effective or the dropout rate will only increase.

63   Mangan, Katherine. "How Gates Shapes State Higher-Education Policy." *Chronicle of Higher Education*. 14 July 2013: n. pag. Web. 21 May 2014.

In this *CHE* Special Report, Mangan examines the influence of private foundations—specifically the Bill and Melinda Gates Foundation—on higher education and developmental course offerings. Mangan outlines the relationship between the Gates Foundation and intermediary nonprofit organizations such as Complete College America (CCA) and Jobs for the Future and explains their roles in the movement to classify developmental coursework as a barrier for students and to tie state funding to retention rates. These organizations promote the elimination of developmental courses, increased supplemental instruction for credit-bearing courses, and the implementation of financial incentives that reward universities for graduating students. Mangan provides testimonies from advocates of the organizations supported by Gates, as well as critiques from developmental educators who suggest that these efforts bypass academic experts and ignore the socioeconomic factors often associated with students who need additional assistance. Mangan concludes her report with a sobering graphic that illustrates the number of states that are members of the CCA alliance and states that have implemented or are transitioning to performance-based funding.

Basic Writers: Who We Teach

64   Adler-Kassner, Linda. "Just Writing, Basically: Basic Writers on Basic Writing." *Journal of Basic Writing* 18.2 (1999): 69–90. Print.

At the University of Michigan–Dearborn, Adler-Kassner and her colleague Randy Woodland interviewed sixteen randomly chosen students about basic writers and basic writing. Adler-Kassner identifies three issues that emerged from the students' responses. First, employing coursework designed to erase the stigma of being labeled a basic writer is a difficult endeavor because most students do not fully understand what that label means. In addition, students in the study tended to equate writing and reading with English courses only and found their composition coursework to be irrelevant to their purpose for attending college. Finally, instead of blaming grammatical conventions for their status as basic writers, these students spoke of an inability to transfer the thoughts in their heads onto paper successfully. Adler-Kassner states that we must address these issues when designing our basic writing courses and that we must first explain to students what this *basic writer* label means. After understanding the label, the students need to work to contest it. This may be accomplished through inquiry-based research during the class.

65   Adler-Kassner, Linda. "Review: Structure and Possibility: New Scholarship about Students-Called-Basic-Writers." *College English* 63.2 (2000): 229–43. Print.

Adler-Kassner discusses five important books that either explore basic writing and basic writers directly (Susan Gardner and Toby Fulwiler's *The Book for Teachers of At-Risk College Writers*, Laura Gray-Rosendale's *Rethinking Basic Writing* [77], and Michelle Hall Kells and Valerie Balester's *Attending to the Margins*) or provide historical and social arguments relevant to theorizing and questioning the concept of basic writing (Bradford T. Stull's *Amid the Fall, Dreaming of Eden* and Paulo Freire's *Pedagogy of Freedom*). Adler-Kassner notes that research about basic writing students has changed from dwelling on what is wrong with basic writers to questioning the academic and social structures that perpetuate the "idea" of a basic writer. She finds that most of these books adopt the latter stance.

66   Bartholomae, David. "The Study of Error." *College Composition and Communication* 31.3 (1980): 253–69. Print.

Bartholomae extends Mina Shaughnessy's hope that teachers, especially basic writing teachers, will examine how they view errors in student writing. For example, he suggests that teachers who cannot understand student prose do not read the prose as complex texts and thus do not find the logic at work in many errors. Bartholomae demonstrates this point by showing the logic behind some student writing, drawing especially from the work of "John," who caught and corrected many of his errors while reading his paper aloud. Bartholomae ultimately offers a glimpse as to the effectiveness of error analysis and what it should accomplish: "It begins with the double perspective of text and reconstructed text and seeks to explain the difference between the two" (265). Overall, basic writing teachers need to separate performance from competence and focus on how to help students create strategies to accomplish each.

67   Bartholomae, David. "Writing on the Margins: The Concept of Literacy in Higher Education." *A Sourcebook for Basic Writing Teachers*. Ed. Theresa Enos. New York: Random, 1987. 66–83. Print.

Marginal writers differ from mainstream writers in the number and kinds of their grammatical errors and also in their methods of organizing, producing, and using texts. The precise nature of the fluency that separates marginal from mainstream academic literacy is explored in this examination of "borderline" texts. Beginning with Mina Shaughnessy's error analysis of basic writers' approximations of conventional sentences, Bartholomae argues that basic writers' use of language follows similar "styles of being wrong" (68). Academic literacy can be measured by the extent to which writers can appropriate the historical and social conventions of an already existing university discourse. Using historical and recent examples, the author analyzes writers' attempts to appropriate the language of the academy and suggests that basic writers should be assigned academic projects that will position them within its accepted discourses. Advanced literacy extends beyond the ability to use academic conventions successfully to a consciousness of speaking through appropriated forms and the capacity to push against them.

68   Bay, Libby. "Twists, Turns, and Returns: Returning Adult Students." *Teaching Developmental Writing: Background Readings*. Ed. Susan Naomi Bernstein. Boston: Bedford, 2001. 167–75. Print.

Bay reports on a research project that she conducted involving students over the age of twenty-four at Rockland Community College in Suffern, New York. Based on responses to questionnaires and one-on-one interviews, Bay concludes that adult students need help dealing with the unique issues they face when returning to school and that faculty and the school itself need help understanding and addressing adult students' needs. She recommends granting credit for adult students' life experiences and requiring a separate orientation to help adult students deal with time management and other issues that they face.

69   Bernstein, Susan Naomi. "A Limestone Way of Learning." *Chronicle of Higher Education*. 10 Oct. 2003: n. pag. Web. 21 May 2014.

Bernstein uses her personal experience in an introductory geology class to argue for the continued importance of basic writing classes at the university level—classes whose place in the college curriculum is being questioned both from within the university and from without. She also uses this experience to suggest how instructors might approach teaching a basic writing class. She explains that her early difficulty with nonverbal learning, in high school science and math classes, might have held her education back significantly had she not been born to a middle-class, suburban family. The benefit of expressive, creative assignments allowed her to capitalize on her writing ability, which either hid or compensated for her other learning difficulties. Bernstein thus argues that the challenge writing presents for students in basic writing classes encourages them to grow, personally and intellectually, just as her geology class challenged her and gave her a lifelong appreciation of the field. Likewise, the challenge for teachers of basic writers is to assume that they are eager and motivated learners and to support a holistic model of learning. Rather than define basic writers by the skills they lack, teachers must look to their strengths and to what they have overcome to reach their current position. Bernstein concludes that the benefits students can gain by being challenged through writing classes extend past the writing classroom to strengthen and enrich their world, both inside and outside the university.

70   Bizzell, Patricia. "Literacy in Culture and Cognition." A *Sourcebook for Basic Writing Teachers*. Ed. Theresa Enos. New York: Random, 1987. 125–37. Print.

Bizzell suggests that literacy scholarship is commonly divided into two main schools of thought: those who embrace the "Great Cognitive Divide" theory, which posits that the acquisition of literacy is a stage in human cognitive development, and those who question this theory and focus instead on literacy as social practice. This latter group demonstrates that literacy ought not be treated monolithically but rather examined within social and cultural contexts. In applying literacy research to the question of whether American college students are literate, Bizzell argues for a definition of academic literacy that takes into account its social context and its specific social purposes. While debate continues about literacy of any kind, functional literacy — "literacy that confers a reasonable degree of education and economic success and political participation" (135) — enables critical reflection on the different relations between social groups and on the educational, economic, and political differences that separate them.

71   DiPardo, Anne. "'Whispers of Coming and Going': Lessons from Fannie." *Teaching Developmental Writing: Background Readings*. 3rd ed. Ed. Susan Naomi Bernstein. Boston: Bedford, 2007. 440–57. Print.

DiPardo's case study of Fannie, a struggling Native American student in a basic writing tutorial program, illustrates the ways in which multicultural writers and linguistic minority students — and often their teachers and tutors as well — must occupy multiple roles as they work together to navigate the terrain of academic literacy. Echoing previous calls by Shaughnessy, Hull, and Rose that entreat teachers both to listen to and learn from their students, the lessons of Fannie and her writing tutor, Morgan, emphasize the importance of relationship-building when working with basic writers. To this end, DiPardo argues that teachers and tutors must be adequately prepared to engage in a process of true collaborative learning: "More than specific instructional strategies, Morgan needed the conceptual grounding that would allow her to understand that authentically collaborative learning is predicated upon fine-grained insight into individual students" (456). Finally, DiPardo notes that reflective practice, including the willingness to interrogate one's approaches and actions critically and consistently, is a key part of such collaborative learning both for the student and the teacher, who must model these strategies in his or her relationship with the basic writer.

72   Eves-Bowden, Anmarie. "What Basic Writers Think about Writing." *Journal of Basic Writing* 20.2 (2001): 71–87. Print.

Eves-Bowden chronicles her study of seven basic writers at a California college, examining how they perceive themselves as writers, how they view their writing processes, and how their writing processes "might limit [their] ability to succeed on a typical college writing assignment" (71). Eves-Bowden discovered that these writers did have a writing process but that it was neither complex nor structured in any way. Most of the students admitted that they had no idea of what to say about an assigned topic, of how to generate any ideas, or of what revision entailed. As a result of her study, Eves-Bowden integrated Linda Flower and John Hayes's "cognitive process model" because of "its easy-to-follow diagram and simple explanations of each recursive step" (76). This particular approach provided her students with a structure from which they could "explore their beliefs, expectations, and perspectives" (81).

73   Fox, Tom. "Basic Writing as Cultural Conflict." *Journal of Education* 172.1 (1990): 65–83. Print.

Fox foregrounds the relationship between basic writing theories and the pedagogies that continue to marginalize students new to universities, including speakers of nonstandard English and, frequently, African Americans. Unfolding the pedagogical ideologies perpetuated by even the most well-meaning teachers, Fox illuminates inequities between the students' use of literacy to negotiate social identities and the institutions' authoritative positioning. He suggests that although recent explorations into discourse communities reveal differences and offer more helpful explanations, resultant pedagogies continue to be ineffective in dislodging the ideologies in which basic writing programs have been grounded. John Ogbu's theory of oppositional culture is offered as a more comprehensive ideological framework that "emphasizes the issues of historically based discrimination and the association of literacy as an instrument of domination" (74). As evidence of a need for a new consciousness in the classroom and political activism within the institution, Fox includes an essay, complete with "errors," written by a student in a basic writing course. He then describes how, in spite of the surface errors, the essay "is a successful piece of academic work" in its use of literacy to "explore and discover connections and conflicts" (80) among the social contexts the student inhabits.

74   Gray-Rosendale, Laura. "Back to the Future: Contextuality and the Construction of the Basic Writer's Identity in *JBW*, 1999–2005." *Journal of Basic Writing* 25.2 (2006): 5–27. Print.

In a continuation of her previous historical review of the *JBW*'s collective construct of basic writing students' identities, Gray-Rosendale asserts that three major shifts now dominate the *JBW*'s scholarly landscape of basic writing students' identity construction. The most important shift in this construction repositions much of the scholarly activity as deconstructing locally contingent and place-specific influences, a move that places identity formation "as *in situ*—or context dependent" (8). The second shift suggests that basic writing students have been cast as reformers of theory, academic discourse, and history. The author synthesizes a growing number of scholars who argue that this construction of identity reveals a growing need to reflect on our own scholarship, and especially those representations of implied and explicit powers held by students to reform institutions and themselves. The third shift in scholarship seems to distract attention away from the construction of students' identities and instead moves toward the formalized study of students' personal habits and practices and asks what these practices reveal about the personal, institutional, and political conditions of the basic writing student and how we might use these studies to enrich basic writing scholarship.

75   Gray-Rosendale, Laura. "Inessential Writings: Shaughnessy's Legacy in a Socially Constructed Landscape." *Journal of Basic Writing* 17.2 (1998): 43–75. Print.

Min-Zhan Lu's 1992 article "Conflict and Struggle: The Enemies or Preconditions of Basic Writing?" [269] inspired a flurry of feminist, Marxist, and poststructuralist reexaminations of Mina Shaughnessy's work. These critiqued Shaughnessy on three counts: for forwarding an "essentialist" conception of language that separates thought from expression and views discourse as a transparent vessel for meaning; for promoting basic writers' accommodation to mainstream linguistic standards and thereby minimizing the political dimensions of language use; and for overlooking materialist considerations such as the economic, social, and institutional issues surrounding basic writers and the teaching of basic writing. Gray-Rosendale systematically explores each of these charges through close readings of critics' and Shaughnessy's texts and ultimately concludes that "Shaughnessy's works render ambiguous if not outright defy many such negative characterizations" (46).

76   Gray-Rosendale, Laura. "Investigating Our Discursive History: *JBW* and the Construction of the 'Basic Writer's' Identity." *Journal of Basic Writing* 18.2 (1999): 108–35. Print.

Focusing on research that has appeared in the *Journal of Basic Writing*, Gray-Rosendale reviews the history of basic writing and describes how this history has influenced the construction of basic writers' identities. She discusses how trends such as the growth, initiation, and conflict metaphors have influenced the way that the scholarship defined basic writers. Lastly, Gray-Rosendale discusses the current state of the basic writer's identity in basic writing scholarship and points toward the future of basic writers in our research.

77   Gray-Rosendale, Laura. *Rethinking Basic Writing: Exploring Identity, Politics, and Community in Interaction.* Mahwah: Erlbaum, 2000. Print.

Gray-Rosendale introduces her study by asking, "Who is the Basic Writer?" Quickly declaring that this question is not useful, she asks, "What can and does the Basic Writer do?" (5). In addressing this generative question, Gray-Rosendale explores students' agency in an array of literacy tasks. She begins by using poststructural, ethnographic, and conversational theories for her analysis of a summer "bridge" course at Syracuse University designed for students considered "at risk by the higher administration" (1) for failure in first-year composition. She then focuses on the interactions of the four students in one peer group in the class, analyzing their conversations about drafts of papers and showing how these students helped each other to make informed and remarkably diverse choices as they composed. After demonstrating some motivations for students' writing, she offers suggestions for teachers, administrators, and legislators.

78   Gray-Rosendale, Laura. "Revising the Political in Basic Writing Scholarship." *Journal of Basic Writing* 15.2 (1996): 24–49. Print.

Gray-Rosendale suggests that focusing on a definition of basic writers interferes with developing a complete, sound pedagogy. She argues that basic writers' definitions of themselves do not match those of basic writing faculty or higher-education administration, that their reflections of self have been largely ignored, and that their constructions of identity must be placed in the forefront. Her analysis of a conversation among four Syracuse University students during a reader review of a politically charged writing assignment demonstrates the complexities of these constructions. Gray-Rosendale recommends that studies of in-class interactions be done to determine how the students "construct new identities" (47). Such extended examination of student interactions is the next step for basic writing as a discipline.

79   Gray-Rosendale, Laura, Loyola K. Bird, and Judith F. Bullock. "Rethinking the Basic Writing Frontier: Native American Students' Challenge to Our Histories." *Journal of Basic Writing* 22.1 (2003): 71–106. Print.

The three authors draw on their own experiences—as an administrator of a program serving many Native American basic writers (Gray-Rosendale), as a Jicarilla Apache Indian formerly classified as a basic writer and currently a graduate student in English (Bird), and as a tutor of Native American basic writers in a boarding high school (Bullock)—to challenge assumptions made about Native American writers and metaphors used in basic writing scholarship. The authors contend that many Native Americans face difficulties with college writing because researchers have ignored them in basic writing research and because the "myth of frontierism" (74) informs both basic writing studies and American ideology. Metaphors like "frontier," "pioneer," and "insider/outsider" (75), frequently used in basic writing, are based on a pioneer mentality in which the civilized university culture tames and assimilates the uncivilized Native Americans. The absence of a sustained critique of these metaphors and of the ways they are used to frame understandings of writers has led to an essentialist view of Native American students of English as foreign language students largely unfamiliar with the culture of the academy. The authors urge teachers, administrators, and scholars to elicit stories from their Native American students by meeting on "Indian land" as "settlers" rather than "pioneers" (83).

80   Gruber, Sibylle. "On the Other Side of the Electronic Circuit: A Virtual Remapping of Border Crossings." *Journal of Basic Writing* 18.1 (1999): 55–75. Print.

Gruber questions the simplistic categorizing of students into majority and minority in this case study of an African American student's participation in a basic writing class's online discussions. Depending on the context of the discussion, the student occupies multiple subject positions—an ethnic minority, a majority male, and a minority homosexual—while recognizing the connection between being a gay black man in a white, patriarchal, homophobic society. Gruber argues that teachers must avoid homogenizing nontraditional students and must recognize the multiple and complicated subjectivities reflected in their language use in online communities.

81   Harrington, Susanmarie. "The Representation of Basic Writers in Basic Writing Scholarship, or Who Is Quentin Pierce?" *Journal of Basic Writing* 18.2 (1999): 91–107. Print.

Harrington examines the research published in volumes 1–17 of the *Journal of Basic Writing* by reviewing trends in research topics. She reveals the tendency in the research to focus on teacher expectations rather than on student needs. The article argues that the research could be enriched by considering students and their voices when conducting and writing research.

82   Hull, Glynda, et al. "Remediation as Social Construct: Perspectives from an Analysis of Classroom Discourse." *College Composition and Communication* 42.3 (1991): 299–329. Print.

Explanations for the low achievement of some students have pointed to deficits within the student (via the student's character, intellect, environment, or culture). Thus instructors working with remedial writers will easily enter a cycle in which they (1) ascribe a student's nonmainstream behaviors to a cognitive or social deficit, (2) construct their interaction with the student in response to that perceived deficit, and (3) limit the kinds of interactions and activities students are allowed in the classroom. Such limitations subsequently serve to eliminate discourse and activities that would disprove the deficit label or move the student and teacher beyond it. Evidence of this cycle is offered through analysis of classroom interactions between June, a well-trained writing instructor, and Maria, a student whose style of conversational turn-taking does not match that valued by June. This case, in which June constructs Maria as a remedial, scattered thinker—despite the cogency of much of Maria's commentary and her history of achievement in academic and literary pursuits—shows that teachers must pay closer attention to the complex dynamics surrounding classroom talk to avoid making misleading judgments about students' abilities and deficits.

83   Kutz, Eleanor, Suzy Q. Groden, and Vivian Zamel. *The Discovery of Competence: Teaching and Learning with Diverse Student Writers*. Portsmouth: Heinemann, 1993. Print.

Over a ten-year period, the authors collaborated on a research project that engaged their urban basic writing students, whose primary language was not English, in the work of an academic community. In this book, the authors focus on how language is acquired; how teachers can facilitate students' development of this acquisition; how culture is represented through language; how thinking, speaking, and writing develop; how active inquiry facilitates these understandings; and how curricula can provide the necessary context for this learning to occur. Through their research, the authors recognized that students learn the structure of writing and language through active engagement and practice with written language in a collaborative environment in which they are expected to build on their knowledge and reflect on their learning processes.

84   Lunsford, Andrea A. "Cognitive Development and the Basic Writer." *College English* 41.1 (1979): 38–46. Print.

Based on her study of basic writers at The Ohio State University, Lunsford argues that basic writers have not attained the level of cognitive development required to succeed at college-level work. Because they have not developed the cognitive ability to decenter themselves to perform tasks that require synthesis and analysis, basic writers have difficulty articulating abstract concepts. Lunsford recommends that basic writing teachers use various strategies, ranging from grammar- and sentence-building activities to essay assignments, to engage students in inferential reasoning rather than in isolated drill exercises and rule memorization. Working in small group workshops, basic writing students should be allowed to practice analyzing, generalizing, and then abstracting, all of which are skills that they need to succeed in college.

85   Minot, Walter S., and Kenneth R. Gamble. "Self-Esteem and Writing Apprehension of Basic Writers: Conflicting Evidence." *Journal of Basic Writing* 10.2 (1991): 116–24. Print.

The notion that self-esteem and writing apprehension can define basic writers as a distinct homogenous group is challenged by the results of an empirical study. Basic writing programs do not seem to acknowledge that basic writing students are a heterogeneous population with diverse, individual writing difficulties; instead, it labels them as a predictable, constant group. This study looked at sixteen sections of regular composition and three sections of basic writing, and the data gathered indicate the potential that self-esteem and writing apprehension may have in writing situations. Remarkably, one basic writing section "had lower writing apprehension and higher self-esteem than sixteen classes of regular composition" (121). These results suggest that conflating self-esteem and writing apprehension limits the affective, cognitive, developmental, social, and cultural influences and expectations that basic writers bring to their writing. Rather than dismissing self-esteem and writing apprehension, however, this study calls for more research and writing on the "emotional atmosphere" (122) that surrounds the different writing situations of basic writers and on the role of teachers within this affective space.

86   Mutnick, Deborah. *Writing in an Alien World: Basic Writing and the Struggle for Equality in Higher Education.* Portsmouth: Boynton, 1996. Print.

Mutnick profiles four older, urban, minority basic writing students who take an intensive six-credit basic reading and writing course for two terms. Each case study focuses on a piece of writing the student chooses and on related interviews with the student, the instructor, and sometimes other instructors. The papers, handwritten or typed, are reproduced in the book with instructor comments. Both students and teachers are asked to read the papers aloud and comment on the text while reading. Thus a dialogue "between the written texts and the 'metacommentary'" (xxi) is created. Student writers and writing teachers are asked similar questions about their family backgrounds, educational experiences, roles as student or teacher, and what "being a writer" and "learning to write" mean to them. Mutnick also describes her own background and attitudes. In essence, the study compares the "readings" of the various participants: the basic writing students who composed the texts, instructors' readings of those texts, and Mutnick's readings of the texts and of the overall situation.

87   Piorkowski, Joan L., and Erika Scheurer. "'It Is the Way That They Talk to You': Increasing Agency in Basic Writers through a Social Context of Care." *Journal of Basic Writing* 19.2 (2000): 72–92. Print.

The authors conducted interviews and designed a questionnaire to portray two kinds of basic writers: those who became more confident in acquiring agency over their work and those who remained relatively distrustful of available assistance. Susan McLeod's work on the role of affective factors in writing and Chris M. Anson's interpretation of William Perry's categories of cognitive development of college-level students are used to back up the authors' findings that students' perception of their instructors' care is as important to students' success as their understanding of feedback and acceptance of assistance with their work. The study also reveals how students use other sources (friends, peers) when they do not trust the ones that are available in writing centers. Students' responsibility for their writing, the authors conclude, comes in response to a surrounding context that includes care.

88   Rose, Mike. "Narrowing the Mind and Page: Remedial Writers and Cognitive Reductionism." *College Composition and Communication* 39.3 (1988): 267–300. Print.

Rose summarizes trends in cognitive science—field dependence and independence, brain hemispherics, Jean Piaget's stages of cognitive development, and orality and literacy—and discusses their implications for writing instruction. His social constructivist perspective drives this analysis, and he reveals severe limitations for the practical application of any of these cognitive theories, which have caused stereotyping and the privileging of certain styles because of cultural biases, to writing instruction. Rose's research clarifies the problems associated with attempting to read writing through the limited lens of clinical psychological research. Class, race, gender, and other differences must be considered in the results, since social factors such as these "should not automatically be assumed to reflect 'pure' cognitive differences but rather effects that may well be conditioned by and interpreted in lieu of historical, sociopolitical realities" (297).

89   Shaughnessy, Mina P. "Diving In: An Introduction to Basic Writing." *College Composition and Communication* 27.3 (1976): 234–39. Print.

In the partnership between teachers and basic writers, the basic writer is perceived as the party who progresses. Discussion thus centers on student needs and attitudes rather than teacher changes that may be the key to student progress. Teacher transformation at various stages of working with basic writers is described through metaphor in a developmental scale. In the stage called Guarding the Tower, teachers are committed to protecting academic tradition from unprepared interlopers; in Converting the Natives, teachers come to perceive basic writers as empty vessels capable of learning the mechanics of language and essay structure; in Sounding the Depths, teachers shift from studying the students to studying writing as a behavior, error as a revealing logic, and the role of teacher as pedagogical planner; and in Diving In, teachers realize and accept the need to remediate themselves regarding the needs and learning styles of basic writers.

90   Sternglass, Marilyn S. "The Changing Perception of the Role of Writing: From Basic Writing to Discipline Courses." *Basic Writing e-Journal* 2.2 (2000): n. pag. Web. 21 May 2014.

Drawing on a six-year longitudinal study at an urban university, Sternglass uses the comments of several students to show how they used writing to learn. Students revealed that writing was helpful to memory tasks. Writing, they reported, helped them with critical tasks, such as criticism, analysis, and assessment. Students' comments and results from the study suggest that critical abilities develop gradually. Exposing the students to and having them use academic language helped basic writing students develop the analytical abilities expected in upper-level courses. When students commented on how the process of learning through writing helped throughout their college years, they discussed how early reliance on textbook language led to their later ability to put their own ideas into words. Sternglass suggests writing assignments that allow basic writing students to practice analytical tasks. She also suggests reading assignments that relate general issues to students' own experiences and writing tasks that help students understand concepts as well as language.

91   Sternglass, Marilyn S. *Time to Know Them: A Longitudinal Study of Writing and Learning at the College Level.* Mahwah: Erlbaum, 1997. Print.

Sternglass's book is a six-year study of college writers enrolled in one of three courses at the City College of New York in the fall of 1989: two levels of basic writing and one first-year composition course. Fifty-three students initially agreed to participate in the study. Sternglass provides extensive background information for nine students and detailed case studies of five of these students. In a heartening report that counters negative assessments of at-risk students' success rates, Sternglass reports that by June 1996, 66 percent of these students had either graduated from college or were still enrolled. The case studies focus both on the complex, arduous path that students must take through college and on students' encounters with writing and learning in their college courses. Based on these observations, Sternglass encourages composition teachers to develop courses and assignments that fully articulate how facts and details support claims. The institutional and instructional contexts for student learning also receive careful attention. Sternglass demonstrates the importance of teacher commentary that addresses surface-level issues but also focuses on the rhetorical realms of content, ideas, and complexity. Sternglass observes courses across the disciplines and suggests that supportive but rigorous instruction will encourage students to succeed.

92   Stygall, Gail. "Resisting Privilege: Basic Writing and Foucault's Author Function." *College Composition and Communication* 45.3 (1994): 320–41. Print.

Michel Foucault's author function becomes a conceptual structure to show how basic writers are constructed and inscribed by institutions. Teachers of basic writers should resist reinscription of institutional norms through questioning and challenging how the author function positions basic writers in the English department and in the university. Specifically, Stygall explores how certain discursive practices support the academically privileged and how those discursive practices are ignored or used specifically to privilege a certain group. Stygall describes a research project that studied correspondence between graduate student teachers in the author's teacher development class and basic writing students from a different university. This research began with the hope that teachers could avoid reinscribing basic writers by becoming aware of the discursive practices that reinforced this notion. The research explored the social and institutional pressures that basic writers and the teachers faced with such a correspondence. Stygall concludes the essay with a reflection on the research project as well as some information about what the teachers in this study have done to change their perceptions of basic writers.

93   Tinberg, Howard. "Teaching in the Spaces Between: What Basic Writing Students Can Teach Us." *Journal of Basic Writing* 17.2 (1998): 76–90. Print.

Tinberg points out that both the political right and the intellectual left have criticized the basic writing enterprise. Basic writing students are largely silent during these debates, even though the outcomes directly impact them. In writing about literacy and education, Tinberg's basic writers demonstrate an understanding of the complexity of the terms and teach him to "reconsider the value of non-school learning" (83). Basic writing instruction must challenge and respect the unique knowledge and logic that basic writers bring to the classroom. A productive turn for basic writing research, Tinberg suggests, would be to begin asking the crucial question, "Whose responsibility is it to promote broad-based literacy in this nation?" (89).

94   Villanueva, Victor. "Theory in the Basic Writing Classroom? A Practice." *Journal of Basic Writing* 16.1 (1997): 79–90. Print.

Villanueva argues that teachers should view their basic writers not as cognitively deficient but, instead, as individuals who need to connect what they know with what the academy wants them to know. When Villanueva began scholarship in composition, most studies of basic writers reflected a cognitivist perspective. This research made claims about basic writers, suggesting they were basic because of their lack of cognitive abilities. The author questions this notion and considers how he could encourage basic writers, help them believe in their abilities with writing and language, and show them respect for who they are as learners, thinkers, and writers. To demonstrate his approach to basic writing, he provides a script of the first day of class. He is careful to show various student responses to his script and hopes that the ones who stay realize that, as college students, they need to learn certain conventions.

95   Virtanen, Beth L. "Brad, Sean, and James: Saying What They Mean in Voices That Sound Like Themselves." *Open Words: Access and English Studies* 1.1 (2006): 9–26. Print.

Virtanen shares a case study of three students in order to foreground an otherwise silenced and erased perspective from higher education — that of working-class students. Virtanen traces the students' entrance to college after earning GEDs; all three students attended open-enrollment institutions and then later transferred to four-year universities. Working-class students, as Ira Shor and Mike Rose attest, often undergo negotiations between home culture language use and the middle-class discourses and argumentation they encounter in higher education. For Brad, Sean, and James, negotiation enables them to experience a process of becoming accepted members of higher education, partly a process of self-acceptance, without having to erase their home histories and values. Virtanen raises important questions about curriculum design, student audience, and access to higher education. She asks how teachers can function as a bridge between curriculum and students to make the classroom meaningful to multiple learners, including those who have historically been denied access to higher education.

Literacy and Basic Writing

96   Bernstein, Susan Naomi. "Material Realities in the Basic Writing Classroom: Intersections of Discovery for Young Women Reading *Persepolis 2.*" *Journal of Basic Writing* 27.1 (2008): 80–104. Print.

At the end of open admissions in the University of Cincinnati, students in a first-year, first-quarter basic writing class explore the intersectionality of their own lives as they relate to Marjane Satrapi's experience portrayed in *Persepolis*. The article begins by looking at literacy and reading in the work of Deborah Hicks and Tami K. Dolan in studying younger girls' reading practices near the university. It highlights and discusses the work of five women in the class who find recognition of their own narratives through close reading, writing, and designing curricula with the instructor. Although similarities between Marjane and the students in this class are hard to find, the resonance of her character as one of "resilience and resistance" allows students to make assertions about their own identity and how they move within the larger world of family, work, and the academy through writing.

97   Biser, Eileen, Linda Rubel, and Rose Marie Toscano. "Be Careful What You Ask For: When Basic Writers Take the Rhetorical Stage." *Journal of Basic Writing* 21.1 (2002): 52–70. Print.

The authors argue that if basic writers are to effect social change through their writing, they must be taught how to read critically the range of social, economic, political, cultural, and ideological perspectives of their audiences—intended and unintended—and how to explore the limitations and benefits of textual forms available for response. Noting that basic writers are also basic readers who apply only a personal interpretive frame to texts, the authors analyze a deaf student's failed attempt to effect social change on her campus and conclude that the student's attempt failed because they, her instructors, failed pedagogically to move beyond a romanticized notion of effecting public change through public rhetorical acts.

98   Brammer, Charlotte. "Linguistic Cultural Capital and Basic Writers." *Journal of Basic Writing* 21.1 (2002): 16–36. Print.

Brammer suggests that basic writers are linguistic outsiders who lack the cultural capital for success in academe because they use oral-discourse patterns that reveal their ethnic, geographic, and economic backgrounds. She argues that instructors should accept Standard Written English as a dialect and mine second-language acquisition studies and literacy studies to better teach linguistic variations. Brammer contends that students need explicit instruction in language variation and in rhetorical strategies that are part of academic discourse but that might be different from students' own oral strategies. She recommends that writing instructors focus on metacognitive activities; strategies at the essay, paragraph, and sentence levels that will support students; and critical reading and analysis, syntactic cohesion, and grammar.

99   Bruch, Patrick L., and Thomas Reynolds. "Critical Literacy and Basic Writing Textbooks: Teaching toward a More Just Literacy." *Basic Writing e-Journal* 2.1 (2000): n. pag. Web. 21 May 2014.

Bruch and Reynolds examine two texts (*Creating America: Reading and Writing Assignments*, by Joyce Moser and Ann Watters, and *Cultural Attractions/Cultural Distractions: Cultural Literacy in Contemporary Contexts*, by Libby Allison and Kristine L. Blair) to assess the possibility for a "more just literacy" (par. 2) through the influence of cultural studies on basic English. Calling on the definition and discussion of critical literacy put forward by James Berlin and Michael Vivion in *Cultural Studies in the English Classroom*, they suggest that cultural studies theory provides the means to discover gaps in cultural representation but does not automatically provide a satisfactory remedy. Turning to the two selected textbooks, Bruch and Reynolds contend that they and many others fail to examine "institutionally valued literacies and justifications for racial hierarchies" (par. 19). Adding material to a textbook is insufficient if literacy itself, or the valued forms of writing taught to students, remains unexamined. Thus, Moser and Watters's addition of minority authors, for example, does not change what counts for literacy.

100   Carter, Shannon. "Redefining Literacy as a Social Practice." *Journal of Basic Writing* 25.2 (2006): 94–125. Print.

In this essay, Carter deplores the pervasive skills-based instruction in basic writing classes, as well as the ubiquitous "teach to the state-mandated standardized test" pedagogy that all too many basic writing classes have. She proposes a "pedagogy of rhetorical dexterity," informed by New Literary Studies and activity theory, through which basic writing students "develop the flexibility and skill necessary to negotiate multiple, always changing literacies." The article includes assignments and student writing for those assignments.

101   Collins, James. "'The Troubled Text': History and Language in American Basic Writing Programs." *Knowledge, Culture, and Power: International Perspectives on Literacy as Policy and Practice*. Ed. Peter Freebody and Anthony R. Welch. London: Falmer, 1993. 162–86. Print.

Collins situates a study of two basic writing courses within the broader tensions surrounding the role of education. He begins by tracing the birth of the liberal arts curriculum as an attempt to inculcate students into the values reflected in the curriculum and to stifle public debate. As a result of twentieth-century attacks on this original purpose of the liberal arts, universities have moved to "cafeteria-style" approaches where writing is often the only core "skill" that runs throughout. Yet basic writing courses and programs disrupt the elite character of the university. Next, Collins describes two basic writing classes that reflect the "skill-based" nature of writing and basic writing's potential. In one class, students wrote primarily from and about experience and were confused about vague assignments that provided little guidance about how to read "experience" within broader contextual frameworks. In the other class, the instructor developed assignments rooted in specific experiences of race, and students became invested in the assignments and wrote copiously. This course was also challenging because of the limitations imposed by institutional constraints—both the instructor's time and the limits of acceptable discourse within institutions. Collins then places both approaches within a broader context of literacy and literacy crisis, suggesting that instructors must be attentive to the institutional and social contexts that shape how literacy is defined and enacted in various contexts.

102   Deming, Mary P. "Reading and Writing: Making the Connection for Basic Writers." *Basic Writing e-Journal* 2.2 (2000): n. pag. Web. 21 May 2014.

Deming views writing and reading as complementary components in basic writing courses. She contends that programs that eliminate the teaching of critical reading from their basic writing curriculum need to reexamine this practice. Drawing from Robert Tierney and P. David Pearson's "Toward a Composing Model of Reading," Deming applies their process model of composition to reading patterns by citing specific classroom examples. The four steps of this reading model—planning, drafting, aligning, and revising—illustrate Deming's argument that the structures of reading comprehension and process writing are too closely linked to be separated. True critical interaction between the students' lives and their worlds is a goal of a college education; for students to achieve this goal, both reading and writing instruction need to be expanded at all levels of college.

103   Dickson, Marcia. "Learning to Read/Learning to Write." *Basic Writing e-Journal* 1.1 (1999): n. pag. Web. 21 May 2014.

Basic readers in college already know how to read well for pleasure, but they lack the schemata and experience to read challenging nonfiction texts in a critical way. Dickson notes that since many basic college readers approach texts from the formulaic topic sentence/support structural pattern, they often misread or dismiss texts that rely on subtle organization or sarcastic tones. Dickson outlines typical problems that basic readers have with text perceptions and lists practical teaching steps that can help instructors lead students toward more complex and critical reading comprehension. She also includes a helpful list of possible "non-textbook" reading texts and their corresponding classroom goals.

104   Goto, Stanford T. "Basic Writing and Policy Reform: Why We Keep Talking Past Each Other." *Journal of Basic Writing* 21.2 (2001): 1–20. Print.

Goto contends that the argument over the place of basic writing programs in universities is the result of the disparate world views of supporters and critics of those programs. Each, he says, espouses a different
philosophy of education. Goto suggests that until those who teach basic
writing learn to use the language of the policy makers to convey the
importance of basic writing classes, programs for basic writers will be
cut. Through an analysis of the literature, Goto shows that basic writing critics believe it is not possible to maintain high standards while
allowing open access. These critics view education as a vertical or
linear construct where students master information at one level before
moving on to a higher level of learning. Goto suggests that critics, be-
lieving that it is up to the student to adapt to the university, have not
attempted innovative practices to help basic writers reach the expected
level of writing skills. Equally important, these critics use statistical
or quantitative methodologies to assess the success or failure of basic
writing students, often analyzing any data they gather in terms of cost
benefits. Supporters of basic writing, on the other hand, believe that
these programs maintain both access and standards. They see education
as horizontal, as a matter of width, not depth. They have instituted new
instructional practices because they view students who need remediation not as deficient but as requiring different strategies to learn. They
use qualitative methodologies to describe the success rate of basic writing students, and they present the individual success of students as the
real benefit of the programs. This new method of viewing the critics
and supporters of basic writing programs should be used to improve the
discussion of the value of basic writing programs.

105   Hodges, Russ, Michele L. Simpson, and Norman A. Stahl, eds. *Teaching Study Strategies in Developmental Education: Readings on Theory, Research, and Best Practice*. Boston: Bedford, 2012. Print.

The strengths of this text are its comprehensive coverage of material addressing the importance of supplemental instruction and the
impact it can have on all students—developmental students in particular—whether these courses are taught as an adjunct course or
embedded in course content. The text addresses the issue that many of
the students entering postsecondary institutions do not know how to
learn in the postsecondary environment, as it requires different study
methods from high school courses. The text highlights the current need
for postsecondary learning institutions to shift from an instructional
paradigm, which places the responsibility for learning completely upon
the student, to a learning paradigm, whereby the institution takes responsibility for meeting the needs of an ever-increasing diverse body of
learners, providing strong evidence that learning-based instruction is
a key to more successful students. While the readings can at times get
bogged down by statistics, researchers and educators both benefit from
the invaluable material and sample offerings of strategies to be incorporated not only by the institution but also in the classroom.

106   Hourigan, Maureen M. *Literacy as Social Exchange: Intersections of Class, Gender and Culture*. Albany: State U of New York P, 1994. Print.

In her initial historical review, Hourigan demonstrates that the literacy crises of the 1970s and 1980s were not new phenomena and that paying attention to a history of literacy problems in America can help to avoid repetition of old remedies that did not work. She then argues that academe must more thoughtfully consider the intersections of class, gender, and culture when thinking of basic writers and their various needs. Hourigan explores the field of basic writing as a site where important work gets done in relation to the literacy debate. However, she notes that discussions of basic writers as outsiders often come from researchers at highly competitive institutions where basic writers, who would be mainstreamed in less competitive schools, are often admitted with "special" status. The result is a skewed portrait of basic writers. Hourigan advocates research at two-year schools to provide a more accurate profile of other basic writing students. Hourigan also examines gender as a marginalizing aspect of literacy crises. Here, she argues that pedagogies focused on gender often ignore and further marginalize nontraditional and non-Western students. She then focuses on intersections between feminism and basic writing pedagogies as well as pedagogies that give voice to students from a variety of cultures. She suggests that all compositionists should attend to intersections of race, class, and gender.

107   Lu, Min-Zhan. "Redefining the Legacy of Mina Shaughnessy: A Critique of the Politics of Linguistic Innocence." *Journal of Basic Writing* 10.1 (1991): 26–40. Print.

Despite the importance of Mina Shaughnessy's *Errors and Expectations* [126], Lu argues that Shaughnessy's pedagogical intentions would have been better served by a theory of language that eschews essentialism and the "politics of linguistic innocence" (27). While pedagogies motivated by the idea of an inherent deep structure of meaning successfully pose the dual challenges of becoming familiar with conventions and of gaining authorial confidence, they fail to offer students a chance to respond to "the potential dissonance between academic discourses and their home discourses" (27). Lu observes that the process of writing in a political and linguistic context of academic convention tends to determine the contingencies of meaning produced by a given student writer. Rethinking the essentialist premises of *Errors and Expectations* allows the possibility of extending Shaughnessy's original open-ended purpose of using the writing classroom to respond to social inequality and cultural marginalization. Therefore, the article goes on to criticize the uses to which Shaughnessy's work has been put by E. D. Hirsch in his New Right rhetoric.

108   Lunsford, Andrea. "Politics and Practices in Basic Writing." *A Sourcebook for Basic Writing Teachers*. Ed. Theresa Enos. New York: Random, 1987. 246–58. Print.

Lunsford responds to the so-called literacy crisis with an overview of the history of "literacy crises" in American universities, a review of certain practices that Lunsford views as "unacceptable or harmful responses" (253) in the education of basic writers, and a review of the practices that she believes constitute a more appropriate response to the condition of basic writers. Lunsford explores the way that basic writing practices have, for more than a century, been overdetermined by "economic, social, and political power" (253) and that, indeed, the so-called current literacy crisis is hardly more than a historical practice of domination and hegemony. Her critique of "bad practices" focuses on a mistaken oversimplification of basic writing courses and an over-attention to correctness, error detection, and unethical labor practices. She endorses challenging students, collaboration, critiquing error within specific writing contexts, requiring smaller class sizes, and customizing the curriculum to learner needs.

109   McCrary, Donald. "Represent, Representin', Representation: The Efficacy of Hybrid Texts in the Writing Classroom." *Journal of Basic Writing* 24.2 (2005): 72–91. Print.

Creatively utilizing techniques from both academic discourses and those discourses too long excluded from our classrooms, such as African American Vernacular, McCrary argues that today's basic writing teachers need to do far more than pay lip service to the value of students' own linguistic competencies. Analyzing popular urban magazines, newspaper articles, scholarly essays, and literary nonfiction, McCrary reveals that we must also make students' home literacies integral components of our writing curricula. To best accomplish this, he contends that more hybrid texts that weave together the autobiographical languages of our popular hip-hop urban landscape with traditional academic languages must be brought into our classrooms. McCrary suggests that doing so will not only go a long way toward actually supporting the linguistic expertise of students long marginalized by the academy; it will also help to foster crucial communities among students from radically different cultural backgrounds. Real basic writing student success will come from hybridization—combining our students' home literacies with those literacies traditionally valued by academic environments, combining popular cultural texts with standard academic texts.

110   Ong, Walter J. "Literacy and Orality in Our Times." *ADE Bulletin* 58 (1978): 1–7. Print.

Describing differences between speaking and writing, Ong sets up a dichotomy between orality and literacy and uses this distinction to explain some of the challenges that students face when developing skills in literate practices. He describes oral culture as loosely structured and emotional and literate culture as analytical and logical. Additionally, Ong sets up a distinction between primary orality, which has not been affected by literate practice, such as the orality of nonliterate cultures, and secondary orality, which is not separate from literate practices but is dependent on them, such as radio and television. He argues that students must move from the spoken form of thought to the written form of thought and explains that because of the influence of oral culture, student writing might resemble the loosely structured form of conversation. Moving to the written form of thought, however, enables students to participate in intense analysis that is not possible in primary oral culture.

111   Robinson, Heather M. "Writing Center Philosophy and the End of Basic Writing: Motivation at the Site of Remediation and Discovery." *Journal of Basic Writing* 28.2 (2009): 70–92. Print.

At the York College Writing Center, the only place where the college does remediation, Robinson surveys basic writers to understand how they use writing centers and how writing centers can best serve them. She finds that they begin extrinsically motivated, concerned with spelling, grammar, and punctuation to obtain the external award of a higher grade. However, repeat sessions allowed basic writers to become more intrinsically motivated, concerned with reading comprehension and invention to better represent their ideas. Because Robinson saw this shift occur at three sessions, she concludes that writing centers can best help basic writers only when the first visit becomes a second visit. Therefore, writing centers should allow basic writers to get their grammar "fixed," as it is a less vulnerable way to ask for help. Robinson concludes that writing center philosophy may not be as useful for supporting basic writers because it does not recognize that sentence-level work can help them enter the discourse community of college from a safe place and eventually lead them to intrinsic motivation, which is Robinson's goal.

112   Roozen, Kevin. "Comedy Stages, Poets Projects, Sports Columns, and *Kinesiology 341*: Illuminating the Importance of Basic Writers' Self-Sponsored Literacies." *Journal of Basic Writing* 31.1 (2012): 99–132. Print.

Students' extracurricular writing has been offered little consideration in basic writing scholarship. After conducting a five-year study on a writing student named "Charles," Roozen finds that this student's upper-division writing—specifically in a kinesiology class—is greatly enhanced by Charles's self-sponsored literacies—that is, in sports journalism, comedy routines, and poetry. Roozen argues that greater attention must be paid to the productive potential of intertextuality between academic and nonacademic literacies. Yet, rather than adopting the attitude that students' self-sponsored literacies ultimately serve their academic interests, Roozen reminds us that these literacies help "basic writers inhabit, remake, reconfigure, even productively disrupt, the densely textual landscapes they traverse throughout the undergraduate curriculum and, more importantly, throughout their lives" (124). Roozen's article is a valuable addition to basic writers' literacy and discourse studies, as well as literacy ethnography.

113   Scott, Jerrie Cobb. "Literacies and Deficits Revisited." *Journal of Basic Writing* 12.1 (1993): 46–56. Print.

Scott identifies two main factors that contribute to the perpetuation of deficit theories in basic writing pedagogy. The first factor is tied to traditional definitions of literacy that focus on the ability to communicate using certain types of privileged discourses. The result of this limited definition is often a pedagogy that oversimplifies content, is boring and irrelevant, and labels marginalized students as deficient. Scott maintains that a broader definition of literacy—one that allows for multiple literacies existing in multiple ways—protects teachers from bringing deficit theories into their instruction. The second factor involves the concept of "uncritical dysconsciousness" (46), the conscious or unconscious "acceptance of culturally sanctioned beliefs that, regardless of intentions, defend the advantages of insiders and the disadvantages of outsiders" (46). Scott argues that there is a resistance to change in pedagogical practices that stems from a lack of change in attitude toward marginalization. She concludes that a "higher level of critical consciousness" (55) can help bring about different approaches to teaching marginalized students that do not focus on deficits. She closes the essay with "think abouts" (55) for readers, intended as strategies for moving toward pedagogical approaches and writing programs that do not depend on deficit models.

114   Soliday, Mary. *The Politics of Remediation: Institutional and Student Needs in Higher Education*. Pittsburgh: U of Pittsburgh P, 2002. Print.

Taking an in-depth look at the history of remediation from the late 1800s through the 1990s, Soliday posits that remediation exists to serve institutional needs and "to resolve social conflicts as they are played out through the educational tier most identified with access to the professional middle class" (1). For students, remedial programs provide extra reading and writing instruction, whereas for institutions, the programs assist with the crisis in admission standards and keep up enrollment when perennial budget problems tighten departmental belts. To illustrate this claim, Soliday constructs her arguments beside a chronological discussion of the transformation of educational institutions, providing relevant examples from her experiences at the City College of New York. In each chapter, she breaks down the history of a central issue while providing the conversation contemporary to each time period. Soliday also brings in other basic writing researchers' work to illustrate the overarching argument that remediation is not new, even when each time period reconceives it as such. Soliday ends the book by raising several more questions to be considered in the field.

115   Stevens, Scott. "Nowhere to Go: Basic Writing and the Scapegoating of Civic Failure." *Journal of Basic Writing* 21.1 (2002): 3–15. Print.

Stevens argues that mandates to reduce remediation rates at California State University campuses have been heralded publicly by administrators as a return to standards but that these mandates result in expelling basic writers. Detailing the local options facing these students, Stevens proposes that the lack of educational choices available to such students is analogous to the institutionalized absence of alternatives for basic writing programs. Moreover, Stevens analyzes the contradictory rhetoric of official policy, linking the elitist return to standards with the ongoing underfunding of public education in California that started in the 1970s and continues today.

Resources

116   Bernstein, Susan Naomi. "BWe 2007: Practice, Professional Development, and Favorite Books." *Basic Writing e-Journal* 6.1 (2007): n. pag. Web. 21 May 2014.

In this introduction to the issue, Bernstein lists some of the favorite readings of basic writing instructors. Essentially comprising a brief annotated bibliography, texts are listed for use in developmental writing classes, in basic writing pedagogy courses, and in a program of individualized, continued professional development of composition faculty. The annotations themselves are notes from instructors who use the texts, describing the nature of the various successes. Also included is a link to a more extensive list of resources inside CompPile.

117   Carter, Shannon. "Graduate Courses in Basic Writing Studies: Recommendations for Teacher Trainers." *Basic Writing e-Journal* 6.1 (2007): n. pag. Web. 21 May 2014.

Carter reviews several graduate-level courses in basic writing studies and finds that one key strategy in designing effective assignments and discussion activities for these classes is to "emphasize both the practical in the theoretical and the theoretical in the practical." She suggests that an "equally important strategy is to present the political in the personal and the personal in the political," and she notes that any involvement in basic writing pedagogy has political implications. Her essay provides overviews of the courses and links to sample syllabi and other materials.

118   Enos, Theresa, ed. *A Sourcebook for Basic Writing Teachers*. New York: Random, 1987. Print.

This collection of forty-two essays (some previously published; others written specifically for this text) includes essays that focus on issues of literacy and cognition, definitions of what basic writing is and how to teach it, ways that error and grammar fit into basic writing classrooms, and pedagogical strategies. The text includes essays by David Bartholomae, Anne E. Berthoff, Patricia Bizzell, Kenneth Bruffee, Robert Connors, Lisa Ede, Paolo Freire, Karen Greenberg, Patrick Hartwell, Glynda Hull, Andrea Lunsford, Sondra Perl, Mike Rose, Mariolina Salvatori, Mina Shaughnessy, Lynn Troyka, and others. As Theresa Enos writes in her preface, "The *Sourcebook* aims to build upon Shaughnessy's contributions to the study of basic writing by gathering together the best of contemporary research, theory, and practice on the subject" (v).

119   Fox, Tom. *Defending Access: A Critique of Standards in Higher Education.* Portsmouth: Boynton, 1999. Print.

Fox argues that contemporary calls for "standards" work against providing broader, more equitable access to higher education. The book is divided into five chapters, with the first three developing a critique of standards in both historical and contemporary contexts and the second two sketching how work for access can be carried out in both pedagogy and writing program administration. The book concludes with a brief comment on the need for perseverance in committed educators—that is, "staying around is half the battle" (114)—and four observations about change: stubborn persistence is necessary; alliances are important; preparation for confrontation helps student survival; and survival is possible with strategic choices about which battles to fight.

120   Halasek, Kay, and Nels P. Highberg, eds. *Landmark Essays on Basic Writing.* Mahwah: Erlbaum, 2001. Print.

The essays in this volume speak directly to the debilitating assumptions that place basic writing students and teachers, and the discipline itself, on the margins of educational, economic, and political localities of influence. The collection is designed to present readers with various previously published essays that depict the fundamental and shifting theoretical, methodological, and pedagogical assumptions of basic writing instruction over the past two decades. Beginning with essays published between 1987 (after the publication of *A Sourcebook for Basic Writing Teachers* [118]) and 1997, the book is arranged roughly chronologically, from Adrienne Rich's "Teaching Language in Open Admissions" [123] to Jacqueline Jones Royster and Rebecca Greenberg Taylor's 1997 "Constructing Teacher Identity in the Basic Writing Classroom" [36]. The collection seeks to historicize the preceding decades of scholarship and also anticipate the future of the field. Essays examine such issues as defining basic writers, the phenomenology of error, cognitivism and writing instruction, the social construction of remediation, and the politics of basic writing pedagogy in a postmodern world. They collectively speak to some of the most enduring and important debates in the field of basic writing. At the same time, they illustrate that neither the basic writing classroom nor recent scholarship need be intellectually marginalized locations. The contributors claim the "margin"— the basic writing classroom—as a borderland, a site of contention and negotiation that allows for a cultural and pedagogical reflection and critique not available to them in more centrally located sites in English departments.

121   Kasden, Lawrence N., and Daniel R. Hoeber, eds. *Basic Writing: Essays for Teachers, Researchers, and Administrators.* Urbana: National Council of Teachers of English, 1980. Print.

This germinal book provides important perspectives in the history of basic writing research. It includes essays by Sondra Perl, Arthur Dixon, Milton Spann and Virginia Foxx, Patrick Hartwell, Harry Crosby, Nancy Johnson, Rexford Brown, Constance Gefvert, Kenneth Bruffee, and E. Donald Hirsch. Each contributor focuses on different elements of basic writing and basic writers, from cognitive studies to examinations of writing programs and writing center practices.

122   Moran, Michael G., and Martin J. Jacobi. *Research in Basic Writing: A Bibliographic Sourcebook*. New York: Greenwood, 1991. Print.

This text is most useful now as a resource documenting the state of basic writing scholarship in the late 1970s and mid-1980s. Although the book bears a publication date of 1991, its ten bibliographic essays (and appendix) are heavily weighted with research and scholarship considerably earlier than the date of publication. The *Sourcebook* was written when basic writing was experiencing a resurgence; thus it extensively documents the dominant approach to basic writing. Woven into many of the chapters are emphases on linguistics, "new grammars" and sentence combining, cognitive psychology, and the City College of New York "origins" of basic writing interest and instruction, a claim that has been contested. Nevertheless, the *Sourcebook* constitutes a useful artifact of a certain period in basic writing scholarship.

123   Rich, Adrienne. "Teaching Language in Open Admissions." *Landmark Essays on Basic Writing*. Ed. Kay Halasek and Nels P. Highberg. Mahwah: Erlbaum, 2001. 1–13. Print.

Rich brings a narrative vision and quality rarely found in scholarship on basic writing. Through her experiences, we see the "graffiti-sprayed walls of tenements" (8) and "the uncollected garbage" (3) on the streets of New York, and we witness the lives of students and teachers as they come together to make sense of the circumstances of their collective educational endeavors in the Seek for Evaluation, Education & Knowledge (SEEK) program at the City College of New York in 1968. Rich describes the larger social, political, and human contexts of that time and formulates many of the questions that continue to demand attention in basic writing scholarship. Rich articulates a condition of education that is characterized by institutional racism and classism. She cites Paulo Freire, insisting that students need to learn to use language for critical reflection, and calls on educators to reassess their methods and materials for teaching. At the same time, her narrative demands that basic writing scholars work at their own critical self-reflection.

124   Rose, Mike. *Lives on the Boundary: The Struggles and Achievements of America's Underprepared*. New York: Free, 1989. Print.

This examination of the idea of "underpreparedness" in a range of schools and educational systems also explores Rose's own experiences as a student who was erroneously placed in the vocational education track. He suggests that lower-track classes create a self-fulfilling prophecy for most students who might, if challenged to succeed, do well in

advanced classes. Among the issues Rose discusses are the problems
encountered by students whose backgrounds provide little context for
the ideas and language they encounter in the academy. By explaining his personal challenges and his experiences with various mentors,
Rose illustrates how he worked to master academic language and ideas.
Rose uses his experiences as a student and a teacher as evidence for a
critique of conceptions of literacy used in contemporary education. He
suggests that students labeled "underprepared" are inexperienced with
the expectations of the academy, that literacy crises running through
the nineteenth and twentieth centuries were manufactured and deflect
other concerns, and that schools must work with students differently.

125   Shaughnessy, Mina P. "Basic Writing." *Teaching Composition: Twelve
Bibliographic Essays.* Ed. Gary Tate. 1976. Fort Worth: Texas Christian
UP, 1987. 177–206. Print.

Rejecting the remedial/medical metaphor, Shaughnessy articulates varied definitions of basic writers and writing among institutions and over
time. She establishes 1964 as the year when the "new" remedial English began. The essay defines the population of basic writing students,
characterizes instructors and instructor training, and notes that little
had been published before 1976 on this rich area of potential research.
The essay identifies three major components of research to that point
and suggests readings on these: classroom environment, methods of
instruction, and focus on prewriting. Throughout, Shaughnessy emphasizes the challenges faced by students who are identified as basic writers
and suggests that traditional instructors rethink their approaches to
better accommodate these students. The essay closes with an in-depth
discussion of selected readings for instructors on classical studies of
language, on grammar, on language in various social settings, and on
writing. Most of the cited articles remain classics in the field. Shaughnessy sums up the main point of the essay: "The 'remediation' of basic
writers' teachers may, in fact, be the most important education going
on today" (167).

126   Shaughnessy, Mina P. *Errors and Expectations: A Guide for the Teacher of
Basic Writing.* New York: Oxford UP, 1977. Print.

Shaughnessy takes teachers through writing problems such as poor
handwriting and punctuation, syntax, common errors, spelling and
vocabulary errors, and lack of idea development. While her focus is
primarily on error, it is underscored by a sensitive understanding of the
reasons behind the rhetorical and linguistic difficulties discussed and a
strong belief in the inherent intelligence of learners described as "basic
writers." Shaughnessy's claims about the difficulties faced by basic writers are supported by examples from thousands of student papers. Examples of many kinds of errors are provided. Each chapter also includes
suggestions for the teacher on how to reduce the particular kind of error
discussed in that specific chapter. Shaughnessy also explains why these
errors occur by examining the rules that are manifested in students'

writing. The book also contains suggestions for placement essay topics and suggested readings for the teacher of basic writing.

127   Smoke, Trudy. "What Is the Future of Basic Writing?" *Journal of Basic Writing* 20.2 (2001): 88–96. Print.

Writing as coeditor of the *Journal of Basic Writing* (first with Karen Greenberg and then with George Otte), Smoke surveys seven years of *JBW* (1994–2001), a time when the journal became "more theoretical and political" (88). Looking back, Smoke highlights some of the most important issues in basic writing: the demise of open admissions at the City University of New York, tracking versus mainstreaming, a reappraisal of Mina Shaughnessy's work, and the elimination of basic writing programs (and hence basic writers). Smoke asserts that research in the field has entered into "meta-analysis" and that scholarship has begun to "historicize" basic writing. Smoke concludes with a tribute to *JBW* and its role as she turns over her editorship to Bonne August.

Pedagogical Issues

Composing Processes

128 Ashley, Hannah. "The Art of Queering Voices: A Fugue." *Journal of Basic Writing* 26.1 (2007): 4–19. Print.

Ashley argues that teaching reported discourse in the traditional way—as a set of conventions for quoting, paraphrasing, and citing sources—encourages basic writers to try to pass as academic insiders by hiding, or "closeting," their outsider status and perspectives. Teaching students how to "queer" reported discourse conventions, by which the writer means using them in playful, disruptive, and unexpected ways, offers students an opportunity to develop openly hybrid, insider-outsider authorial voices. Ashley offers a compelling model of what reported discourse looks like when it is queered and a thorough analysis of how queered discourse works. (She refers readers to another article for advice about how to teach it.) The article is written as a demonstration of queered discourse: the academic arguments are collaged with snippets of confessional narrative, dictionary definitions of musical forms, and quotes from the DSM-IV diagnostic manual.

129 Bernstein, Susan Naomi. "Seeing beyond the Ordinary: Imagination and the Work of Teachers and Students in Basic Writing." *Modern Language Studies* 34.1/2 (2004): 84–91. Print.

Bernstein suggests that standardized and skills-based pedagogies at the elementary level operate much the same way in the post-Fordist university. She argues that by the time students reach college, they have been "exposed to basic skills training for years" (87). Thus Bernstein "understand[s] the teaching of writing as a continuum" (86), suggesting that her experiences teaching imaginative writing through metaphor to elementary students helped her to imagine how figurative language might create similar dissonance in her university-level basic writing courses. Bernstein affirms that providing contexts and spaces for students to re-imagine their lives through metaphor and figurative language moves student learning beyond skill and drill to meaningful, critical, and personal engagement with language and the material conditions of the writing classroom.

130 Biser, Eileen, Linda Rubel, and Rose Marie Toscano. "Mediated Texts: A Heuristic for Academic Writing." *Journal of Basic Writing* 17.1 (1998): 56–72. Print.

Mediated text is defined as written text produced with second- and third-party assistance in its drafting and final production. Because the Americans with Disabilities Act requires accommodation for deaf college students, mediated texts produced with second- and third-party assistance help deaf college students successfully complete writing courses. Biser, Rubel, and Toscano identify the function of mediated texts as a useful drafting technique for English as a second language (ESL) students and for basic writers as well. Although they address philosophical and pedagogical implications of second- and third-party participation, mediated texts as heuristic devices may benefit many students in their drafting and revision.

131   Cody, Jim. "The Importance of Expressive Language in Preparing Basic Writers for College Writing." *Journal of Basic Writing* 15.2 (1996): 95–111. Print.

Cody argues that basic writers should develop their own voices and not just imitate others', which will result in language that is "more sensitive to multicultural concerns" (109) and "more openly accountable for the damage caused from academia's privileging of dominant discourses" (109). To this end, Cody urges a move away from "pedagogies of imitation" (108), in which students must adapt to existing formulas and standards, reject familiar discourses, and "hide the evidence" (101) of their lives outside academia—lives that often involve "oppression, marginalization, deprivation, and suppression" (101). Instead, he endorses a pedagogy that encourages students to use their own experiences and discourses in academic writing. This approach also helps students become aware of audience and purpose, affords them the experience of having readers pay attention to their work, and transforms academic language into a more representative discourse. Cody argues that instructors and students can work from such "expressive" language toward more "linear modes" used in academe without betraying their own discourses.

132   Collins, James L. "Basic Writing and the Process Paradigm." *Journal of Basic Writing* 14.2 (1995): 3–18. Print.

Collins contends that an unquestioned acceptance of the process approach to teaching writing may fail basic writers because of the myths that inform the implicit instruction in this paradigm—that "writing development is natural and that teaching is primarily the facilitation of development" (5). Collins also notes that process literature promotes a structuralist, binary approach to writing instruction. He recommends a more poststructuralist appreciation of "differences among discourses" (5).

133   De Beaugrande, Robert, and Mar Jean Olson. "Using a 'Write-Speak-Write' Approach for Basic Writers." *Journal of Basic Writing* 10.2 (1991): 4–32. Print.

The authors begin with a dilemma: linguists emphasize the primacy of speech over writing, but this causes problems with labeling dialects. De Beaugrande and Olson refute the linguistic premise that restricted speech, such as that identified by Basil Bernstein as spoken by the British lower class, is an indicator of psychological and linguistic deficits, and the authors question the connections between speech and writing. They also argue that formal correctness is not a prerequisite for effective communication. They describe a pilot project in which student athletes were asked to create a narrative about three of their games—one week in writing, one week later in speech, and the third week in writing (the Write-Speak-Write Approach). Each student was asked to use the first written draft and an annotated, typed transcript of the speech to compose the final draft. Final drafts were longer and clearer than the initial versions. A change of approach to teaching basic writing in elementary and secondary schools could greatly ease the problems we are now facing at the college level, which often cannot be fully remedied in one or two semesters. Writing instructors should support the human freedom of access to knowledge through discourse.

134   Gunter, Kimberly K. "Braiding and Rhetorical Power Players: Transforming Academic Writing through Rhetorical Dialectic." *Journal of Basic Writing* 30.1 (2011): 64–98. Print.

This engaging example of a braided text recaps basic writing theoretical debates of Bartholomae and Elbow via an imagined Steel Cage Death Match between the compositionists and argues that flaws in basic writing pedagogy are suggested by each scholar's views. Citing other compositionists and basic writing curricular traditions (expressive narrative assignments ease students into transactional/academic texts), the essay suggests braided assignments can foster a "rigorous subjectivity" more likely to engage students with the social action (not just accepted formats) of their own intellectual and academic experiences. Basic writing populations include many students (of color, low income, and other demographics) whose language and sociopolitical experiences are already in opposition to the academic discourse such classes ultimately teach students to perform, and such students have long practiced knowledge within their own "counter rhetorics." The essay concludes by analyzing how braided writing assignments in a queered writing class allowed one student, a lesbian ROTC candidate in the Don't Ask/Don't Tell military, to move beyond both military and GLBTQ coercive discourse to careful, intellectual/personal questioning and powerful personal/transactional texts.

135   Hebb, Judith. "Mixed Forms of Academic Discourse: A Continuum of Language Possibility." *Journal of Basic Writing* 21.2 (2002): 21–36. Print.

In challenging Patricia Bizzell's negative characterization of hybrid discourses, Hebb claims that instructors should view them not simply as a mix of the academic and nonacademic but as part of a continuum of discourses for which no solid boundaries differentiate academic discourse from others. At one pole of the continuum is mainstream academic discourse, and Hebb argues that privileging "academic discourse" reinforces dominant ideology. At the other pole is the idiosyncratic and unintelligible. Hybrid discourses fall between these two poles, which represent impoverished forms of discourse that "reflect neither the complexity and multi-vocality of group nor the individual voice(s) of self" (28). Instructors can help their students negotiate their passage into various academic discourse communities by assuming no hierarchy of value, offering students linguistic resources rich in their ideational and expressive possibilities, and encouraging them to produce hybrid discourses that perform intellectual work.

See: Patricia Bizzell, "Basic Writing and the Issue of Correctness, or, What to Do with 'Mixed' Forms of Academic Discourse" [5].

136   Hull, Glynda, and Mike Rose. "'This Wooden Shack Place': The Logic of an Unconventional Reading." *College Composition and Communication* 41.3 (1990): 287–98. Print.

Contemporary pedagogies that call for an integrative approach to reading and writing in the "remedial" classroom increase the likelihood of divergence between students and instructors along the lines of literary interpretation. Instructors' readings tend toward conventions socialized by training during their undergraduate and graduate study of English, while personal history strongly influences the logic of a basic writer's response to literary texts. To show that basic writers benefit from immersion in the intellectual task of generating new interpretive perceptions, Hull and Rose analyze the discourse surrounding one student's reading of "And Your Soul Shall Dance," a poem by Garrett Kaoru Hongo. The ensuing reinterpretation of the poem demonstrates that "deficit-oriented assumptions about the linguistic and cognitive abilities of remedial students" (296) need reexamination. The more student-centered and "knowledge-making" model of pedagogy that would result might create moments of uncertainty or hesitancy for the instructor, who must nevertheless stand ready to provide guidance, focus, structure, and accountability.

137   Hunter, Paul, and Nadine Pearce. "Basic Writers: The Writing Process and Written Products." *Teaching English in the Two-Year College* 14.2 (1987): 252–64. Print.

Focusing on studies utilizing transcribed audiotapes as a method of researching basic writers' writing processes, Hunter and Pearce question if those processes could be understood by an analysis of think-aloud protocols. After observing the writing processes of eight basic writers, the authors conclude that writing assignments should be designed to minimize "premature editing" (stopping and starting) and that many basic writers do not have at their disposal the kinds of knowledge or language "to respond comfortably and effectively to traditional academic writing tasks" (263).

138   Kirch, Ann. "A Basic Writer's Topoi for Timed Essay Tests." *Journal of Basic Writing* 15.2 (1996): 112–24. Print.

Basic writers have difficulty generating ideas while taking timed essay tests. Patterned after James Berlin's approach—a "positivistic, behavioral epistemology that focuses on steps in processes and descriptions of external reality" (113)—Kirch advocates that basic writers respond to the essay's prompt by asking themselves how other people might respond to the topic. This pedagogy helps students examine the topic more objectively, including their and others' insights, thus making them better able to respond to the topic. Through this technique, basic writers are enabled to "discover the political and social topoi" and "completely reposition the timed writing tests" (123).

139   Kraemer, Don J. "On Whether to Convert from a Rhetorical to a Psychoanalytic Pedagogy." *Journal of Basic Writing* 29.2 (2010): 5–30. Print.

Although psychoanalytic and rhetorical pedagogical approaches have been in conversation with one another, they fundamentally differ, making it difficult to come to a reasonable synthesis. The central problem that partitions them relates to the subject's relationship to conflict, audience, and identity. That is, while, on the one hand, psychoanalysis concerns itself with how the subject's repressed desires impede her writing, distorting and demonizing the Other, rhetoric, on the other hand, understands audience and conflict as a location for invention and negotiation. For psychoanalysis, thus, language becomes a means through which a stable and consistent identity manifests. This positivist stability runs in direct conflict with a rhetorical understanding of language and identity as contextual and negotiated. Ultimately, though psychoanalysis can and should be employed as a means to directing students toward a more nuanced understanding of their desires, and in turn a more careful and informed knowledge of the Other and the Symbolic, to convert entirely away from a rhetorical pedagogy risks losing the very processes associated with garnering, rather than objectively discovering, meanings and truths.

140   Kroll, Barry M., and John C. Schafer. "Error-Analysis and the Teaching of Composition." *College Composition and Communication* 29.3 (1978): 242–48. Print.

Process-based error analysis from ESL studies offers insights into the errors native speakers make in written composition. The process-analytic approach views errors as necessary stages in all language learning, the product of intelligent cognitive strategies, and potentially useful indicators of the processes a student uses. The error analyst investigates the sources of error to help students reach target forms and levels of discourse. Like Mina Shaughnessy's work, this approach sees errors as the product of learning and thinking. Error analysis does not dictate any single teaching device, and instructors should avoid simple exercises or explanations. Instead, they should view teaching as hypothesis testing, look for systematicity and pattern in student error, individualize materials and strategies for particular errors, and explain sources of errors to students.

141   Leary, Christopher. "Meshing Digital and Academic Identities in Basic Writing Classrooms." *Basic Writing e-Journal* 10.1/11.1 (2011–2012): n. pag. Web. 10 Jan. 2014.

By reversing the established order (publisher products consumed by students) and having students craft their own course reader, Leary holds up "macrocomposition"—the selection and assemblage of other peoples' texts—as a pedagogy fundamental to learning how to compose one's own. Rather than writing individual texts "from sketch," the act of composing (patch-writing) an entire anthology of readings enables students to enter literate conversations running full-speed, empowered to manipulate them with expert intent. Asking students to moderate the whole before producing parts-that-fit reverses traditional linear notions of how writing skill develops. Based soundly in firsthand classroom experience, Leary proves once again that writing ability is acquired in complex communal settings—through the strategic, playful repositioning of found texts. Less a byproduct of grammatical control, writing in today's "information-thick" world requires subtractive, editorial skill (capturing, assembling, curating). The well-documented links Leary offers here between his anthology assignment and related macrocomposition practices definitively close the gap between classroom instruction and the digital world where students live, empowering both to converge authentically on shared (deliberately meshed) academic goals.

142   McAlexander, Patricia J. "Developmental Classroom Personality and Response to Peer Review." *Research and Teaching in Developmental Education* 17.1 (2000): 5–12. Print.

McAlexander conducted a study of two developmental writing classes to investigate which form of peer review—oral or written—most benefitted students. The class she describes as composed of intermediate developmental writers reported a strong preference for oral feedback, with students stating that oral review comments were far more helpful and enjoyable than written comments, especially those written by classmates they did not know. In contrast, students from the class that McAlexander notes demonstrated lower levels of academic and social skills reported that neither method was helpful or enjoyable. McAlexander concludes that the personality of the class is largely responsible for student experiences with peer review. Thus instructors cannot make assertions about student experiences with peer review without first taking into consideration the levels of student self-confidence and motivation and the level of social interaction observed in the particular classroom.

143   Miller, David. "Developmental Writing: Trust, Challenge, and Critical Thinking." *Journal of Basic Writing* 21.2 (2002): 92–105. Print.

Miller argues that basic writers are likely unaware of their own critical thinking skills and that teachers must demonstrate to them how to apply those skills in their own writing. Because students often distrust their own experiences and abilities, Miller suggests that teachers have an obligation to validate students and give them a sense of safety within the physical space of the classroom, for only when students feel safe will they partake in the cognitive activities associated with critical thinking. Miller also stresses the importance of challenging students and describes his own use of difficult texts by Annie Dillard and Mark Twain. Miller concludes by suggesting that engaging students in critical thinking about their own work and the work of others leads them to experience and understand critical thinking as a more "natural" process.

144   Parisi, Hope A. "Involvement and Self-Awareness for the Basic Writer: Graphically Conceptualizing the Writing Process." *Journal of Basic Writing* 13.2 (1994): 33–45. Print.

Basic writing students benefit from conceptually mapping their own writing processes. This activity gives students the opportunity to identify and classify, spatially, their own writing behaviors. Writing students of all ability levels often do not recognize the correlation between their successes and failures as writers and the decisions they make when writing, but this problem is experienced most frequently by students who are less acculturated to the college learning environment. As a metacognitive task, mapping highlights the movement from idea to idea or from task to task that all writers undertake, both independently and through collaboration. Various student experiences of mapping are presented in detail. Examples of student maps are also provided.

145   Parisi, Hope, and Lara Rodriguez. "'Why Are You Here?': Troubling Legitimacy for Basic Writers and Their Instructors in the Community College." *Open Words: Access and English Studies* 7.1 (2013): 5–20. Web. 21 May 2014.

Parisi and Rodriguez encourage a critical reevaluation of the prototypical start-of-semester question "Why are you here?" Frequently used as an introduction or goal-defining activity, the authors caution that uncritically deploying this or similar questions of academic initiation/welcome "may compound negative self-beliefs and assumptions by which community college students enter college; replicate and sustain asymmetrical power relations between instructor and student; and ultimately limit possibilities for both teacher and student self- and re-definition" (7). Though usually well-intentioned, the authors argue, questions of "Why" do not often yield the authentic reflective answers instructors desire. Instead, Parisi and Rodriguez encourage changing questions of "Why" to "How and What of it" (15). This change, the authors say, relieves students from defensively proving their legitimacy and encourages them to focus on their own social and political locations within and outside of the community college.

146   Perl, Sondra. "The Composing Processes of Unskilled College Writers." *Research in the Teaching of English* 13.4 (1979): 317–36. Print.

Perl summarizes her 1975–1976 study of the composing processes of five unskilled college writers at Eugenio Maria de Hostos Community College of the City University of New York. Perl argues that, prior to this work, little was done to study basic writers and their "observable and scorable behaviors" (318) in the composing process. One specific goal of the study was to provide a mechanism for documenting composing processes: research in a "standardized, categorical, concise, structural, and diachronic" (320) format. Perl developed a code for what students do in their composing processes. "Miscues" in students' own reading and writing work were also noted in a standardized format. The discovery that the students' composing processes were consistent, even when the resultant writing appeared to have been done in a haphazard or arbitrary manner, supports the research Shaughnessy did in the late 1970s. Perl argues that basic writing faculty must look at students' internalized processes to make decisions about instruction.

147   Perl, Sondra. "A Look at Basic Writers in the Process of Composing." *Basic Writing: Essays for Teachers, Researchers, and Administrators*. Ed. Lawrence N. Kasden and Daniel R. Hoeber. Urbana: NCTE, 1980. 13–32. Print.

Perl uses Janet Emig's 1969 work on "composing aloud" to set up this study of five students at Eugenio Maria de Hostos Community College of the City University of New York in 1975 and 1976 and to create a formal, standardized approach to viewing the work that basic writers do as they complete writing assignments. The findings show that the student writers, though often unskilled, had consistent strategies for composing. While the students spent little time on prewriting, there was no indication that this created subsequent problems. Students discovered meaning as they wrote in a process that was recursive, discursive, and decidedly nonlinear. Editing created most of the problems for the students, as they often hypercorrected or began to correct before writing enough to untangle what they wanted to say. Perl argues that these students do know how to write and have stable composing processes. She suggests a "loosening" of the writing process: "readying oneself to write, sustaining the flow of writing, shaping the discourse for oneself, readying the discourse for others" (31–32) as a consideration for basic writing instruction.

148   Purves, Alan. "Teaching People Who Don't Write Good." *Journal of Basic Writing* 14.1 (1995): 15–20. Print.

Purves suggests that composition is a complex business that is in a constant state of change. We expect students to come to the university with a certain level of prowess with composition, but perhaps that expectation is unrealistic. Part of the problem is that we are sometimes unsure of what we should teach students. What genres are important? Are we more concerned with grammar or content, style or voice? Do we want students to challenge the academy or become part of its discourse community? Technology complicates the matter further. Composition is evolving into a complex manipulation of images for a rhetorical effect—images including graphemes, punctuation marks, paragraphs, typefaces, illustrations, pictures, and sound effects. Perhaps in this new digital world we are all neophytes. Rather than worry about teaching students how to write well, Purves says, perhaps we should question the very nature of writing.

149   Rodgers, Johannah. "Defining and Experiencing Authorship(s) in the Composition Classroom: Findings from a Qualitative Study of Undergraduate Writing Students at the City University of New York." *Journal of Basic Writing* 30.1 (2011): 130–55. Print.

Rodgers interviewed ten of her former students, working adults studying at CUNY's Center for Worker Education, to explore their definitions and applications of the terms *author* and *writer*, their academic writing histories, and their experiences with audience and publishing. In her analysis, Rodgers divides her interviewees into two groups: "writers" and "non-writers, not-yet writers, and sometimes-writers" (142). The former drew on a process model of authorship and internalized audience as dialogic, a back-and-forth between themselves and their imagined readers, while the latter, blurring notions of author and writer, constructed their audience as monologic, an external "controlling authority" (145). Given the versions of authorship circulating as students learn to write, these interviews reveal that invested and authoritative writing positively influences the student/audience relationship, but teacher responses to student texts can work at cross-purposes. As students write, their identities are under construction and best supported by writing contexts with a clear purpose and audience. Rodgers calls for a pedagogy based on enactment and modeled on conversation, one that articulates students' current positionalities but also offers them prospective possibilities.

150   Rose, Mike. "Rigid Rules, Inflexible Plans, and the Stifling of Language: A Cognitivist Analysis of Writer's Block." *College Composition and Communication* 31.4 (1980): 389–401. Print.

This study of students and writer's block finds important differences among writers. Five case studies form the basis of the study, which includes a thorough discussion of writer's block and the challenges student writers face when their performance as writers does not accurately reflect their abilities. Rose concludes that the blocking these writers faced was caused by "writing rules or . . . planning strategies that impeded rather than enhanced the composing process" (390). Acknowledging the complexity of the writing process, Rose proposes that writer's block can in many cases be alleviated if the rigid rules and plans that seem to control writers' performances can be discovered. The essay contains both interview data and writers' self-reports of their composing processes. In interdisciplinary fashion, the essay also contains a survey of "several key concepts in the problem-solving literature" (390) that undergird Rose's analysis.

151   Shafer, Gregory. "Negotiating Audience and Voice in the Writing Center." *Teaching Developmental Writing: Background Readings*. Ed. Susan Naomi Bernstein. Boston: Bedford, 2001. 354–64. Print.

Shafer addresses the fundamental tension between students' self-expression and the conventions of academic discourse taught in composition courses. Shafer compares vivid examples of three students' emotionally charged yet nonstandard writing with the correct but bland academic writing often said to be valued in composition courses. In doing so, he critiques David Bartholomae's pedagogy by asking, "Who is really being served in a pedagogy that elevates prescription over critical dialogue?" (359). Shafer refers to Paolo Freire, bell hooks, Mina Shaughnessy, Louise Rosenblatt, Peter Elbow, and Donald Murray as he develops an argument against "a contrived discourse that serves to exalt the academic community over the students it is supposed to empower" (357). He also supports students' efforts to accommodate their writing to the instructors' and institutions' requirements, even if these tend to stifle voice, by helping students focus on audience analysis.

See: David Bartholomae, "Inventing the University" [2].

152 Shaughnessy, Mina P. "Some New Approaches toward Teaching." *Journal of Basic Writing* 13.1 (1994): 103–16. Print.

In general, writing teachers are people who did well in school, enjoyed English, and got high grades on everything they wrote. They use internalized models of their past composition successes to evaluate the work of their students, a system that always puts the basic writing student at a disadvantage. Students learn to write by writing, and the teacher who interferes with this process by imposing too many conditions must recognize that the goal of instruction is to guide students to be self-sufficient. Teachers must be sensitive to the details of the various difficulties students may have in handwriting, spelling, punctuation, grammar, and making and ordering sentences. Each student is an individual who will follow a unique, nonlinear path of development. The teacher-student relationship is best described as one in which two people learn from each other.

153 Sirc, Geoffrey. "*The Autobiography of Malcolm X* as a Basic Writing Text." *Journal of Basic Writing* 13.1 (1994): 50–77. Print.

Sirc addresses several issues: subject positions, student ability, and the debate about whether basic writing should focus on teaching "academic writing" or recasting the academic standards of appropriate writing. Mentioning composition's stringent focus on writing process, Sirc endorses the last choice from the above list. The power of revision—both by readers and writers—in the tweaking of meaning forces writers into closure. Sirc prefers Malcolm X's flexible philosophy from the end of his autobiography to be used as a model for basic writing instruction. Most students began reading Malcolm X's story with a fairly stable notion of identity, a closed notion of who people are and how they engage with the world. Sirc claims that most students remained in that mind-set. However, some students demonstrated change, and Sirc believes that many will not remain solely within that reductionist framework. By endorsing this approach to the classroom, Sirc opens the possibility for students to learn the positive force that literacy can have in their lives.

154   Sommers, Jeff. "Reflection Revisited: The Class Collage." *Journal of Basic Writing* 30.1 (2011): 99–127. Print.

Students in basic writing or first-year composition classes are often assigned end-of-semester reflections in which they analyze their cognitive development throughout the course; however, composition research has found that reflection must be practiced in order to work effectively. When students are asked to reflect only once, they may be unable to perform the necessary metacognitive work demanded by the task. In place of traditional reflections, Sommers suggests that students engage in ongoing reflective work on their beliefs about writing, revising, and writing courses. He assigns students to write credo statements, which are compiled at the end of the semester into a class collage; students analyze the collage in their final reflections. This assignment is beneficial because (1) students often describe concurrent transfer of learning, (2) students can examine out-of-school learning and experiences, (3) teachers can use the reflections for outcomes assessment, and (4) teachers learn from the reflections what is and is not working well in their teaching. This assignment is particularly useful for basic writers, who might need a scaffolded approach to reflecting.

155   Yood, Jessica. "Present-Process: The Composition of Change." *Journal of Basic Writing* 24.2 (2005): 4–25. Print.

Yood finds the process theory of writing to be in a state of "paradigm-paralysis" (8–9), a problem she traces back to Maxine Hairston's misreading of Thomas Kuhn. Proposing the term *social movement* as an alternative to *paradigm*, Yood attempts to resurrect process, not as a "big theory," but as a way of "understanding knowledge making in our complex world as a circular, feedback loop" (13). She endorses "autopoesis," or observing systems and making processes visible, as a conceptual way for writing scholars to reflect upon the "how" of composing (13) and to enact change. As an example of a "present-process movement," Yood highlights the new Writing Across the Curriculum (WAC) program at the City University of New York, a program that took shape after basic writing and remedial writing were dispensed with along with open admissions.

Invention, Reading, Prewriting, and Collaboration

156   Launspach, Sonja. "The Role of Talk in Small Writing Groups: Building Declarative and Procedural Knowledge for Basic Writers." *Journal of Basic Writing* 27.2 (2008): 56–80. Print.

Focusing on a case study, Launspach explores the role of talk in underprepared students' acquisition of academic discourse. Conversation analysis as a linguistic framework is used to examine the interactions of students participating in a small writing group. Tracing the progress of one student's paper, the essay explores how students' participation in small writing groups allows them, in Claus Faerch and Gabriele Kasper's terms, to build declarative knowledge and negotiate strategies they can apply to their procedural knowledge of writing. The small writing groups, led by a teaching assistant, expose underprepared students to the practices and values of the academic discourse community. A systematic look at how students' talk is structured and what topics they focus on offers important insight to instructors into aspects of student writers' learning processes and suggests additional pedagogical approaches.

157   Shafer, Gregory. "Using Letters for Process and Change in the Basic Writing Class." *Teaching Developmental Writing: Background Readings.* Ed. Susan Naomi Bernstein. Boston: Bedford, 2001. 46–59. Print.

Wanting his assignments to be informed by real-world relevance, Shafer had his students write personal letters to anyone of their own choosing. Shafer participated in the assignment by sharing a letter he wrote to his recently deceased father and came to understand the anxieties that students feel when sharing their writing with others. As an audience, his students broke free of their normal error seeking, evaluated his letter's essence, and revised instead of edited. The next class meeting demonstrated that students themselves were becoming writers. Many arrived in class with letters that had been revised multiple times. Letter writing, Shafer argues, paired with a writing or literacy club, is "invaluable not only for its short, holistic character but also for the many political and liberating opportunities it offers" (53).

158   VonBergen, Linda. "Shaping the Point with Poetry." *Journal of Basic Writing* 20.1 (2001): 77–88. Print.

VonBergen argues that expressivism does not belong in the basic writing classroom because students have not internalized a sufficient array of narrative models and are likely to produce expressive essays that are heavy on extraneous detail and light on main point. Drawing on David Bartholomae's "Inventing the University," she claims that allowing students to write without making a point is a disservice and that instructors should help students to imitate and appropriate the forms of academic discourse. To that end, VonBergen suggests using poetry to provide students with a model on which to base their essays. Key for VonBergen is that the discursive aims of this assignment are not expressive (emotional) but referential (referring to a concrete reality). She provides a sample assignment that uses Countee Cullen's poem "Incident" as a model for a personal essay. The three stanzas of the poem, she says, are models for three parts of an essay: the context for the incident, the events that happened, and the author's reactions to those events. Using this model, she contends, students are much less likely to produce personal essays in which no point is made or in which a point is made but only incidentally.

See: David Bartholomae, "Inventing the University" [2].

Response and Revision

159   Bartholomae, David, and Peter Elbow. "Responses to Bartholomae and Elbow." *College Composition and Communication* 46.1 (1995): 84–92. Print.

In these responses to each other's longer *College Composition and Communication* articles (also published in issue 46.1), Bartholomae and Elbow further explain their differing views of how to teach students and respond to their writing. Bartholomae advocates teaching students to take a critical stance toward dominant discourses and taking a critical stance when responding to students' papers. His goal is to help see "the ways their writing constructs a relationship with tradition, power and authority—with other people's words" (86). Elbow advocates "hold[ing] back" criticism of students' work to "let them make as many decisions as they can about their writing" (90). He recognizes that they "may be written by the culture" (90), but he values "the long-range benefits of helping students achieve their goals" (91).

160   Butler, John. "Remedial Writers: The Teacher's Job as Corrector of Papers." *A Sourcebook for Basic Writing Teachers.* Ed. Theresa Enos. New York: Random, 1987. 557–64. Print.

Butler suggests that the markings that a teacher puts on a basic writer's paper mean little to the writer. The writer already knows that he or she is a weak writer, and these marks confirm this fact. While the comments are meaningful to the instructor, they are not meaningful to the writer. This essay encourages instructors to use comments on each student essay as a chance to encourage the writer and to meet one-on-one with students to help the student with specific problems in his or her writing.

161   Conrad, Susan M., and Lynn M. Goldstein. "ESL Student Revision after Teacher-Written Comments: Text, Contexts, and Individuals." *Journal of Second Language Writing* 8.2 (1999): 147–79. Print.

The authors analyze the effect written feedback has on the revision processes of three ESL college students. Researching drafts of student papers, written comments by teachers, and transcripts of teacher-student conferences, Conrad and Goldstein conclude that "the crucial variable that influenced the effectiveness of revisions was the type of problem students were asked to revise" (160). Students generally seemed to successfully revise problems related to lack of details or examples, coherence, cohesion, purpose, paragraphing, or lexical choice. Students were usually unsuccessful, however, in revising problems related to explanation, explicitness, and analysis. Additionally, the authors identify contextual factors that affect the revision process (teacher and student beliefs, roles and assumptions, content knowledge, and time constraints). Three pedagogical implications are drawn: the need for different instructional strategies appropriate to the context, the benefits of explicitness when giving feedback, and the benefits of composition classrooms that are designed around the content about which students will write (174).

162   Gay, Pamela. "Dialogizing Response in the Writing Classroom: Students Answer Back." *Journal of Basic Writing* 17.1 (1998): 3–17. Print.

Teacher commentary on student-written texts usually yields emotional reactions from students. For teachers to gain perspective on how students react to their comments, Gay advocates a written dialogic interaction between teacher and student. Students should respond to teacher commentary immediately upon receiving their drafts, even if their reactions include anger, frustration, or confusion. In addition, students should be encouraged to initiate teacher commentary by writing a letter to the teacher in which they identify their goals for their text and their own perceived weaknesses and strengths as writers. Through this exercise, students learn to appreciate the dialogic nature of language and to appreciate a range of reader reactions to their written texts.

163   Grobman, Laurie. "Building Bridges to Academic Discourse: The Peer Group Leader in Basic Writing Peer Response Groups." *Journal of Basic Writing* 18.2 (1999): 47–68. Print.

Basic writers are traditionally located outside the realm of academic discourse, which makes peer-response activities problematic for them because they do not feel that they have sufficient authority to criticize other writers' work. Grobman attempts to correct this problem by introducing a peer-group leader—a sophomore who offers assistance and guidance to the students—into her first-year class's peer-response activities. Grobman concludes with a discussion of the pros and cons of employing such a leader in the basic writing classroom.

164   Hanson, Sandra Sellers, and Leonard Vogt. "A Variation on Peer Critiquing: Peer Editing as the Integration of Language Skills." *A Sourcebook for Basic Writing Teachers*. Ed. Theresa Enos. New York: Random, 1987. 575–78. Print.

Students entering universities under open admissions typically did not possess the language skills necessary to participate in the analysis of writing required in traditional peer critiquing. Therefore, Hanson and Vogt created a model of peer editing that develops language skills through the integration of speaking, listening, reading, and writing. Although the peer-editing procedure begins with a focus on content and structure, three-member peer groups spend extensive time on editing. Each writer reads his or her paper aloud, stopping after each sentence for peer comments on grammar and mechanics. Through the process of peer editing, reviewers and writers begin to recognize discrepancies between the writer's verbal representation of his or her text and the text itself and thus learn to catch their own errors. The integration of language skills involved in the process of peer editing allows writers to see the changes they need to make in their writing. The ability to distinguish one's own errors gives basic writers a critical voice and autonomy in their own learning.

165   Horner, Bruce. "Rethinking the 'Sociality' of Error: Teaching Editing as Negotiation." *Rhetoric Review* 11.1 (1992): 172–99. Print.

Compositionists generally agree that what counts as an "error" in writing is often a failure to adhere to a set of arbitrary conventions—socially agreed-on ways to make notations that create meaning. However, the history of the regularization of these conventions suggests that they favor the syntactic form of dialects spoken by the dominant social groups; that correctness in writing has to do with power, status, and class; and that pedagogies can contribute to a sense of powerlessness in speakers of nonstandard dialects. It might be more productive, then, to understand errors as representing flawed social transactions and a failure on the part of both the writer and the reader to negotiate an agreement about the significance that should be attributed to the written notations offered. Such an understanding would allow power to operate dialectically, and basic writers would make changes not to appease their instructors but to communicate particular meanings to particular readers.

166   Hull, Glynda. "Research on Error and Correction." *Perspectives on Research and Scholarship in Composition.* Ed. Ben W. McClelland and Timothy R. Donovan. New York: MLA, 1985. 162–84. Print.

Hull surveys research on and attitudes toward error and suggests pedagogical approaches to error. Acknowledging that the role of research in this area is to help provide access for underprepared students, Hull discusses the changes in attitudes toward error that make possible an informed pedagogy focused on inclusion. Revision is reformulation rather than surface polishing. Research is beginning to focus on error as a cognitive process. Hull identifies key articles on the history of attitudes toward error; the relationships among power, status, race, and class; and the desire of inexperienced writers to conform to conventions. There has been "a movement away from a concern solely for correctness and toward an interest in rhetoric" (171). The article categorizes and analyzes research on the mental processes involved in making errors. It includes research on error counts, error categories, and possible sources of error, arguing that errors should be treated from a developmental perspective. Another subtopic is research on editing, which typically includes protocol analysis and interviews. Research demonstrates that "students can learn to edit through repeated acts of locating errors and imagining alternatives to them in contrast to learning about errors in the abstract in hopes of somehow inhibiting them" (181). The article ends with recommendations for further research on error that will increase the access of "outsiders."

167   Shor, Ira. "Critical Pedagogy Is Too Big to Fail." *Journal of Basic Writing* 28.2 (2009): 6–27. Print.

Shor responds to Danielewicz and Elbow's work proposing the use of unilateral grading contracts in writing courses (CCC 61:2). Shor disagrees with their B-minimum grade because they presume a writing proficiency that is not standard across socioeconomic lines. More important, he critiques the contradiction between the terms *unilateral* and *contract*, claiming that their contract is not a contract at all. It is, instead, a consumer guarantee that is unintentionally patterned after a neoliberal ideal of education that imposes power and discipline on students in order to produce human capital. In lieu of unilateral contracts, Shor proposes a grading contract that "involves the co-authoring of mutual obligations" to allow students to experience the "civic foundation of strong democracy" (13). For Shor, the experience of strong democracy through grading contracts is central to the project of critical pedagogy because mutually agreed upon contracts allow students to learn about negotiation and power as it relates to their own experience. Ultimately, Shor's essay both explains the use and value of grading contracts for writing classrooms and reasserts critical pedagogy practices as necessary for empowering democratic education.

Reading and Using Texts

168   Armstrong, Sonya, Norman A. Stahl, and Hunter R. Boylan. *Teaching Developmental Reading: Historical, Theoretical, and Practical Background Readings*. 2nd ed. Boston: Bedford, 2014. Print.

Armstrong, Stahl, and Boylan present an edited collection that provides an overview of key issues in the field of developmental reading. Drawing from foundational work in the field as well as current research, this collection is divided into eight thematically focused chapters. These chapters include analyses of diverse student readers, curricular models, pedagogical strategies for teaching developmental reading, reading in the disciplines, cross-level discussions, placement and assessment, faculty development, and a collection of interviews with leading scholars in the field. Some of the more current research in the collection addresses timely issues such as the implementation of the Common Core Standards, contextualized basic skills instruction, and accelerated courses.

169   Bernstein, Susan N., and Pete Johnson. "Writing to Learn: The Nickel and Dimed Project." *Research and Teaching in Developmental Education* 20.2 (2004): 59–75. Print.

The participant inquiry research of a critical literacy project in a linked developmental reading and writing course suggests that students engaged in real-life mathematics, reading, and writing can gain content knowledge, critical literacy, and appreciation of the roles math and literacy may play in their lives. The assignments for the linked classes were based on Barbara Ehrenreich's book *Nickel and Dimed*. Literacy lessons included multiple, guided close readings and rereadings of the book as well as note-taking lessons and writing assignments, such as reactions to insights gained while rereading the book. Mathematical lessons included a re-creation in the students' Houston area of

Ehrenreich's efforts to survive on a minimum wage salary. Students combined mathematical and literacy insights, and the authors offer poignant evidence of students' maturation.

170   Cummings, Martha Clark. "*Someday This Pain Will Be Useful to You*: Self-Disclosure and Lesbian and Gay Identity in the ESL Writing Classroom." *Journal of Basic Writing* 28.1 (2009): 71–89. Print.

Cummings decided to use the book *Someday This Pain Will Be Useful to You* in her ESL classroom in New York, knowing that the book's main character questions his sexual orientation. She knew that the book might also bring up an opening for her to discuss her own sexual orientation in the classroom. She uses writing from her students' journals to discuss their reactions to different situations in the book. She watched for the "golden moment" to disclose her own sexuality and found that the moment took the form of discussing the continuum of sexual orientation and bringing awareness of different sexual orientations to her students. She concludes by stating that her students "experienced the way homophobia affects everyone" in the novel, which in turn affected their "sociosexual attitudes" (85). Cummings will continue to watch for "golden moments" in her teaching and will be prepared to address issues of sexual orientation and homophobia when the moment arises, which could in turn lead to "new understandings of identity" (86) for both her and her students.

171   Falk, Jane E. "Shaped by Resistance: Work as a Topical Theme for the Composition Classroom." *Open Words: Access and English Studies* 1.2 (2007): 49–61. Print.

Falk traces the use of work as a topical theme through several semesters of first-year composition at The University of Akron. A former manufacturing hub, Akron experienced a severe decline in its rubber industry, and a high percentage of University of Akron students reported having at least one part-time job while they attended the university. In her composition classroom, the author utilized summer reading texts such as Barbara Ehrenreich's *Nickel and Dimed*, Yvonne Thornton's *The Ditchdigger's Daughters*, and Joyce Dyer's *Gum-Dipped*. Assignments ranged from personal narratives of a work experience, rhetorical analyses of American Dream narratives, critical analyses of employer-employee relationships, and comparisons between student work experiences and those of fictional characters in film and television. Collaborative projects involving field research furthered the inquiry into work issues. While many students showed critical thinking and raised awareness of issues, student resistance often acted as a catalyst for assignment revisions and prompted the use of reflective journals. In particular, students debated the depressing nature of some work-related topics, their perceptions of the summer reading texts, and the ethical issues involved in conducting research in one's own workplace. Falk concludes that, "despite initial resistance to the topic, I believe that the study of students' working lives enables growth, furthers lively discussion and critical thinking about the commodified and class stratified world in which we live, and has present and future relevance for students at The University of Akron" (60).

172   Jones, Billie J. "Are You Using? Textbook Dependency and Breaking the Cycle." *Basic Writing e-Journal* 2.1 (2000): n. pag. Web. 21 May 2014.

Jones argues that while textbooks stabilize courses often organized at the last moment for adjunct instructors, help instructors link reading and writing, and are safe in their familiarity, they also often place needless philosophical and monetary restraints on teachers and students alike. These textbooks rarely fit an instructor or class population completely and are often directed at traditional-age first-year college students rather than returning learners. Jones calls for close analysis of textbook dependence in basic writing classes and a knowledgeable choice about when to use them. The author suggests that by examining often unconscious dependencies on textbooks in basic writing classrooms, instructors will be able to creatively reexamine classroom activities and more closely approach course goals.

173   Levy, Ronna J. "Literature Circles Go to College." *Journal of Basic Writing* 30.2 (2011): 53–83. Print.

After struggling with engaging her students in reading as a process, Levy discovered and implemented Harvey Daniels's Literature Circles in her basic writing classroom. Usually employed at the elementary level, these small reading discussion groups provide scaffolding and structure in a social context for reading. Students are given roles that define a purpose for reading, such as questioning, connecting, or summarizing, and then gather to discuss the text. Citing the awareness that reading is seldom taught beyond the elementary level, yet basic writing students are also basic readers, Levy concludes that reading pedagogy needs to be developed for the basic writing classroom. Levy's article describes her classroom approach, student reactions, and variations on the traditional literature circle structure. It also includes appendices containing roles and reading reflection prompts.

174   Maxson, Jeffrey. "'Government of da Peeps, for da Peeps, and by da Peeps': Revisiting the Contact Zone." *Journal of Basic Writing* 24.1 (2005): 24–47. Print.

Maxson discusses ways to advance contact-zone pedagogy for basic writing students. Based on his teaching of a hybrid basic/first-year writing class at a midsize public university, Maxson focuses attention on the subject matter of a writing classroom: academic language and students' (assumed) position of outsiders to academic discourse. In the first exercise, students translate a challenging text into a recognized form of slang. In the second exercise, students compose a parody of academic language and genre. The students' writing explores the power dynamics at play in both academic texts and writing classrooms. Maxson argues that these two exercises challenge the idea that basic writing students cannot participate in productive critiques of academic discourse.

175   McCrary, Donald. "(Not) Losing My Religion: Using *The Color Purple* to Promote Critical Thinking in the Writing Classroom." *Journal of Basic Writing* 28.1 (2009): 5–31. Print.

Religion is a private arena through which many students learn to navigate the landscape of critical analysis and interrogation of public discourses. McCrary privileges religious discourse through the literary vehicle of Alice Walker's *The Color Purple* for learners who may identify socially and culturally with the novel's central characters. By making public the typically private (or nonacademic) discussion of religion, students become more adept at recognizing the need for awareness of ideological underpinnings that necessarily accompany discourse analysis. McCrary draws from studies in reader response, African American religious studies, and literary analysis to inform his conclusion that, in part, "[e]xploring private discourses is critical for student writers, particularly for basic writers" (29) as both creators and critics of public discourses. Example essays from several students illustrate the interrogation of the text and underlying assumptions and ideologies while giving voice to the student writer at the center of the exploration.

176   Moran, Mary Hurley. "The Connection between Reading Aloud and Stylistic Improvement for Basic Writing Students." *Journal of Basic Writing* 16.2 (1997): 76–89. Print.

Moran explores the hypothesis that students who read their writing aloud produce more successful drafts than students who do not. Moran notes a correlation between reading ability and the efficacy of this activity. Reading drafts aloud was beneficial to students with adequate or good reading skills but did not make any significant difference in the case of poor readers. The first stage of the research involved investigating students' writing processes. Poor writers often wrote a single draft of a paper and made only superficial changes during the revision process. Stronger writers, by contrast, completed more drafts, revised more thoroughly, and began by revising content and style before looking at issues of mechanics and structure. The second stage involved secondary research about the relationship between drafting and revising aloud, and Moran mentions that the findings of much of the research agree with her hypothesis. In the third stage, Moran describes a classroom experiment that was designed to test the validity of her hypothesis that the more proficient readers would read their drafts aloud and score higher on the essay and that the experimental group would read their drafts aloud more often than students in the control group. The first assertion was not definitively proven; however, the second seems to have been correct. As a result of her experiment, Moran was convinced that reading essay drafts aloud is beneficial to basic writers who are also proficient readers but is not beneficial to students who do not engage in reading with any degree of frequency.

177   Salvatori, Mariolina. "Reading and Writing a Text: Correlations between Reading and Writing Patterns." *A Sourcebook for Basic Writing Teachers*. Ed. Theresa Enos. New York: Random, 1987. 176–86. Print.

Basic writers tend toward what Wolfgang Iser calls "consistency build-ing" (179), seeking main ideas and familiar concepts rather than at-tending to multiple interpretations and textual inconsistencies. Thus reading instruction that includes analysis of how readers construct meaning and interact with texts is integral to the basic writing class. As writers become more actively involved in constructing textual mean-ings through reading, their writing begins to exhibit recognition of in-consistencies, alternative interpretations, and disagreement. Salvatori's research suggests that reading has a greater impact on writing than previously thought.

178   Smith, Cheryl Hogue. "'Diving In Deeper': Bringing Basic Writers' Thinking to the Surface." *Journal of Adolescent & Adult Literacy* 53.8 (2010): 668–76. Print.

This article is more than a clever play on Shaughnessy's title; it con-fronts the issues of error and error analysis in a whole new light. While Shaughnessy emphasizes the errors within a writer's sentences, Smith acknowledges the "errors" that basic writers make while reading. How-ever, according to Smith, these are not "errors" at all, but like Shaugh-nessy claims, they are logical misinterpretations based on the inexperi-ence of the student. Referring to cultural literacy, transactional reading theories, and the differences between learning versus performance goals, Smith offers a compelling argument that the internalized "fail-ure" students feel in the academy is not their fault, but indeed a natural struggle of learning. Furthermore, Smith discusses that by acknowledg-ing the roots of reading and thinking "errors" made by basic writers, instructors can support students through these challenges of not only thinking about external texts, but how they read and revise their own writing. The most important take-away from Smith's article is not only that the typical criticism of basic writers not thinking is inaccurate, but that they are actually thinking harder than more experienced learners.

179   Smith, Cheryl Hogue. "Interrogating Texts: From Deferent to Efferent and Aesthetic Reading Practices." *Journal of Basic Writing* 31.1 (2012): 59–79. Print.

This article presents an instructional strategy for scaffolding students' reading of complex texts. Beginning with a solid overview of basic writ-ing scholarship on reading theory, Smith comes to terms with Louise Rosenblatt's transactional reading theory, defining efferent versus aes-thetic reading stances, and then argues that an additional stance, the deferent, typifies basic writing students who narrow reading tasks to finding the correct answer. Accordingly, the deferent stance belies the process of rereading because readers perceive confusion to be evidence of deficiency in themselves rather than a productive step for engaging texts. To move beyond a deferent reading stance, Smith describes a reading workshop method, influenced by Sheridan Blau, wherein a series of questions prompt students in small groups to reread a text with increasingly complex levels of depth and analysis. It is a great resource for teachers of basic writing and scholars interested in reading theory.

180   Spigelman, Candace. "Taboo Topics and the Rhetoric of Silence: Discussing *Lives on the Boundary* in a Basic Writing Class." *Journal of Basic Writing* 17.1 (1998): 42–55. Print.

Spigelman explores basic writing students' resistance—expressed largely through silence—to Mike Rose's *Lives on the Boundary* [124]. Using Rose's text, Spigelman encouraged her students to explore and critique educational and institutional inequities such as those Rose faced and that many of the students likely also faced. While in their essays many students identified personally with Rose's struggles, they resisted larger cultural critique: they rejected any notion that the system was to blame and read *Lives on the Boundary* as an American success story. Interpreting her students' refusal to speak about the failures and exclusions of education as rhetorics of silence, Spigelman argues that despite students' confusion and discomfort, compositionists should not abandon the ethical and political implications of writing instruction, but neither should we ignore the implications of those silences. Finally, citing a discussion she had with Rose, Spigelman urges compositionists to address these contradictions and conflicts through creativity and imagination—first by helping students to see inequalities and then by helping students reimagine alternatives.

Acceleration

181   Adams, Peter, et al. "The Accelerated Learning Program: Throwing Open the Gates." *Journal of Basic Writing* 28.2 (2009): 50–69. Print.

Adams's description of his efforts to ensure that developmental classes are "more path than gate" to college success are detailed in this article. After examination of the data, he determined students were not successfully completing college if their postsecondary careers began in developmental writing classes. During the 1992 Fall Conference of Basic Writing, which Adams was chairing, the idea of "mainstreaming" developmental writers was first introduced. The keynote speaker, David Bartholomae, unbeknownst to Adams, had basically the same idea. The detailed chronological summary of Adams's efforts to improve the success rates of developmental students began in January 2007 with a proposal for the Accelerated Learning Program (ALP). Beginning at the Community College of Baltimore County by securing administrative support and compiling two years of data, Adams explains the nine reasons ALP is successful and provides a path to college success for developmental writing students.

182   Edgecombe, Nikki, Elaine DeLott Baker, and Thomas Bailey. "Acceleration through a Holistic Support Model: An Implementation and Outcomes Analysis of FastStart@CCD." *Community College Research Center*. Teachers College, Columbia University. Feb. 2013. Web. 21 May 2014.

FastStart, launched in 2005 at the Community College of Denver (CCD), allows students to complete multiple developmental education courses within a single intensive semester. Originally designed for students who test into at least two levels of developmental education in a particular subject area, FastStart is a compressed course program. The program combines multiple semester-length math or English courses into a single intensive semester. Unlike traditional courses, FastStart also provides case management, career exploration, and educational planning services for enrolled students. This report discusses the development of FastStart, its program features, and student perspectives. It presents specific findings from a quantitative analysis of the FastStart math program. The authors find that, in addition to providing opportunities for students to benefit from innovative curricula in a time-extended course, student participation is associated with higher rates of enrolling in and passing college-level math courses. The analysis suggests that FastStart makes it possible for students to complete the developmental math sequence and required gatekeeper math course more quickly than would otherwise be possible, without harming other long-term academic outcomes. This study finds, however, that FastStart is not associated with increased persistence or with increased accumulation of college-level credits.

183   Rose, Mike. "Standards, Teaching, Learning." *Journal of Basic Writing* 28.2 (2009): 93–102. Print.

Standards for student work remain part of our task in evaluating students. Perhaps too often we accept standards without understanding or evaluating why or how they have been constructed. Teachers should shift to a "dynamics of development" (97). Such a shift would allow teachers to recognize the provisional nature of standards and be more mindful of "access and equity versus excellence" (98). Moreover, teachers could be more aware of the reasoning behind selecting certain readings: What are the goals from this reading? How might the students understand a reading based on their experience? What do I as the teacher want them to take away from this reading? What experience do I have as a reader of this piece? Perhaps most of all, what is the educational philosophy that is influencing the standards we are upholding? By answering questions such as these, teachers can better articulate standards and the theoretical basis behind them.

184   Webb-Sunderhaus, Sara. "When Access Is Not Enough: Retaining Basic Writers at an Open-Admission University." *Journal of Basic Writing* 29.2 (2010): 97–116. Print.

In this article, Webb-Sunderhaus argues persuasively that as scholar-teachers of basic writing, we "must devote as much critical attention to offering basic writers equality of success as we do to offering [them] equality of access" (99). We may do this, she argues, by taking into account studies on student retention, persistence, and departure and, in light of their findings, "asserting more forcefully that access is not enough" (99). While the values commonly enacted by basic writing pedagogy and curricula—"access, inclusion, equity, and respect for student knowledge"—are crucial, Webb-Sunderhaus contends, we also need to examine more carefully "*how* actual students," and particularly those from marginalized populations, "invent the university and succeed in it" (101, 109). Ultimately, listening to the college success stories of "real" basic writing students will demonstrate that their success does not hinge just upon access, but also upon strong institutional support for "multiple support structures that go beyond a writing program," such as "writing centers, advising, . . . bridge programs, services for students with disabilities, . . . childcare and financial aid" (111).

Basic Writers and Technological Literacy

185   Alexander, Kara P., Beth Powell, and Sonya C. Green. "Understanding Modal Affordances: Student Perceptions of Potentials and Limitations in Multimodal Composition." *Basic Writing e-Journal* 10.1/11.1 (2011–2012): n. pag. Web. 30 Dec. 2013.

Alexander, Powell, and Green examine traditional, nontraditional, and basic writing students' perceptions of the affordances of multimodal composing by collecting questionnaires from fifty first-year composition students who completed both a print and a multimodal essay. Questionnaires given before and after students completed these writing assignments on the same subject surveyed their perceptions about integrating and employing modal affordances in their compositions. Students perceived potentials in multimodal texts that included layering, implicit persuasion, and a clearer understanding of audience, creativity, and affective appeals. Conversely, students perceived the construction of a clear, well-supported thesis as a limitation. The authors argue for incorporating multimodal composition assignments because it helps basic writers enter the academic world, benefits students, and adds value to the composition classroom. However, they suggest that the concept of thesis may need to be expanded to multimodal texts, so instructors should provide students with additional instruction on how to develop theses, assertions, arguments, and claims. The authors conclude with pedagogical recommendations for implementing multimodal assignments in composition courses.

186   Ashley, Hannah. "Social Justice and Multimodal Writing for Basic Composition, Really? A Post-Process Framework." *Basic Writing e-Journal* 10.1/11.1 (2011–2012): n. pag. Web. 30 Dec. 2013.

In this interactive Prezi, Ashley responds to Matthew Heard's "What Should We Do with Post-Process Theory?" and encourages writing faculty to examine their classroom practices. Ashley contends writing teachers must move beyond the idea that writing is a "codifiable, a stable, transmittable body of knowledge" and a skill to be mastered to the idea that writing is a fluid, public act of encoding and decoding messages. Since "writing is paralogical—it cannot ever be fully predicted or codified"—teaching writing in the twenty-first century requires a shift toward multimodal writing, which exposes students to "MANY communication scenarios." Ashley argues faculty must transition from the idea that they are graders and experts to the idea that they are coproducers of discourse, who can encourage students to think metacognitively about their decisions as writers. Multimodal writing allows students to establish connections between the classroom and their communities and allows them to explore multiple discourses.

187   Crank, Virginia. "Asynchronous Electronic Peer Response in a Hybrid Basic Writing Classroom." *Teaching English in the Two-Year College* 32.2 (2002): 145–55. Print.

Crank reports on a peer-response experiment that began when she converted her traditional composition classes to a hybrid of online and traditional models. She discovered that asynchronous electronic peer response helped students become better responders to each other's texts and created a "new kind of composing community" (147) in her classes. Asynchronous peer response offered certain strengths lacking in synchronous electronic or traditional peer response. Students engaged with the texts as genuine readers took more time and care in composing responses, responded with more specificity, wrote to one another rather than to the instructor, and valued the flexibility they had when they responded in the asynchronous environment.

188   Cummings, Martha C. "'Because We Are Shy and Fear Mistaking': Computer-Mediated Communication with EFL Writers." *Journal of Basic Writing* 23.2 (2004): 23–48. Print.

Cummings reports on an online writing course she taught at a Japanese university. She used Nicenet.org to set up the classroom. Her study analyzes the extent to which computer-mediated communication alleviates the stress students in Japan feel when using English as an interactive tool with native speakers of English and its impact on the quantity and quality of student output. Results suggest that although students in the computer-mediated course did not produce texts of a higher quality than those of traditional students, they did develop a more positive attitude "toward writing, learning English, accuracy, and communicating with each other, their instructor, and native speakers of English in general" (36). Students valued three aspects of the computer-mediated classroom: learning from one another, the possibility of communicating with real native speakers, and communicating with the instructor. At the same time, some missed the benefits of face-to-face instruction. The computer-mediated classroom also had a positive effect on the author, who found out things about her students she would not have learned in the face-to-face classroom, causing her attitude toward them to change for the better.

189   Grabill, Jeffrey T. "Technology, Basic Writing, and Change." *Journal of Basic Writing* 17.2 (1998): 91–105. Print.

Grabill asserts that writing teachers commonly think of adapting curricula to meet the needs of students to effect change but that true change in curriculum, institutions, and students will not result until the institutional view of basic writing is altered radically. He demonstrates that the level of technology available for basic writers reveals the lowly position of basic writing in the institution. However, for basic writing to gain a more important position in academia, developmental writing students need meaningful access to technology, and their courses must be credit-bearing. Grabill used his institution's emphasis on access to technology for all students as an "institutional wedge" to attempt to improve the position of basic writing. The introduction of advanced technology into the basic writing courses changed the attitude of the instructors and the students: both saw the class as an intellectually stimulating course that "counts." The university has yet to make the class credit-bearing, but some movement toward change has been possible because of technology.

190   Grobman, Laurie. "'I Found It on the Web, So Why Can't I Put It in My Paper?': Authorizing Basic Writers." *Journal of Basic Writing* 18.1 (1999): 76–90. Print.

Because Internet sources are easily accessible to students, basic writing instructors should consider the influence of the Web in the context of their pedagogical practices. The Internet enables basic writers to join the "conversation of ideas," thereby authorizing them as members of an academic community. Part of this authorization is based on writers' abilities to evaluate and question the credibility of Internet sources and on their use of critical reading and thinking skills, even though the Internet "necessitates" a reexamination "of the relationship between authority, academic discourse, and basic writers" (77).

191   Henry, Thomas, Joshua Hilst, and Regina Clemens Fox. "Remembering Basic Composition: The Emergence of Multimodality in Basic Writing Studies." *Basic Writing e-Journal* 10.1/11.1 (2011–2012): n. pag. Web. 12 Jan. 2014.

This essay explains why and how print-focused *basic writing* instructors should embrace multimodal *basic composition* instruction and how they can do so without jettisoning all aspects of the Mina Shaughnessy–inspired basic writing paradigm. Beginning with a cogent history of how and why the field of composition has incorporated the multimodal change while continually sharing key rhetorical lessons of knowledge making, persuasion, and social participation, the essay moves beyond defining technology as a tool to consider how "digital natives" deserve to be taught from and about their "digital comfort zone." Brief definitions of orienting terms (multimodality, affordance/s, modes, medium/media) introduce lesson suggestions that rely on those terms while considering nontraditional and traditional students' "digital communication needs" for future academic, workplace, social, and civic writing and engagement. The lessons reviewed also embrace and expand multimodal experiences students bring to college writing/composition classes. Such a shift to multimodal basic composition that includes lessons about written, visual, and aural/oral rhetoric may save threatened basic writing programs.

192 Jaggars, Shanna Smith. "Online Learning: Does It Help Low-Income and Underprepared Students? (Assessment of Evidence Series)." *Community College Research Center*. Teachers College, Columbia University. Jan. 2011. Web. 21 May 2014.

Jaggars analyzes thirty-six studies comparing online and traditional courses to determine whether online courses meet the needs of low-income and underprepared students. Her research review concludes that current online practices impede progress for these students. Jaggars then explores online obstacles for students, including technical difficulties, lack of social connection, loose structure, and insufficient student support. Jaggars notes that many low-income households do not have the technology necessary for online coursework, and while online courses are flexible and convenient, they do not lower the costs of tuition and fees. In addition, some students seek fully online degrees rather than individual online courses, and options are limited. To improve access and progression for low-income and underprepared students online, Jaggars suggests reducing tuition and technology costs by restructuring financial aid requirements, creating more fully online degree programs, teaching online learning skills, improving faculty training, providing stronger student support, and investing in ongoing research to identify how to better serve low-income and underprepared student populations in the online environment.

193 Jonaitis, Leigh. "Troubling Discourse: Basic Writing and Computer-Mediated Technologies." *Journal of Basic Writing* 31.1 (2012): 36–58. Print.

Jonaitis identifies and analyzes several discourses surrounding basic writers and technology. Drawing from scholarship in the fields of basic writing and computers and writing, the author argues that decisions regarding the role of technology in a basic writing context are influenced by locally contexualized politics that shape perceptions of access, student ability, and what constitutes a "remedial" education. By positioning the discussion using Bertram Barton's framework for understanding the relationship between technology and teaching, Jonaitis outlines "oppositional" and "skeptical" positions on teaching with technology on one hand, as well as "utilitarian" and "transformational" stances on the other. Jonaitis urges readers to consider a view of literacy in which technology and writing are closely integrated and socially situated, reminding her readers throughout to consider the political and ideological nuances inherent in decisions about where and how technology might fit in a basic writing curriculum. The article ends with a call for additional research into the effects of technology on teaching basic writing.

194   Kish, Judith Mara. "Breaking the Block: Basic Writers in the Electronic Classroom." *Journal of Basic Writing* 19.2 (2000): 141–59. Print.

Kish uses her 1997–1998 computer-assisted "stretch" class at Arizona State University as a case study to explore connections between the difficulties of basic writers and the difficulty of writer's block. Connections between the two—problems with genre and problems with the linearity of texts—are identified. To help to alleviate the students' problems, hypertext and basic hypertext theory were introduced to the class, a method that proved to be useful in helping students with their writing difficulties.

195   Klages, Marisa A., and J. Elizabeth Clark. "New Worlds of Errors and Expectations: Basic Writers and Digital Assumptions." *Journal of Basic Writing* 28.1 (2009): 32–49. Print.

Klages and Clark provide an overview of the rationale, implementation, and outcomes of the E-Portfolio Program at CUNY in the basic writing program, with an empathetic analysis of the barriers erected by educational institutions and of the deep insecurities that can cripple basic writers. Implementation of an E-Portfolio program engages struggling writers, challenging them to find their authentic voice while increasing digital technology skills to negotiate and thrive by critically analyzing not only their own work for revision, but also by commenting on the public artifacts created by their classmates. As students write for public consumption, they are demonstrating understanding of audience and purpose, and negotiating understanding in an authoritative voice that rises above the rhetoric used for social media. This transforms the author with an understanding of the expectations of a digital culture while becoming literate cyber-citizens.

196   Lay, Ethna Demsey. "Welcome e-Burdens: New Media Projects in the Basic Writing Classroom." *Basic Writing e-Journal* 10.1/11.1 (2011–2012): n. pag. Web. 10 Jan. 2014.

Lay muses about the problem of "remediating" (restructuring/reconstructing) traditional textual composition assignments as multimodal products. In a substantive discussion of two students' collaboratively produced video submitted in lieu of a traditional composition, Lay praises the students' ingenuity, technical expertise, and rhetorical flair but glosses over their obvious rejection of the academic expectations for basic and first-year writing. Lay suggests that we embrace students' preference for electronic communication venues; however, she doesn't illustrate how expertise in e-world venues equates to competence in traditional writing. Lay's term *e-burden* encapsulates ambivalence about substituting aptitude in effective electronic communication for competence in traditional written communication. Lay scaffolds her discussion on well-chosen supporting concepts from practitioners and theorists including David Bartholomae, Bruno Bettelheim, and Paolo Freire. She ends by asserting that the academic essay needs reconsideration in light of electronic composition and concomitant reconstructions of textuality.

197   Lutkewitte, Claire. "The First Digital Native Writing Instructors and the Future Multimodal Composition Classroom." *Basic Writing e-Journal* 10.1/11.1 (2011–2012): n. pag. Web. 20 Jan. 2014.

Lutkewitte believes digital native students have been discussed thoroughly in professional literature but that digital native instructors (DNIs) have not, positioning her article in that gap. She argues that instructors "who were born after 1980 and grew up interacting daily in networked digital technologies" (1) read, write, and compose through different methods than those of "digital settlers and digital immigrants" (2) from previous generations. Lutkewitte argues that DNIs can, will, and should have new-to-academe ideas about the definitions and creations of writing, text, research, and authorship. She envisions future composition courses teaching not only the composition of these new and multimodal methods but the associated technical skills, ethics, and online safety concerns as well. She also admits that basic writing classrooms will face particular challenges, as students who struggle with standard literacy also often struggle with technology and information literacy. Finally, Lutkewitte argues for DNIs to take—and be allowed to take—the lead on their campuses and across the profession in creating these future pedagogies, texts, and discourses.

198   Otte, George. "Computer-Adjusted Errors and Expectations." *Journal of Basic Writing* 10.2 (1991): 71–86. Print.

Otte examines papers written by his basic writing students, who have failed the City University of New York Writing Assessment Test, for patterns of error and the students' ability to correct them. As a reader of the test, Otte knows that a high incidence of error causes students to fail. Using a computer program called Error Extractor, he developed a list of eighteen categories of errors he found in his students' papers. With the program, which coded errors in their papers, Otte had students go through their essays, editing errors they found. Their successes and failures to edit were then recorded by the program and could be tabulated both synchronically and diachronically throughout the term. Otte found that using handbooks or covering in class the general types of errors he saw in the students' papers did little to help students edit. Instead, individual conferences, during which he discussed a particular student's particular errors, aided his students in editing their papers. Statistics gathered over the term indicate that students did become better editors of their own writing through the conferencing method: when retested, 79 percent of his students passed the Writing Assessment Test.

199   Otte, George, and Terence Collins. "Basic Writing and New Technologies." *Basic Writing e-Journal* 1.1 (1999): n. pag. Web. 21 May 2014.

In a two-part essay, Otte and Collins describe Web resources available for teachers of basic writing and English as a second language. Otte offers a link and directions for using the Currtran Database, a collection of innovative teaching-with-technology practices and ideas for use in basic writing and other courses. Collins provides a collection of links to

Web sites that offer grammar resources, e-journals, and reference works for ESL teachers.

200   Pavia, Catherine Matthews. "Issues of Attitude and Access: A Case Study of Basic Writers in a Computer Classroom." *Journal of Basic Writing* 23.2 (2004): 4–22. Print.

Most research that considers the use of computers in basic writing classrooms emphasizes technology's positive pedagogical value for students and teachers. Pavia urges teachers to consider student attitudes and access to computers before they "jump on the technology bandwagon" (20). She asks, "What happens when basic writers, who by definition lack experience in writing, also lack experience with computers?" (14). Through case studies of two basic writing students with limited access to technology, Pavia concludes that computers both "create opportunities" and "accentuate differences in opportunity" (15). Students who have had few chances to work on computers at home or in previous schools may appreciate the exposure to technology, but they will not necessarily transfer that positive attitude about computers to their writing (12). In addition, Pavia notes that students will need much more than equipment to truly access computer literacy; some students will struggle to write effectively on computers if they lack typing skills or a familiarity with word processing (18). Therefore, basic writing instructors who use computers should assume neither that their students are computer literate nor that presenting students with computers will ensure that they become computer literate. Rather, Pavia suggests that teachers take steps to understand and address the disadvantages some students may face when using computers in a basic writing classroom. First, she recommends assigning a technology narrative at the beginning of the semester that asks students to reflect on their relationships to and histories with technology. Then, she suggests teachers make use of the information they gather about student backgrounds from the technology narratives to build flexibility and balance into the curriculum. Computers should neither overshadow writing instruction nor hinder student learning. Rather, technology should be understood as a tool that teachers and students can choose to access when it will help them best meet their goals in the writing classroom.

201   Shapiro, Rachel. "The Word on Hope and Dread: Multimodal Composition and Basic Writing." *Basic Writing e-Journal* 10.1/11.1 (2011–2012): n. pag. Web. 20 Jan. 2014.

According to Shapiro, the digital sphere is such an important site of knowledge-making that basic writing instructors should provide direct, critical instruction in digital literacies as an essential part of the curricula in their basic writing classrooms. To help instructors overcome their potential fears about digital work in their classrooms, she offers a framework for assignment design that includes digital and multimodal projects. Shapiro's webtext includes a candid overview of the lessons learned from a multimodal Upward Bound project, as well as the specifics of a multimodal assignment sequence that uses PostSecret,

Prezi, and Picnik. Once basic writing instructors address their fears and expectations, Shapiro asserts they can create complex, multimodal assignments that will help prepare basic writers to respond to the contemporary moment.

202   Spina-Caza, Lillian, and Paul Booth. "Video Unbound: Have You Vlogged Lately? Infusing Video Technology in the Composition Classroom." *Basic Writing e-Journal* 10.1/11.1 (2011–2012): n. pag. Web. 20 Jan. 2014.

The use of digital video as a writing tool in the composition and basic writing classrooms has the potential to increase students' rhetorical awareness, critical eye toward mainstream ideologies, and active participation in the production and distribution of their ideas. Much like print, video production asks students to engage in recursive literacy practices to develop ideas for particular audiences, but it also challenges students to move beyond alphabetic literacy. Through digital video — a "fluid and malleable communication tool" — students also cultivate an "oral-aural" literacy. By using digital video in the classroom, students can examine contemporary cultures, analyze "their own places in their culture," and construct arguments. Through carefully designed assignments like vlogging, mashup videos, autobiographical sketches, and documentaries, composition faculty offer students rich opportunities to refine their understanding of words, motion, interactivity, and visuals. Using digital video in the composition and basic writing classroom does not mean replacing the traditional essay. It means developing students' multimodal thinking in ways that are relevant to both the purpose of composition pedagogy and the lived experiences of the students.

203   Stine, Linda J. "The Best of Both Worlds: Teaching Basic Writers in Class and Online." *Journal of Basic Writing* 23.2 (2004): 49–69. Print.

In her discussion of the incorporation of computer technology and online resources into the composition classroom, Stine begins with an overview of both the potential problems instructors could encounter and the benefits this transition could bring to the classroom. Rather than favoring online instruction over classroom instruction, Stine argues for a "hybrid" environment, one in which students can benefit from both forms of learning while avoiding their negative aspects. Using her experience in classroom curricula as an example, Stine establishes seven principles for teaching effectively in a curriculum that is heavily reliant on online spaces and resources. As the teacher of a first-year composition course comprised primarily of nontraditional students, most of whom commute to campus, Stine offers a unique perspective into the benefits of online resources such as e-learning and chat rooms.

204   Stine, Linda J. "Teaching Basic Writing in a Web-Enhanced Environment." *Journal of Basic Writing* 29.1 (2010): 33–55. Print.

Stine asks, "How does online learning change the teaching role, what kinds of assignments are appropriate to this medium, and what tools/

methods may best encourage the sort of student self-reflection so important to academic success?" (34). She answers these questions through
both research review and personal teaching experience. Guided by
well-known online education theorists from Palloff and Pratt to Cynthia Selfe and her own work teaching basic writing to returning adult
students, Stine specifically discusses different Web-enhanced methods
for the writing classroom: chat rooms, wikis, and blogs. She advocates
an involved, responsive online writing pedagogy of "continuous innovation" (38). Stine argues that hybrid-style classes are the best
Web-enhanced method of basic writing instruction because they allow
professors to assist students with course technology as well as course
content. She also exhorts basic writing teachers to contribute more to
the literature and national conversation regarding Web-inclusive basic
writing instruction.

205   Wuebben, Dan. "Synesthetic White Noise: Translating, Transforming, and Transmitting Affect/Text." *Basic Writing e-Journal* 10.1/11.1
(2011–2012): n. pag. Web. 20 Jan. 2014.

Tentatively drawing from psychological theories of synesthesia, Wuebben argues that composing multimodal texts can help students develop
more than one form of literacy simultaneously. In particular, Wuebben
focuses on an "affective" engagement with texts that can enable students to develop technological and academic literacies. He does this
by providing opportunities for students to relate to texts in multiple
ways. In this article, he describes a course in which students used writing, voice, image, and video to respond to Don DeLillo's *White Noise*.
Students collaborated on this project both inside and outside the
classroom and were able to contribute their own different perspectives
and expertise. Wuebben concludes that by asking his students to relate
to a text in different ways through multimodal composing, they were
able to make connections between technological and academic literacy
practices.

Style, Grammar, and Usage

206   Connors, Robert J., and Andrea Lunsford. "Frequency of Formal Errors
in Current College Writing, or Ma and Pa Kettle Do Research." *College
Composition and Communication* 39.4 (1988): 395–409. Print.

In their analysis of three hundred samples of writing from first- and
second-year college composition courses across the United States, Connors and Lunsford wanted to identify the most common patterns of student writing errors and the patterns that were marked most consistently
by American teachers (397). Topping the list of fifty-four identified
types of errors were spelling (450 errors), no comma after introductory
element (138 errors), comma splices (124 errors), and wrong words
(102 errors). They found that "what constitutes a serious, markable
error var[ies] widely" from teacher to teacher and that "teachers do

not seem to mark as many errors as we often think they do" (402). In addition, what constitutes an error is largely an individual judgment, the kinds of errors students make may be a result of cultural trends, and students are probably not making any more errors in their writing than they did decades ago.

207   D'Eloia, Sarah. "The Uses—and Limits—of Grammar." *Journal of Basic Writing* 1.3 (1977): 1–20. Print.

The analytical study of grammar is of limited value for basic writers, but D'Eloia suggests that other approaches to grammar are useful. Basic writing instructors benefit from grammatical expertise since it gives them tools to identify, explain, and design appropriate exercises for student error. Students benefit when they are taught grammar economically and as part of the writing process. Instructors should use minimal, simple terminology to teach students as much grammar as they need to make standard English predictable. Students should complete grammar exercises that help them transfer abstract principles into the production of correct writing, such as dictation, focused proofreading, paraphrasing, and imitation. A discovery approach, in which students move inductively to grammar rules, can be more helpful, though time consuming. D'Eloia provides sample exercises and a syllabus for teaching the verb phrase.

208   Fearn, Leif, and Nancy Farnan. "When Is a Verb? Using Functional Grammar to Teach Writing." *Journal of Basic Writing* 26.1 (2007): 63–87. Print.

This article outlines the results of teaching two sections of tenth-grade students with a focus on what words do in sentences, rather than on the more traditional focus on what those words are called. Fearn and Farnan compare their results for those two sections with another section taught with a focus on identification, description, and definition (IDD). Their results indicate that while all students scored about the same on mechanical accuracy and a grammar test, their two classes did better on holistically graded writing.

209   Flores, Nelson. "Beyond Charity: Partial Narratives as a Metaphor for Basic Writing." *Journal of Basic Writing* 29.2 (2010): 31–49. Print.

The debates about the work of Mina Shaughnessy and Min-Zhan Lu sparked a spirited debate in the 1990s. While this debate seems far from over (and sometimes misunderstood), it can now be seen through a different perspective—a "pedagogy of partial narratives." Based on the work of Elizabeth Ellsworth, partial narratives are narratives that allow for the partiality of all discourse. They "challenge composition teachers to accept the inherently political nature of language and discourse and to make it part of their pedagogical relationship with students." Such a position regards knowledge within a dynamic of power that we cannot escape. The underlying potential for basic writing classrooms is for students and teachers to work in concert to find ways to master, partially through resistance, an academic writing style. With this acknowledgment and acceptance, we understand the realities of the colonizing effect and/or oppression of academic discourse, while still finding ways to embrace the historical nature of basic writing and its radical history.

210   Gray, Loretta S., and Paula Heuser. "Nonacademic Professionals' Perception of Usage Errors." *Journal of Basic Writing* 22.1 (2003): 50–70. Print.

Gray and Heuser update the survey that Maxine Hairston created for her groundbreaking article, "Not All Errors Are Created Equal: Nonacademic Readers in the Professions Respond to Lapses in Usage." Hairston correctly assumed that readers would consider some errors more egregious than others. To determine what errors would be the most bothersome, Hairston surveyed professionals who were not English teachers. The survey consisted of sixty-six sentences, each with a single mistake. Nonacademics were to choose from the following options: "Does not bother me," "Bothers me a little," or "Bothers me a lot." Gray and Heuser added a "No Error" answer and some grammatically correct sentences to the survey and represented each error by at least two sentences. The survey revealed that respondents were often inconsistent or incorrect in applying grammar rules. Overall, the revised study results suggest that while nonacademics are less bothered by usage errors, the errors that they find most bothersome are still common dialectical features. Gray and Heuser argue for a comprehensive grammar curriculum so that students may learn metalinguistic skills to understand the ways that language usage norms vary among communities.

211   Harris, Muriel, and Katherine E. Rowan. "Explaining Grammatical Concepts." *Journal of Basic Writing* 8.2 (1989): 21–41. Print.

Harris and Rowan suggest that editing is a complex problem that is perceived as having many steps, especially for basic writers. While such students do not "need to be able to spout grammatical *terminology*," they do need to "understand fundamental grammatical *concepts*" to successfully edit their writing (22). Harris and Rowan suggest drawing on "concept learning research"—an approach that focuses on explaining a student's "most frequent misunderstandings" (23). The authors explain and outline in detail four key steps to understand and explain concepts: recalling background knowledge, controlling all the critical features of a concept, recognizing new instances of a concept, and discriminating apparent from real instances of a concept. The authors also make suggestions on how to implement their ideas. They conclude that no one method works for all students and all problems; however, they suggest using a combination of approaches.

212   Hartwell, Patrick. "Grammar, Grammars, and the Teaching of Grammar." *College English* 47.2 (1985): 105–27. Print.

To demonstrate how misunderstandings in the debate over grammar instruction have rendered it largely useless for producing effective strategies for teaching writing, Hartwell identifies five definitions of grammar: the arrangement of words, the study of rules about the arrangement and use of words, judgments based on the use and arrangement of words, school grammar, and stylistic grammar. He argues that instructors often confuse the more useful definition of grammar (how language works) with power-imbued definitions of grammar (school rules for writing correctly). Too often, teachers conclude that students are poor writers because they don't know the school rules for writing when, in fact, students often have great command over how language works. Hartwell concludes that our theories and research studies should teach us that student involvement with language is always preferable to any direct instruction on the "rules" of that language.

213   Kenkel, James, and Robert Yates. "A Developmental Perspective on the Relationship between Grammar and Text." *Journal of Basic Writing* 22.1 (2003): 35–49. Print.

Citing the long-standing awareness of the limitations of teaching formal grammar to developmental students, Kenkel and Yates propose viewing student errors from a developmental perspective—not as evidence of ignorance or carelessness but as "principled attempts to manage information" (45). Expanding on the earlier work of Charles Fries, Mina Shaughnessy, Patrick Hartwell, Robert De Beaugrande, Rei Noguchi, Charles Coleman, and Eleanor Kutz, the authors suggest that some nonstandard constructions can be explained as students' "difficulty fitting complex ideas into the correspondingly more complex syntactic structures" (39). The authors assert that assignments should be constructed to encourage mature shifting of focus (something that a personal narrative, for example, does not do) and "making explicit comparisons between student texts and mature texts" (46). These types of nonstandard constructions are not performance errors, they contend, cannot be easily self-corrected, and will not disappear after extensive reading and writing.

214   Lauren, Ben, and Rich Rice. "Teaching Style in Basic Writing through Remediating Photo Essays." *Basic Writing e-Journal* 10.1/11.1 (2011–2012): n. pag. Web. 20 Jan. 2014.

Lauren and Rice remind us that those students born after 1980 are "natural" to the "social digital technologies," and we must incorporate these digital technologies into our basic writing curricula through the use of the photo essay. The photo essay allows students to better visualize the stylistic elements of an essay. An explanation of a photo essay assignment is included along with a student's reflection after completing a photo essay assignment. The student realizes "blurry photos or blurry words can confuse an audience," thus acknowledging revision is necessary. Two student examples of annotating a peer's photo essay are also included. The first example illustrates how a basic writing student "struggling to understand the importance of clarity of writing" is able to articulate an essay by looking at the photos, thus "demonstrating understanding." In the second student example, the students can quickly identify gaps between photos and holes in the story, which "demonstrates other areas of confusion that require re-envisioning."

215   Lees, Elaine O. "Proofreading as Reading, Errors as Embarrassments." *A Sourcebook for Basic Writing Teachers*. Ed. Theresa Enos. New York: Random, 1987. 216–30. Print.

Lees argues that a social view of proofreading and error explains why basic writers have difficulty correcting their own writing. Joseph Williams's work on the complexities of perceiving error shows that errors are located not in texts or writers but in the reader's experience. Proofreading is not a mechanical process of correcting the physical features of a text but a critical interpretation carried out within a cultural group. Skilled proofreaders use texts to construct meanings that support conventional judgments of literacy. Unsuccessful proofreaders do not possess the interpretive frameworks to organize the features necessary for revealing errors. Errors are flaws in social display that embarrass writers by revealing their imperfect mastery of behaviors considered appropriate in communities they wish to join. Some basic writers have trouble leaving behind their original interpretive community for that of Standard Edited American English and might always need help when editing their work.

216   Neuleib, Janice, and Irene Brosnahan. "Teaching Grammar to Writers." *Teaching Developmental Writing: Background Readings*. Ed. Susan Naomi Bernstein. Boston: Bedford, 2001. 91–97. Print.

Neuleib and Brosnahan argue that for teachers to use approaches like sentence combining and error analysis in the classroom, the teachers themselves must know grammar better than they currently do. The authors tested twenty-four teacher-certification students in a required upper-level grammar course and found that most of these prospective teachers had had grammar instruction at three or more levels (elementary, junior high, high school, and college) but that few knew grammar as well as they thought they did. Neuleib and Brosnahan attribute this gap in perception to fuzzy definitions of grammar that are not informed by the history of language. To help students edit for grammar, teachers "need to be able to work out exercises of the types illustrated by Shaughnessy and D'Eloia, exercises patterned to individual students' language problems" (118). Better grammar instruction at the teacher-training level will enable teachers to apply grammar instruction effectively in their own classrooms.

See: Sarah D'Eloia, "The Uses—and Limits—of Grammar" [207].

217   Newman, Michael. "Correctness and Its Conceptions: The Meaning of Language Form for Basic Writers." *Journal of Basic Writing* 15.1 (1996): 23–38. Print.

Basic writers are sometimes overly preoccupied with grammatical concerns because they are "trying to send the message that they belong to the academic world they have come to join" (35). Surface-level errors are best approached with students through acknowledging this perspective and working with them on how their texts might fit in best with the expectations of register or genre. Newman posits that teaching language conventions from a perspective that views many usage edicts as based on logic or another language's grammatical rules does students little good; nor does denying the appropriateness of the above-mentioned usage edicts, as so many sociolinguists do. These edicts carry weight because they are based on myth, not science, and the myths of prescriptivism are an attempt to make clear what is not. Instead, instructors may do best by focusing on register variations, approaching tasks with students by working with them to best fit their texts into those already in the genre. In this way, instructors would not just be teaching grammar but would be focused on helping students "acquir[e] a new way of meaning" (38).

218   Noguchi, Rei R. *Grammar and the Teaching of Writing: Limits and Possibilities*. Urbana: NCTE, 1991. Print.

Citing a long line of research from anti- and pro-grammarians, Noguchi suggests that writing teachers navigate the middle ground by using grammar in a way that works to improve student writing. This sort of grammar instruction addresses a manageable collection of a select few rules and rubrics based loosely on generative grammar and common-sense editing models that can help writing students help themselves. Noguchi addresses grammar more as an editing tool than as a generative tool. To further circumvent a reductive traditional approach, Noguchi suggests an editing and revising model based on students' innate and cultural grammatical and syntactic knowledge.

219   Truscott, John. "The Effect of Error Correction on Learners' Ability to Write Correctly." *Journal of Second Language Writing* 16.4 (2007): 225–72. Print.

In the last decade, much research about error correction has presented one-sided discussions, offering a favorable view of error correction. In this small-scale meta-analysis of the effect of error correction on learners' ability to write accurately, Truscott comes to the conclusion that error correction actually has a small negative effect on learners' ability to write accurately. Error correction is defined as correcting errors of all types, such as spelling errors and grammatical errors. Six controlled and six uncontrolled experiments are selected for synthesis. All of the controlled experiments suggest that correction has small, harmful effects on students' ability to write accurately, and the uncontrolled studies indicate small gains in accuracy made by correction groups. However, Truscott points out two biasing factors that may lead to the gains shown in correction groups in the uncontrolled studies: (1) the same setting of correction and testing and (2) avoidance. The first factor means the break between the correction and the measurement of accuracy is very short, and thus long-term effects remain unknown. The avoidance factor explains the phenomenon that students tend to avoid using situations corrected before, thus leading to deceptive gains in accuracy. A discussion of factors that may have biased previous studies as well as meta-analysis of key studies of controlled comparisons between those who received correction and those who did not and of absolute gains made by correction groups reveal the ways that previous studies have overestimated the effectiveness of correction and underestimated the harmfulness of correction.

220   Weaver, Constance. "Teaching Style through Sentence Combining and Sentence Generating." *Teaching Developmental Writing: Background Readings*. Ed. Susan Naomi Bernstein. Boston: Bedford, 2001. 119–29. Print.

Weaver offers four mini-lessons for preservice and inservice teachers in a course on grammar or the teaching of grammar. The lessons help teachers to view themselves as writers and to model techniques of teaching grammar in context. The first lesson encourages students to include narrative and descriptive details in their writing. The second lesson encourages students to write "I am" poems that metaphorically equate themselves with things that reflect their interests. The third lesson encourages students to identify present participle phrases, past-participle phrases, and absolute phrases and to use all three of these free modifiers in their writing. The fourth lesson encourages students to find effective examples of absolute constructions in literature and to appreciate absolute constructions as a means of conveying descriptive detail.

221   Williams, Joseph. "The Phenomenology of Error." *College Composition and Communication* 32.2 (1981): 152–68. Print.

Williams explores how educated readers read and react to perceived errors based on the complex interplay of text, reader, and intention. Williams shows how differently texts are read when they are read not for error but for their message. He does this by highlighting passages taken from style guides that break the very rules they posit. He argues that error cannot be defined only as either a violation of a grammatical rule or a breach of social expectations because the significance of an error depends on our response to it. Williams challenges his readers to realize that "if we read any text the way we read freshman essays, we will find many of the same kind of errors we routinely expect to find and therefore do find" (159). Williams discusses the range of responses we have to "errors" that are often lumped together in style guides and common wisdom as "nonstandard," showing how errors that mark class (nonstandard verb forms, for example) provoke much higher negative responses than errors of usage (the use of *irregardless*, for example).

Curriculum Development

Course Development

222   Bartholomae, David. "Facts, Artifacts, and Counterfacts: A Basic Reading and Writing Course for the College Curriculum." *A Sourcebook for Basic Writing Teachers*. Ed. Theresa Enos. New York: Random, 1987. 275–306. Print.

This article details how Bartholomae and Anthony Petrosky came to design a course for basic writers. It discusses their approach to the course (one based on close reading and written responses to specific texts), the ways in which such reading strategies are critical for basic writers, and the specific curriculum goals of their basic reading and writing course. Their course concentrates on literacy and writing from a social constructionist perspective and seeks to teach academic discourse to basic writers. Bartholomae offers a critical synopsis of their textbook, outlining the methodologies and pedagogical philosophies surrounding Bartholomae and Petrosky's course. He takes up questions of epistemology in basic writing pedagogy and examines issues of authority as they are presented within basic writers' prose.

223   Bartholomae, David, and Anthony Petrosky. *Facts, Artifacts, and Counterfacts: Theory and Method for a Reading and Writing Course*. Portsmouth: Boynton, 1986. Print.

Bartholomae and Petrosky present curriculum, theoretical framework, and rationale for teaching "students outside the mainstream—students unprepared for the textual demands of college education" (4). Their course disrupts many of the previous constructions of basic writing courses by suggesting that basic writers be challenged intellectually rather than given rote exercises. Drawing from contemporary theory and social constructionist philosophies, the authors reveal how teaching thoughtful, critical reading can help basic writers to utilize and comprehend academic discourse. The book includes a brief discussion of the problems basic writers face, pragmatic suggestions about how to teach reading and writing skills to basic writers, the procedures basic writers undertake when completing reading and writing, a case study of one basic writing student, an explanation of the implications of reading and writing assignments, and a discussion of error and editing and the complexities teachers face while teaching these issues to basic writers.

224   Bruch, Patrick L. "Universality in Basic Writing: Connecting Multicultural Justice, Universal Instructional Design, and Classroom Practices." *Basic Writing e-Journal* 5.1 (2004): n. pag. Web. 21 May 2014.

Bruch addresses the challenges of reinvigorating universality for basic writing by bringing together the notions of multicultural justice and Universal Instructional Design. He "proposes an understanding of universality that links the work of Basic Writing to recent political philosophy and the pedagogical movement Universal Instructional Design." (The term *Universal Instructional Design* comes from architecture and refers to the movement to make buildings accessible to those with physical disabilities while enhancing the quality of the design for all users.) Bruch presents assignments created for his basic writing class that his students have redesigned and enhanced to address their diverse needs as learners. Bruch suggests that implementing Universal Instructional Design to the theory and practice of basic writing pedagogy "is a way of equipping ourselves to explain the project of Basic Writing—the project of enabling participation in transforming cultural and material obstacles to educational equity." He offers an example of the ways in which Universal Instructional Design provides opportunities for him to collaborate with his students in revising a summary assignment so that it is more inclusive of students' multiple learning styles, emphasizing opportunities for students "to participate in creating alternative designs for texts." Such strategies, Bruch argues, offer students insight into conversations generated by texts and give students a chance to "lear[n] about literacy work by doing the work of literacy."

225   Carter, Shannon. *The Way Literacy Lives: Rhetorical Dexterity and Basic Writing Instruction.* Albany: State U of New York P, 2008. Print.

Drawing on activity theory and New Literacy Studies, Carter advocates teaching rhetorical dexterity, "a meta-awareness of the ways in which literacy functions in a familiar community of practice as a first step in reading and negotiating an unfamiliar one" (63). Carter proposes a basic writing curriculum whose subject is literacy itself, as students analyze their own literacies of work and leisure before studying the rules for academic literacies. She begins by contextualizing her own institutional position as a composition director in Texas and by examining how high-stakes testing has shaped her university's writing program. She then illustrates the implications of reductive definitions of literacy with a compelling narrative of how her brother's highly literate behaviors remained unrecognized and invisible in Texas public schools. Claiming that the era of accountability has limited the effectiveness of the kind of critical pedagogy proposed by David Bartholomae and Anthony Petrosky, Carter argues that bringing high-stakes testing and schooled literacy into the classroom for critique can be both politically and pedagogically effective. Later chapters demonstrate what a course teaching rhetorical dexterity would look like. The book includes a course overview, classroom materials, and analyses of student writing.

226   Cleary, Michelle Navarre. "How Antonio Graduated on Out of Here: Improving the Success of Adult Students with an Individualized Writing Course." *Journal of Basic Writing* 30.1 (2011): 34–63. Print.

Cleary describes the Writing Workshop, a course created at DePaul University's School for New Learning, which provides support for student writers as they move through the university. The course draws on Peter Adams's Accelerated Learning Program (ALP) model, writing center pedagogy, and a Studio approach, offering individualized, ongoing, and direct writing instruction that explicitly coaches students in academic writing conventions and in the management of their ongoing development as writers. Using numerical data as well as examples from one of her classes, Cleary argues the Writing Workshop has led to improved retention of its students and higher GPAs. She further contends the Writing Workshop is an especially important resource for adult and nontraditional students, who are far less likely to persist towards graduation.

227   Connors, Robert J. "Basic Writing Textbooks: History and Current Avatars." *A Sourcebook for Basic Writing Teachers*. Ed. Theresa Enos. New York: Random, 1987. 259–74. Print.

Textbooks specifically for developmental writers first appeared in the 1890s, as mainstream composition authors such as A. S. Hill and John Genung responded to growing cultural and institutional concerns about linguistic correctness with basic treatments of college-level writing. By the advent of open-admissions policies in the late 1960s, basic writing texts had slowly developed into standardized forms such as the simplified rhetorics and basic handbooks and workbooks still seen in large numbers today. Simplified rhetorics as a whole portray the sentence and paragraph as the primary units of discourse and reduce writing to an algorithmic, rule-governed process. Basic writing handbooks and workbooks offer prescriptive lessons on mechanics and pages of fill-in-the-blank and multiple-choice exercises for which students provide correct answers. By isolating and diagnosing discrete grammatical problems through repetitive drills and simplified rules, these texts ignore most of what compositionists currently know about the phenomenon of writing—that it consists of saying something to someone in context. They also reflect a basic writing community that has not progressed as much as a reading of professional books and journals would indicate.

See: Joseph F. Trimmer, "Basic Skills, Basic Writing, Basic Research" [44].

228   Curtis, Marcia, and Anne Herrington. "Writing Development in the College Years: By Whose Definition?" *College Composition and Communication* 55.1 (2003): 69–90. Print.

Curtis and Herrington examine their book, *Persons in Process: Four Stories of Writing and Personal Development in College* (2000), to "explore more closely" their invocation of development and the relationship between writing development and personal development. At a moment when postmodern theories that figure the individual as constructed by discourses, or as shaped by biological or environmental factors, have placed the entire developmentalist project in question, the authors align themselves with theorists who view development as "multidirectional, not unidirectional" and who are interested in the "interplay between the individual and historical/contextual factors in shaping change" (70–71). In response to cautions about college writing focused on personal matters and attention to self, Curtis and Herrington focus on the five-year journey of a student featured in their longitudinal study to show that both writing development and personal development are characterized by "positive change that carries with it into the present clear threads of the past . . . and [an] inescapable link between public and private" (73). They focus on six essays written by "Lawrence/Steven" to illustrate that when writers are provided with opportunities to write about personal/private concerns, they can discover and explore public/academic interests. For the students in their study, "writing development and personal development were furthered by class projects" that provided "specific and varied frames that gave a focus to students' self-reflections as well as connection with public interests" (85). In answer to the question posed in the title, Curtis and Herrington question an emphasis on skills assessment that narrows the concept of development and its measurement to a focus on grammar and syntax and on expository or argumentative writing. Concerned that measurement of skills might become confused with measurement of development, the authors argue for a broad, multidimensional view of writing curricula that draws on several developmental models of writing (they name Applebee's "Alternative Models of Writing Development").

229   Darabi, Rachelle L. "Basic Writers and Learning Communities." *Journal of Basic Writing* 25.1 (2006): 53–72. Print.

The positive impact of learning communities on student success and retention is well established, but there has been minimal examination of composition courses in such contexts. Darabi's study focuses on a Learning Community Pilot Program implemented at Indiana University–Purdue University Fort Wayne (IPFW), where the retention rate between the first and second year had been at 65 percent. A study by the IPFW Office of Academic Affairs found a strong correlation between passing basic writing and remaining in school. The pilot program was designed to structure a first-year learning community experience that linked together three skills-based courses that included basic writing. Attendance improved, Drop-Fail-Withdrawal (D-F-W) rates markedly decreased, and retention rates for students who participated in the program increased to 82 percent. Given these findings, Darabi suggests that basic writing courses may produce better results when taught within a learning community than in isolation. Students make strong connections with each other in the learning community context. This bonding carries over into their work with basic writing on many levels: the improved quality and completion of assignments as well as enhanced ownership of the writing process. In turn, collaborative work with writing strengthens the quality of student interactions in other classes, helping to make the shift from the more socially based interaction of high school to the learning-based interaction of college.

230   Davi, Angelique. "In the Service of Writing and Race." *Journal of Basic Writing* 25.1 (2006): 73–95. Print.

Davi argues that the incorporation of service learning allows underprivileged students to develop the necessary critical reading and writing skills needed in college. But more important, service learning also provides these students with the opportunity to recognize their own contributions to the community while simultaneously learning how to speak critically about race, class, and gender. Using her own experience as a teacher of underprivileged and underperforming students, she explores the benefits and drawbacks to service learning, pointing out that one of the common criticisms of this approach is that many students view service learning as their way of "feeling good about themselves," which prevents them from engaging in critical thought. To avoid this patronizing sentimentality, she asks her students to talk about what was difficult about service learning rather than just telling the "feel good" stories. By writing about their experiences in service learning and in the educational system, students learn to think critically about race, class, and gender.

231   Delpit, Lisa. "The Silenced Dialogue: Power and Pedagogy in Educating Other People's Children." *Landmark Essays on Basic Writing.* Ed. Kay Halasek and Nels P. Highberg. Mahwah: Erlbaum, 2001. 83–101. Print.

Delpit uses the process versus skills debate, as well as other examples, to uncover and critique larger societal and educational cultures of power that inform US classrooms. Progressive and liberal educators, Delpit argues, do significant and irreparable damage to black and poor students who are not participants in the culture of power by ignoring or denying that cultures of power exist and, in turn, by not articulating for students the rules of that culture. Delpit, however, does not advocate a simple, unself-reflexive return to direct instruction. She recognizes that students need to use their knowledge and to write for real audiences and purposes at the same time that they are taught and use the conventions and expectations of academic discourse. Delpit's narrative analysis, coupled with the chorus of teachers she quotes, constructs a look into the cultural divide that exists in classrooms in which white teachers, even those with the best of intentions, do not recognize themselves as part of the institutional and cultural forces constructed to ensure the continued success of middle-class and white students at the cost of further disenfranchisement of poor students and students of color. The pedagogical divide is articulated nowhere more strongly than in Delpit's contrastive descriptions of democratic and authoritarian classrooms.

232   Fleck, Andrew. "'We Think He Means . . .': Creating Working Definitions through Small Group Discussion." *Teaching Developmental Writing: Background Readings.* Ed. Susan Naomi Bernstein. Boston: Bedford, 2001. 220–25. Print.

Fleck became frustrated while teaching a course structured around "Arts of the Contact Zone" by Mary Louise Pratt and an excerpt from Stephen Greenblatt's *Marvelous Possessions*. In his analysis, his students were not arriving at understandings of these complicated texts. His solution was to create discussion groups of three to five students because research in the use of small discussion groups claims that students can better modify and clarify ideas through discussions with other students. Fleck reports that students who had never talked in class participated in the small-group conversations and that students used key-term definitions created by the group while discussing Greenblatt to write more sophisticated essays. Fleck concludes that small-group discussions release students from the anxiety of speaking to the entire class, help them to ask questions and clarify their thinking, and encourage them to engage in more sophisticated discussions of complicated texts.

See: Mary Louise Pratt, "Arts of the Contact Zone" [272].

233   Gleason, Barbara. "Returning Adults to the Mainstream: Toward a Curriculum for Diverse Student Writers." *Teaching Developmental Writing: Background Readings*. 3rd ed. Ed. Susan Naomi Bernstein. Boston: Bedford, 2007. 214–38. Print.

Based on her argument that returning students should not be placed in remedial courses, Gleason presents a case for creating writing courses specific to the working adult student and particularly for using ethnographic writings in these courses. She describes what she does in her courses at the Center for Worker Education, a program within the City College of New York. In addition, Gleason discusses the diversities within an adult population, especially at her academic institution, and how these academic and cultural diversities help the students and teacher to learn from one another and to expose their different levels of abilities and expectations in the academic world. Gleason demonstrates, through the case studies she presents, the connection between older adult students' conversational and oral presentations and their writing skills. She argues that their writing skills often contradict their true abilities and intellects, which are demonstrated in their oral skills. Once students recognize that they are able to tell stories about their own literacy development, they can begin writing ethnographic papers by incorporating their oral interviewing skills; these papers develop into a writing project. Via the sequenced writings, students learn academic writing abilities and forms and gain knowledge that should assist them in becoming successful in their college careers. Gleason argues that adult students do not need to be in remedial courses but need to experience a writing curriculum that allows them to be successful while expanding their literacies.

234   Goode, Dianne. "Creating a Context for Developmental English." *Teaching Developmental Writing: Background Readings*. Ed. Susan Naomi Bernstein. Boston: Bedford, 2001. 71–77. Print.

To motivate learners, Goode asserts, it is necessary to provide a real context for their reading and writing. Goode describes the CONCUR ("CONtextual CURriculum") program at Piedmont Community College in rural North Carolina. The purpose of the program is to provide developmental English students with a context for reading and writing. The CONCUR program models the workings of a publishing house: students choose what to read and what to write, and the term's writing is collected into a class-designed anthology that is published and shelved in the school library. Simply knowing that their writing will be published spurs the students to attend carefully to their course work. Students read fifty to seventy-five pages each week and "reflect, analyze, speculate, [and] evaluate" their reading in a journal shared with the instructor (75). Students also participate in silent reading, book discussions, vocabulary sharing, mini-lessons on reading strategies, and literature circles.

235   Hidalgo, Alexandra. "Group Work and Autonomy: Empowering the Working-Class Student." *Open Words: Access and English Studies* 2.2 (2008): 3–23. Print.

Working-class students often face difficulties when attending college and may feel alienated from academic discourse. Unlike their middle-class counterparts, they may feel as if they do not belong in university classrooms and may feel frustrated in courses like freshman composition. Hidalgo draws on the experiences of scholars like Barbara Mellix, who, as a nontraditional, working-class, African American student, felt she was not "meant to be in those classrooms" and feared her peers and instructors would see her as an "imposter who should not be there" (5). In typical composition classrooms, discussions, writing assignments, and academic language can be quite daunting and intimidating for some working-class students. To empower these students and to make them feel comfortable as members of the academic environment, Hidalgo suggests group work to foster discussion of relevant readings, drafts of assignments, and ideas for improving writing. Group work reflects "community," which is "important in working-class culture" (10). Utilizing group work in writing classes creates a more comfortable atmosphere for working-class students to express themselves, gives them a sense of belonging, and helps them to become a part of the academic discourse community. This leads to success in future classes.

236   Lazere, Donald. "Back to Basics: A Force for Oppression or Liberation?" *Landmark Essays on Basic Writing.* Ed. Kay Halasek and Nels P. Highberg. Mahwah: Erlbaum, 2001. 121–34. Print.

Lazere asks whether liberatory pedagogy, which has come to be defined in the United States in generally Freirean terms, serves the needs of students better than a basic skills approach. "Leftists," he writes, "err grievously in rejecting . . . a restored emphasis on basic skills and knowledge which might be a force for liberation—not oppression—if administered with common sense, openness to cultural pluralism, and an application of basics toward critical thinking, particularly about sociopolitical issues" (123). In arguing his case, Lazere undertakes a Marxist critique of both liberal and conservative motives for pedagogical choices. Lazere launches a critique of James Sledd, Andrew Sledd, and Richard Ohmann, among others, for their refusal to see beyond their own assumptions about the relative value of various approaches to literacy education.

237   Leary, Chris. "'When We Remix . . . We Remake!!!' Reflections on Collaborative Ethnography, the New Digital Ethic, and Test Prep." *Journal of Basic Writing* 26.1 (2007): 88–105. Print.

Leary challenges the common notion in basic writing curricula that students must be taught low-level skills that will merely help them to "pass." Such curricula, he argues, confine students and leave their valuable voices out of the conversation on composition studies. Drawing from his own experience with leading a "collaborative ethnography" project in a basic writing course designed to prepare students to take the ACT writing exam, Leary illustrates two ways in which he worked to resist traditional approaches to teaching basic writing. First, he involved students with the composition of one of his graduate school essays in composition studies, engaging them in the critical reading of scholarly texts and in the written correspondence with another composition theorist, and eliciting their feedback in the writing and revision process of the essay itself. Leary later invited his students to experiment with the ACT writing exam by collaboratively drafting their responses to practice prompts, posting their responses online and hyperlinking their text to related Web sites, and comparing prompts across exams for their cultural implications. These two projects, he found, helped students not only to get involved in an academic conversation about the culture of composition but also to gain access to and be critical about higher-level composition issues, such as textual and digital remixing. This approach to basic writing, he argues, not only helps to foster students' success with the ACT, but it also helps them to reimagine writing as relevant, creative practice.

238   Maas-Feary, Maureen. "Attitude Is Everything, a Developmental Writing Instructor Finds While Teaching Freshman English." *Research and Teaching in Developmental Education* 17.2 (2000): 83–85. Print.

Maas-Feary explores the difference in students' attitudes toward College English (a developmental writing class) and Freshman English (the writing class required for all students at her community college). Students in College English do not take pride in their work and believe that the class should be easy to pass, whereas Freshman English students take the class seriously and produce thoughtful work. Maas-Feary believes these attitude differences can be attributed to the stigma assigned to College English at her school. She concludes that the instructor needs to infuse the developmental writing class with an attitude of purpose by assigning college-level work that challenges students' views of themselves as well as the class.

239   McCurrie, Matthew Kilian. "Measuring Success in Summer Bridge Programs: Retention Efforts and Basic Writing." *Journal of Basic Writing* 28.2 (2009): 28–49. Print.

Surveys conducted while Columbia College Chicago's Summer Bridge program was being revised show that administrators in student affairs, basic writing teachers, and students enrolled in the program defined success in different ways. Administrators defined success by considering how prepared students are for the challenges of the college's curriculum. Basic writing teachers measured success by considering students' academic and social engagement, and thus revised the curriculum to introduce students to collegiate life and the expectations of first-year writing courses. Students defined success by considering the extent to which the courses contributed to living a fulfilling life, particularly through self-efficacy and the pursuit of their own interests. In addition, the article considers the ethical issues surrounding access and gatekeeping at an expensive private institution in an age of reduced financial aid, arguing that such contextual issues require the administrators and basic writing teachers to carefully weigh a generous assessment of students' readiness with the "financial and personal damage to students who are not likely to succeed at the college" (41).

240   Peele, Thomas. "Working Together: Student-Faculty Interaction and the Boise State Stretch Program." *Journal of Basic Writing* 29.2 (2010): 50–73. Print.

Policy changes at the state level led to Boise State University piloting a basic writing stretch program in 2005. It is a two-semester sequence that "stretches" English 101 over two semesters. Subsequent assessments showed student success in terms of proficiency, course completion, retention rates, portfolios, and GPAs. The results mirrored those determined by Gregory Glau in his longitudinal study at Arizona State University, "*Stretch* at 10" [380]. BSU instructors shared a productive and rewarding curriculum structured around a year-long syllabus. Correlating with the work of Pascarella, Terenzini, and other scholarship on student-faculty interaction, results from BSU showed that students who completed the two-semester stretch course with the same instructor statistically performed significantly better than those students who did not. Faculty also benefitted from working with the same students over two semesters. However, the no-credit bearing status caused students concern. Due to conflicting definitions of what constitutes college-level writing, multiple requests to attach college credit to the stretch course have been denied. Peele concludes that institutional structures need to be created to neutralize the outsider status of basic writing programs.

241   Peele, Thomas. "Writing about Faith: Mainstream Music and Composition." *Basic Writing e-Journal* 6.1 (2007): n. pag. Web. 21 May 2014.

Peele reminds readers that composition (and academe writ large) tends to devalue faith and formal religion—particularly when used as evidence. He argues for the inclusion of faith traditions within the curricula of the first-year composition classroom, asserting that the practice of discouraging students from writing about their faith diminishes their potential for examining their beliefs in context with people of other faith traditions. He feels that many basic writing students, in particular, need to have their faith-based experiences affirmed by the academy. To bring discussions of faith into an appropriate academic setting, Peele outlines a pedagogy in which students write about how popular music represents religion and faith—a pedagogy he finds valuable in part because students learn how various discourse communities conceptualize and value religion and faith. He presents a writing project he assigned in one of his classes; the assignment sequence has students use critical discourse analysis as a lens through which to consider issues of intertextuality and tone in lyrics that take up spiritual issues. Ultimately, Peele concludes that this sequence's focus on textual analysis, interpretation, and consideration of multiple perspectives allows students to develop and practice the kinds of intellectual and rhetorical proficiencies valued in the academy. Included in the article are several student responses, as well as links to PowerPoint presentations, thirty-second audio clips of songs used in the writing projects, and the writing assignment sheet given to students at the beginning of the project.

242   Raymond, Richard. "Building Learning Communities on Nonresidential Campuses." *Teaching Developmental Writing: Background Readings.* Ed. Susan Naomi Bernstein. Boston: Bedford, 2001. 204–18. Print.

Raymond describes the process that he and colleagues from the speech and anthropology departments went through to develop and implement a learning community on a campus with a substantial population of commuter and working students. Raymond discusses how the instructors gathered support, planned their classes, and underwent assessment by the college's assessment expert, students, and faculty. He also discusses the assessment tools that he and his colleagues used and includes student writing samples and excerpts from his own assessment journal. Raymond concludes that linked courses can help to demonstrate students' reading, writing, and critical thinking abilities and can help to facilitate student retention.

243   Remler, Nancy Lawson. "The More Active the Better: Engaging College English Students with Active Learning Strategies." *Teaching Developmental Writing: Background Readings.* 3rd ed. Ed. Susan Naomi Bernstein. Boston: Bedford, 2007. 239–45. Print.

Using Charles Bonwell and James Eison's definition of active learning, Remler draws on her own classroom experiences to argue for an approach to teaching college English that emphasizes active learning strategies as the most effective means of facilitating student engagement and fostering understanding of course concepts. She discusses her successes with active learning strategies in both her sophomore literature course and her first-year composition course, where students engage with course material by working in groups and by constructing their own discussion questions using Bloom's taxonomy. When students take on the role of professor and instruct one another, Remler argues, they also take ownership of the class and thereby invest more heavily in the material.

244   Rustick, Margaret Tomlinson. "Grammar Games in the Age of Anti-Remediation." *Journal of Basic Writing* 26.1 (2007): 43–62. Print.

Rustick responds to the ambiguity surrounding grammar instruction for developmental writers, citing a necessary shift in the way basic writing teachers consider contextual differences between written and spoken language. She suggests supplementing grammar instruction with the use of creative games that require students to consider the way sentences are constructed and focus on how meaning and function shift when certain parts of a sentence are rearranged. Rustick argues that her games help students build metalinguistic knowledge through the manipulation of words and sentence syntax that can change the meaning and function of specific elements in a sentence.

245   Uehling, Karen S. *Starting Out or Starting Over: A Guide for Writing.* New York: Harper, 1993. Print.

"Starting out" refers to those "traditional" college students, eighteen to nineteen, who are entering college for the first time; "starting over" refers to nontraditional students returning to college to complete studies started years ago or attending college for the first time in search of a new career. A third target audience for the book is basic writers. The book is designed to break away from a skill-and-drill mode of worksheets and "objective" instruments to help students learn how to write better. Unlike other approaches, which publish complete student essays in tandem with "professional" writers' essays, this text employs student writing of various types, lengths, and quality. Uehling uses these assorted texts to illustrate many of her pedagogical points. For instance, she argues that distinctions between modes of discourse are an artificial way of examining composition because outside the artificial world of the classroom, few paragraphs and virtually no compositions are written exclusively in one mode. Uehling advises student writers about developing a positive attitude, accepting suggestions, letting go of the text and allowing others to read it, building their confidence as writers, and allaying fear. Uehling also spends some time discussing "critique anxiety" and ways to overcome this serious impediment to joining the conversation of the classroom (120–22).

246   Wachen, John, et al. "Contextualized College Transition Strategies for Adult Basic Skills Students: Learning from Washington State's I-BEST Program Model." *Community College Research Center.* Teachers College, Columbia University. Dec. 2012. Web. 21 May 2014.

In this report, Wachen et al. describe a multiyear study assessing the state of Washington's Integrated Basic Education and Skills Training program (I-BEST), an initiative integrating adult basic skills instruction with career-technical education through courses jointly taught by community college basic and technical skills instructors. Designed to improve the completion rates of at-risk community college students such as adult basic education and ESL students, the short-term program is meant to provide students with an "on-ramp" to a career program through initial intensive support with subsequent mainstreaming. Based on their research, Wachen et al. provide a number of recommendations for those seeking to implement similar programs, including recommendations for better articulation between such programs and "next step" programs and for structuring the coordination between instructors in programs seeking to provide integrated and contextualized basic skills instruction (including writing). In particular, the authors draw attention to the often-overlooked but vital component of supporting instructors' joint planning time and professional development. The report also includes a cost-benefit analysis of the program for state- and college-level decision makers.

247   Wiley, Mark. "Rehabilitating the 'Idea of Community.'" *Journal of Basic Writing* 20.2 (2001): 16–33. Print.

Wiley argues that composition studies, and in particular basic writing, can benefit from the present educational reform movement involving learning communities. Practically speaking, learning communities provide environments of peer collaboration and relationship building and can thus facilitate learning and writing development. Moreover, Wiley counters Joseph Harris's conception of the basic writing classroom as a "city" that privileges conflict over consensus and that positions the student as a developing public intellectual. Learning communities help students acquire the "discourse about being a student" (30) through social networks that do not ignore conflict but instead aid students' negotiation of consensus at their "point[s] of need" (31).

248   Wiley, Mark. "Response to Joseph Harris's 'Beyond Community.'" *Journal of Basic Writing* 20.2 (2001): 34–37. Print.

Wiley responds to Joseph Harris's critique of "community" in the Fall 2001 issue of the *Journal of Basic Writing* by emphasizing the materiality of learning communities, the need for both dissent and compromise, and the complementary natures of the concepts of community and public. Wiley rejects the notion that community implies a regressive, naïve, or enclosed space. Rather, he argues that communities, especially learning communities, offer new possibilities for thinking, learning, and writing.

249   Williams, Mark T., and Gladys Garcia. "Crossing Academic Cultures: A Rubric for Students and Teachers." *Journal of Basic Writing* 24.1 (2005): 93–119. Print.

The authors contend that a process-guided rubric, based on Kenneth Burke's dramatist pentad, is especially useful to transition students from the position of *outsider* to academic writing to the preferred position of *insider*. Relying heavily on Burke's "pentad of act, scene, agent, agency, and purpose," Williams and Garcia illustrate through student essays and subsequent analysis the many ways that student writers function as either *outsiders*, *crossers*, or *insiders* to the writing style that the academy demands (96). Acknowledging that traditional rubrics for writing assessment do not allow for cultural differences, the authors propose the process-guided rubric. They write, "We use the rubric to characterize student writers who may be crossing into the more critical terrain of academic culture and to invite fellow teachers to reconsider the values and viewpoints that underwrite our position within the academy" (95). An understanding of the process-based rubric that Williams and Garcia propose is realized through the in-depth analysis of student essays in terms of *outsider*, *crosser*, and *insider* writing. Detailed analyses acknowledge not only the strengths of each stage of writing but also the weaknesses of each stage. Furthermore, the authors suggest ways that those teaching basic writing may proceed in integrating the process-based rubric, support student writing, and learn from their students' writing.

Essays and Personal Writing

250   Bartholomae, David. "Writing with Teachers: A Conversation with Peter Elbow." *College Composition and Communication* 46.1 (1995): 62–71. Print.

Based on ongoing exchanges between Peter Elbow and David Bartholomae, this essay critiques the ideology of expressive writing and Elbow's 1969 text, *Writing without Teachers*. Bartholomae defends his definition of academic writing and defines expressive writing in an attempt to distinguish between the two. While Bartholomae acknowledges ambiguity in the term *academic writing*, he constructs a definition by distinguishing academic writing from what it is not. He claims that since "academic writing is the real work of the academy," there can be no writing that is "without teachers" (63). Bartholomae further asserts that Elbow's text ultimately works to preserve the authority of the student as well as the assumed value of expressive writing. Instead, Bartholomae argues that basic writing as well as other college classes should be spaces in which we investigate the "transmission of power" (66). College writing courses, he says, should teach students about intertextuality as well as the dialogic nature of reading and writing, helping them to recognize that they are writing "in a space defined by all the writing that has preceded them" (64).

251   Berthoff, Ann E. "What Works? How Do We Know?" *Journal of Basic Writing* 12.2 (1993): 3–17. Print.

Berthoff attacks the idea of the five-paragraph essay and writing instruction that focuses on error. Instead, she advocates an approach that "preach[es] the gospel of the uses of chaos and the making of meaning" (5). Using the "us-against-them" approach (the writing instructors versus the deans), she comments that the deans want students to write beautiful, well-organized prose but give little or no thought to how students get there. She argues that students will come to that beautiful, well-organized prose only by combining personal and public discourse.

252   Bloom, Lynn Z. "The Ineluctable Elitism of Essays and Why They Prevail in First-Year Composition Courses." *Open Words: Access and English Studies* 1.2 (2007): 62–78. Print.

Based on an analysis of freshman composition readers published from 1946 to 1996, this article argues that the essay as a genre reflects elitist attitudes and education. Bloom isolates 175 authors who are "canonical essayists" (63) and suggests that they write to an upper-middle-class to middle-class audience, whose intellect and education make sophistication in prose and allusion a given. These canonical essays, even when they include journalism and excerpts from autobiographies, assume that the reader is "along for the pleasure of the ride itself as the essay meanders into engaging byways and scenic overlooks rather than sticking to the superhighway to the main idea" (64). A "common cultural repertoire" (64) among these authors and the anticipated audience constructs a barrier for working-class students to overcome. Bloom notes the lack of innovation in form and the adherence to Standard Written English in contemporary and canonical essays reproduced in textbooks that focus on working-class culture, feminist thought, and ethnic perspectives. She believes that the goal for both textbook publishers and writing programs is to "ensure that the essays, however elitist in form, may be understood in terms of middle-class values and experiences, even those that discuss working-class lives" (70). The glut of textbooks espousing middle-class values accompanies the teaching of first-year writing courses, which is "by and large a middle-class endeavor" (72). She feels that as long as the academy remains middle class, "there will be little incentive to reorient composition pedagogy to challenge these middle-class values and aims" (73). Yet she concludes that "students' cultural horizons" cannot help but be broadened by the readers available for first-year writing courses (73), even though the essays within are written in Standard Written English. This merely reflects the dominant method of writing instruction in college-level reading and writing courses, which Bloom feels is as it should be.

253   Elliot, Norbert. "Narrative Discourse and the Basic Writer." *Journal of Basic Writing* 14.2 (1995): 19–30. Print.

Many experts in the field of basic writing use narrative in their own academic discourse but do not allow their students to use narrative in the classroom. An examination of the academic discourse about basic writing indicates that narrative is used widely as a way to make academic issues relevant to our lives. In light of this, perhaps we should reconsider our skepticism about the value of narrative discourse in the basic writing classroom. Narrative has attributes that foster many of the academic skills we seek to nurture in our students. For one thing, it serves as a form of legitimization—a way for students to establish a position before those who might otherwise dismiss them. Furthermore, narrative can facilitate metacognition. By asking students to distinguish between the story and the presentation of the events, we encourage them to think about the process of thinking. Perhaps most important, narrative can provide access to the mysterious, the spiritual, and the awe-inspiring. Through narrative, students can explore themselves and their place in the world, including the academy. They can discover the relationship between their lives and their ideas.

254   Mlynarczyk, Rebecca Williams. "Personal and Academic Writing: Revisiting the Debate." *Journal of Basic Writing* 25.1 (2006): 4–25. Print.

Hearkening back to a "defining moment in composition studies" (8) — the Peter Elbow–David Bartholomae debates over personal versus academic writing — Mlynarczyk juxtaposes their ideas with the work of psycholinguist Jerome Bruner and linguist James Britton. She argues that there is widespread disagreement today about what type of writing is most appropriate for the composition classroom and the academy. After outlining Bruner and Britton's language theories and reviewing Elbow and Bartholomae's 1995 debate, Mlynarczyk illustrates the similarities between Elbow and Britton's emphasis on expressive language and Bartholomae and Bruner's preference for transactional language. Mlynarczyk sides with Elbow and Britton: if basic writing students are to become comfortable with and adept at academic writing, they are more likely to reach that point via assignments that promote personal writing. To support her stance, Mlynarczyk cites a qualitative study she conducted on the journal-writing experiences of five multilingual students. In particular, one ESL student exemplifies that the personal and expressive writing appropriate to journaling can lead to self-confidence and ability in traditional academic writing. Forming and expressing thoughts in a personal language helps students become more proficient at forming and expressing thoughts in the language of the academy. Mlynarczyk admits there are "caveats" (18): some students do not learn to embrace journal writing; some are uncomfortable with it for cultural reasons; and some do not transcend the inauthenticity of calling what is actually a public product (the journal) private and personal. Nevertheless, Mlynarczyk asserts that the Britton-Elbow concept of expressive language, especially through journaling, is better suited to helping basic writers acquire the thinking and writing discourses expected of them at the academy and beyond.

See: David Bartholomae and Peter Elbow, "Responses to Bartholomae and Elbow" [159].

See: David Bartholomae, "Writing with Teachers: A Conversation with Peter Elbow" [250].

255   Moran, Molly Hurley. "Toward a Writing and Healing Approach in the Basic Writing Classroom: One Professor's Personal Odyssey." *Journal of Basic Writing* 23.2 (2004): 93–115. Print.

Moran outlines how her experience of writing a book about a personal tragedy led her to investigate the fledgling interdisciplinary field of writing and healing. She redesigned her basic writing class to ask students to start by writing on personal and often painful issues, but also to move toward academic genres of writing, connecting those experiences to larger societal issues. Initial survey results indicate that such an approach may help improve students' attitudes about and confidence in their writing; it also appears to help basic writing students develop a "stronger prose style and more authentic voice." Anecdotal reports also indicate a significant level of student engagement from the approach.

256   Rankins-Robertson, Sherry, et al. "Expanding Definitions of Academic Writing: Family History Writing in the Basic Writing Classroom and Beyond." *Journal of Basic Writing* 29.1 (2010): 56–77. Print.

Family writing (that is, writing about family) in basic writing and first-year composition expands the concepts of academic writing, research, and family, and provides a pedagogical space where all three can merge to create personalized writing-with-purpose. In addition, family writing encourages multimodal projects that include historical chronologies, memoirs, manifestos, travel writings, and family- or community-based thematic arguments. While composing family writings, students explore and build upon nontraditional concepts of family, primary and secondary research, writing for the self, writing for an audience, and academic writing. Furthermore, using family writing in the basic writing and first-year composition classroom creates a less intimidating and more welcoming academic space for novice writers by showing that they and their families, as subjects, are significant inside and outside academia.

Gender, Race, Class, and Ethnicity

257   Adler-Kassner, Linda. "The Shape of the Form: Working-Class Students and the Academic Essay." *Teaching Working Class.* Ed. Sherry Lee Linkon. Amherst: U of Massachusetts P, 1999. 85–105. Print.

Adler-Kassner argues that some students' issues with the expository essay "extend to a disjuncture between students' own values, reflected in their literacies, and the values and literacy reflected in the shape of the essay itself, as a genre" (86). She traces the history of the form of the expository essay through the work of Progressive Era compositionists like Fred Newton Scott. She notes that while they helped to transform expository writing into an act at least somewhat related to students' experiences, they also insisted that the form (and language) of the essay reflect particular conventions, which themselves reflected particular values of their culture. These conventions and their accompanying values remain intertwined with the expository essay to the current day, but students who do not share these values sometimes have issues with the expository essay for this reason. To make this point, Adler-Kassner examines writing by working-class students and proposes three possible solutions to pedagogical problems arising from this clash between cultures: move toward hybrid texts, design assignments that invite student experience, and allow hybrid language and form into the essay.

258   Agnew, Eleanor, and Margaret McLaughlin. "Those Crazy Gates and How They Swing: Tracking the System That Tracks African-American Students." *Mainstreaming Basic Writers: Politics and Pedagogies of Access.* Ed. Gerri McNenny. Mahwah: Erlbaum, 2001. 85–100. Print.

A seven-year longitudinal study that tracked the academic progress of sixty-one basic writers provisionally admitted in 1993 to a rural southeastern regional university found that the basic writing course itself did not negatively affect students' lives as much as the invalid assessment system that framed the program did. Although a poorly designed assessment system is detrimental to any student writer at any level, the results of this study suggest that unreliable and invalid writing assessment may contribute to the widely recognized cycle of academic failure and high attrition rates for black students who, on the basis of one timed, impromptu exit essay, can become trapped in noncredit courses. The subjective nature of creating and scoring single-method holistic essays—an assessment system that lacks conceptual validity and interrater reliability—led to a gate-keeping process that was most damaging to African American basic writers whose home speech is African American Vernacular English (AAVE). Excerpts from students' exit essays and a description of the arbitrariness of one holistic scoring session are included as a possible explanation for why almost twice the percentage of black students (31 percent) as white students (17 percent) did not exit basic writing after four attempts. Four failures to pass the exit essay excluded students from enrolling in any state-supported postsecondary institution for the next three years.

259   Bean, Janet, et al. "Should We Invite Students to Write in Home Languages? Complicating the Yes/No Debate." *Composition Studies* 31.1 (2003): 25–42. Print.

The authors work with a variety of populations, including students who speak African American Vernacular English and immigrant and international students, and take "[a shared] interest in helping all [their] students to produce effective and appropriate writing in English for academic contexts and purposes" (26). The authors state that "writers will feel more confident as language-users when their home language is valued and respected" (26). While the article recommends that teachers experiment with assignments that offer students a variety of opportunities for using their home language, the authors review a "list of variables" that complicate writing situations and can derail an instructor's best intentions. The authors consider the differences between home language and home dialect and suggest how the conditions shift, depending on whether (or to what degree) the home language is considered stigmatized. In addition, the authors point to circumstances when it might be valuable for students to use their home dialects for something not converted into standardized English. They emphasize the significance of inviting students to use their own dialects and the possible consequences of that decision. "Linguistic richness and bilingualism" should be valued, the writers argue (37). The article closes with an important reminder from Lucille Clifton, who writes in a poem titled "defending my tongue" that, "what i be talking about / can be said in this language / only" (38).

260   Bloom, Lynn Z. "Freshman Composition as a Middle Class Enterprise." *College English* 58.6 (1996): 654–75. Print.

Bloom argues that freshman composition addresses a number of the major aspects of social class to get students to write and think as good citizens of the academic community and the workplace. One major reason that freshman composition is the only course required of all students remains its reproduction of middle-class values that are thought to be essential to proper functioning of students in the academy. Bloom likens students in freshman composition to swimmers passing through a chlorine footbath before plunging into the pool. Bloom names self-reliance and responsibility, respectability (middle-class morality), decorum and propriety, moderation and temperance, thrift, efficiency, order, cleanliness, punctuality, delayed gratification, and critical thinking as the hallmarks of middle-class identity. Working-class students are often placed in so-called remedial courses like developmental writing because of an unspoken supposition that they will not be successful in freshman composition classes requiring such virtues. In addition, developmental writing teachers are encouraged to move their students in the direction of these virtues.

261   Cochran, Effie P. "Giving Voice to Women in the Basic Writing and Language Minority Classroom." *Journal of Basic Writing* 13.1 (1994): 78–90. Print.

Examining the ways that language affects sex roles, Cochran concentrates on women in English as a second language (ESL) and basic writing classes. She contends that they are often disadvantaged because they do not possess the language skills that allow them to succeed. In addition, males in these classrooms often make it difficult for women to participate. To facilitate women in ESL and basic writing classrooms, Cochran has four suggestions for teachers: use dramatic scenarios or dialogues, become conscious of the nonverbal communication of the instructor and the student, model the use of nonsexist language, and become familiar with the "literature on the topic of sexism and language" (85).

262   Counihan, Beth. "Freshgirls: Overwhelmed by Discordant Pedagogies and the Anxiety of Leaving Home." *Journal of Basic Writing* 18.1 (1999): 91–105. Print.

This study was based on an ethnographic study of three female freshmen who enrolled at City University of New York's Lehman College. Counihan began with high hopes for her subjects, whom she called *freshgirls*, but she went on to see them fail to pass most of their classes. She wonders why this happened—if the girls failed or if the institution failed them. She centers her study around a description of their classrooms to illuminate the problems facing the freshgirls. Counihan explains the background that produced the freshgirls and the problems that they encountered growing up in one-parent or unsupportive homes. In college, these subjects hoped to find a way into the comforts of the middle class, but none wanted to submit to the workings of the educational institution to make that happen. Instead, they bucked the system, and their own grades suffered as a result of their nonconformity. The freshgirls did not possess academic literacy, and they resisted their teachers' efforts to educate and engage them. Based on her observations of the freshgirls, Counihan suggests that "we need a serious reassessment of our rigid views of what a college experience 'should' be" (103). She hopes for the adoption of a flexible pedagogy that might help students like the freshgirls succeed. She concludes her article by explaining what has happened to the freshgirls since their semester at Lehman in Fall 1995.

263   DiPardo, Anne. *A Kind of Passport: A Basic Writing Adjunct Program and the Challenge of Student Diversity*. Urbana: NCTE, 1993. Print.

DiPardo examines the successes and failures of a peer-teaching program at "Dover Park University," a largely white university grappling with issues of racial and cultural equity throughout the campus. She focuses on workshops led by two peer teachers (adjuncts) for students enrolled in a faculty-taught course in basic writing. Through observations, interviews, and teaching logs, DiPardo studies and reports on the dynamics between adjuncts and student writers working together in an intimate workshop setting. The book captures challenges faced by undergraduates who are becoming educators with pedagogical uncertainty and minimal preparation and the development of their teaching self through the day-to-day experiences of working with struggling writers. While she sometimes asserts that both the peer teachers and the university were not curious enough, DiPardo finds that by welcoming equity students and beginning the task of transforming basic writers into mainstream achievers, the students, the teachers, and the institution itself will all be slowly but unquestionably changed.

264   Dunn, Patricia A. *Learning Re-abled: The Learning Disability Controversy and Composition Studies*. Portsmouth: Boynton, 1995. Print.

Dunn presents an overview of current understandings of learning disability theory and a rich discussion about the ways that institutions, writing programs, composition scholars, and faculty privilege certain ways of understanding students' writing problems. Dunn grounds her research in her observations of the extreme difficulty that some students have in learning to use written language proficiently. She notes that composition theory does not fully account for the kinds of errors that some students make, and she suggests that the field has largely ignored neurological causes of writing difficulty and privileged instead research and theory that considers writing difficulty to be a primarily socioeconomic challenge. According to Dunn, "[e]ven if only one student — . . . who may have a difference in learning not related to dialect, social class, or educational background — appears in a composition class, the instructor owes it to that student to be informed" (43). The book focuses on perspectives on and controversies about learning disabilities, the ways that composition has understood writing difficulties, multi-modal pedagogies for students with learning disabilities, interviews with learning disabled (LD) students who describe their frustrations and experiences, and the ways that instructors and administrators can best help LD students demonstrate their intelligence and communicative competence.

265   Gaskins, Jacob C. "Teaching Writing to Students with Learning Disabilities: The Landmark Method." *Teaching English in the Two-Year College* 22.2 (1995): 116–22. Print.

Gaskins discusses teaching methods he learned during a week-long training institute at Landmark College, a school for students with learning disabilities. He presents and briefly discusses ten principles that constitute the "Landmark Method" for teaching writing to students with dyslexia, dysgraphia, attention-deficit disorder, and other learning disabilities. Approaches are phrased as imperatives ("exploit the inter-relatedness of reading, writing, speaking, and listening"; "foster meta-cognition"; "teach to the student's strengths and accommodate learning styles"). Citing the institute's training materials, Gaskins suggests ways that these principles can translate into specific classroom practices.

266   Gilyard, Keith, and Elaine Richardson. "Students' Right to Possibility: Basic Writing and African American Rhetoric." *Insurrections: Approaches to Resistance in Composition Studies.* Ed. Andrea Greenbaum. Albany: State U of New York P, 2001. 37–51. Print.

Gilyard and Richardson survey the core ideas of the 1974 "Students' Right to Their Own Language" (SRTOL) resolution and contend that empirical models of how to implement SRTOL pedagogically are needed. The authors offer a model in the form of a study conducted by Richardson that was designed to evaluate the practicality of using SRTOL principles to teach academic writing to African American students who are placed in basic writing courses. The study asked "to what extent African American speech styles can be instrumental to the development of critical academic writing" (39). Richardson designed and taught a basic writing course focusing on Afrocentric topics and African American rhetoric. Drawing on a modified version of Geneva Smitherman's 1994 typology of black discourse features, the authors perform quantitative and qualitative analyses of forty-seven student essays from this course to conclude that "making the African American rhetorical tradition the centerpiece of attempts to teach academic prose to African American students, especially those characterized as basic writers . . . increase[s] the likelihood that they will develop into careful, competent, critical practitioners of the written word" (50).

267   Gleason, Barbara. "Returning Adults to the Mainstream: Toward a Curriculum for Diverse Student Writers." *Mainstreaming Basic Writers:*

Politics and Pedagogies of Access. Ed. Gerri McNenny. Mahwah: Erlbaum, 2001. 121–43. Print.

Mainstreamed writing courses are especially suitable for returning adults at the City College of New York Center for Worker Education. As is often the case in similar programs, the Center for Worker Education aims to speed up students' academic progress with convenient schedules, life experience credits, and no remedial classes. At the center, all students are placed directly into credit-bearing courses, regardless of their skills or test scores. The curriculum for a first-year writing course is designed for students who have highly diverse competencies. This curriculum features sequenced multitask assignments that offer appropriate challenges for strong writers and opportunities to experience success for weaker writers. Students' oral-language fluencies are the foundation for assignments such as interviewing and ethnographic research. Case studies illustrate the benefits of this curriculum for one weak student and one strong student. Both students wrote ethnographic research reports in the same course, and both experienced growth as writers and success in the classroom.

268   Inman, Joyce Olewski. "'Standard' Issue: Public Discourse, *Ayers v. Fordice,* and the Dilemma of the Basic Writer." *College English* 75.3 (2013): 298–318. Print.

Ayers v. Fordice, a significant desegregation case involving higher education in Mississippi, provides a case study that reveals how public discourse may both contribute to a privileging of conservative beliefs about education and limit the subject positions available to basic writers. Articles from the *Clarion-Ledger* and correspondence between private citizens and government officials demonstrate the influence standards-based conceptual metaphors exert on the development of basic writing programming. Specifically, the artifacts demonstrate the relationship between standards-based metaphors and the development of institutional policies that emphasize and reaffirm the importance of standards in higher education. By emphasizing and reaffirming standards, these metaphors influence the development of subjectivities that silence and exclude basic writers. Institutions of higher education must be freed from these metaphors to facilitate both the inclusion of underprepared students and the ability of those students to achieve self-definition.

269   Lu, Min-Zhan. "Conflict and Struggle: The Enemies or Preconditions of Basic Writing?" *College English* 54.8 (1992): 887–913. Print.

Contemporary theorists of writing, such as Gloria Anzaldúa, Mike Rose, and many others, celebrate the idea that writing takes place at a site of painful yet constructive tension between the academy and the student's original culture. Nevertheless, much basic writing instruction still centers on the relatively isolated mastery of "skills" and discursive conventions, thus failing to acknowledge the inevitable process of ideological repositioning implied in poststructuralist models of language. Lu examines the roots of the basic writing movement that followed the introduction of open admissions at the City University of New York to historicize the conceptual role of conflict and struggle in the writings of numerous educators, including Kenneth Bruffee, Thomas Farrell, and Mina Shaughnessy. In the 1970s, the arguments of other thinkers and writers—Lionel Trilling, Irving Howe, and W. E. B. Du Bois—contextualized the emergence of basic writing instruction as a discipline. Only by accepting conflict and struggle as important parts of the scene of composition can basic writing teachers hope to empower their students to make an authentic move toward the rhetorical position that Anzaldúa characterizes as the "borderlands."

270   Newton, Stephen. "Teaching, Listening, and the Sound of Guns." *Basic Writing e-Journal* 4.1 (2002): n. pag. Web. 21 May 2014.

Deromanticizing the notion of a multicultural classroom as one full of exotic voices, Newton's experiences in a Brooklyn open-enrollment university increased his awareness of the confessional discourse that developmental writers produce. When Newton asked his students to "write about a turning point in their lives" and to include only examples that they would be comfortable sharing with him and the rest of the class, they wrote detailed accounts of their families' painful struggles with poverty and disease. He defines developmental students as having histories that have caused them to create academic personas separate from their authentic selves because "[t]he weight of institutional authority had superseded the reservations they had about revealing the intimate details of their lives" (par. 21). Thus his example serves as a call for teachers to recognize these students' perceptions of the academy and to discover their students' histories so that they do not assume or underestimate the narratives they will produce. Newton also warns against critical pedagogies that ask for such writing because he believes that there is a "very real danger, indeed likelihood of objectifying them, and by doing so dehumanizing the very people we are claiming to serve" (par. 26).

271   Norment, Nathaniel, Jr. "Some Effects of Culture-Referenced Topics on the Writing Performance of African American Students." *Journal of Basic Writing* 16.2 (1997): 17–45. Print.

Norment examines whether and how culture-referenced topics affect the writing of eleventh- and twelfth-grade African American students in response to an urban university placement exam. In this study, "culture-referenced" refers to any topic or prompt that incorporates values, attitudes, or information relevant to African American culture. Further, the topics incorporate a combination of culturally, socially, linguistically, and historically determined aspects of African American culture. The study considers both the overall quality of writing produced by students (for example, its development, content, usage, and mechanics) and the syntactic complexity, organization, and length of resulting essays. Trained raters scored 711 essays holistically, and the essays of twenty-five students were analyzed using an analytical scale measuring the number of words, sentences, and paragraphs; average words per sentence and paragraph; and number of sentences per paragraph. Norment concludes that culture-referenced topics do, in fact, elicit essays of higher quality and should therefore be considered in the development and implementation of writing pedagogies, curricula, and assessment measures.

272   Pratt, Mary Louise. "Arts of the Contact Zone." *Profession* 91 (1991): 33–40. Print.

This germinal essay introduces the term *contact zone*, which has seen widespread use and application in postcolonial and cultural studies, among other fields. Pratt defines *contact zones* as "social spaces where cultures meet, clash, and grapple with each other, often in contexts of highly asymmetrical relations of power, such as colonialism, slavery, or their aftermaths as they are lived out in many parts of the world today" (34). Pratt's essay discusses the bilingual literacy and biculturalism of fifteenth-century Incan Guaman Poma, whose twelve-hundred-page letter to the king of Spain chronicles and critiques the Spanish presence in Peru. Poma's text is an "autoethnographic" text, "a text in which people undertake to describe themselves in ways that engage with representations others have made of them" (35). These texts often speak from the margins of cultures. Pratt also discusses the ethnographic term *transculturation*, noting that the term "describe[s] processes whereby members of subordinated or marginal groups select and invent from materials transmitted by a dominant or metropolitan culture" (36). Many composition theorists have invoked these terms in discussions of disempowered student writers, including basic writing students. Pratt acknowledges that our best opportunities for teaching and learning may take place in the contact zones. The pedagogical arts of the contact zone, based on cultural mediation, must be developed.

273   Reagan, Sally Barr. "Warning: Basic Writers at Risk—The Case of Javier." *Journal of Basic Writing* 10.2 (1991): 99–115. Print.

Instead of defining the basic writer, which usually only generalizes or oversimplifies the complex situations of basic writers, we should begin to examine our intentions and methods as teachers of basic writing, especially the work we do with at-risk students, those lower-level basic writers whose reading and writing practices are shaped by social and cultural forces that create problems outside writing. The case study of Javier represents "the multitude of idiosyncratic factors which may influence our students' feelings and behaviors" (101) about reading, writing, and learning. Moreover, the study suggests that "failure" may not be a student's fault at all. Rather, the "problem may lie more significantly on the approach to teaching and the assumptions behind it" (113). This article suggests that the number of at-risk students will continue to grow as America becomes more diversely populated and that our approaches and assumptions must be reflected upon and revised according to the needs of at-risk students like Javier.

274   Richardson, Elaine. *African American Literacies*. New York: Routledge, 2003. Print.

Richardson explores what it would mean to center African American rhetorics and discourses on individual writing classrooms and on composition curricula at large. She argues that African American students are attempting to learn in an educational system that is still dominated by American standardized English and by the cultural hierarchy that it symbolizes and reinforces. Richardson draws on educational research and the rich history of African American rhetorics to explain how students of African American heritage use African American Vernacular English (AAVE) as a "technology" through which to learn and utilize other languages and literacies, including college-level critical literacies. Because African American students are overrepresented in basic writing courses, Richardson argues that teachers of basic writing need to learn and teach the history and linguistic features of AAVE rhetorics and discourses in their writing classrooms. Richardson contends that, "for the most part, America continues to teach us to accept the status of lower achievement for Black students as the norm. Under the present system, we are set in motion to replicate the paradigm and the results" (8).

275   Ryden, Wendy. "Conflicted Literacy: Frederick Douglass's Critical Model." *Journal of Basic Writing* 24.1 (2005): 4–23. Print.

Ryden calls the literacy narrative, a common assignment in basic writing, into question as a tool for critical pedagogy. Frederick Douglass's slave narrative, she notes, is commonly used as an urtext of the genre, but she goes on to critique its representation to students by teachers. She argues, through a discussion of numerous writers, that it is the literacy myth—that literacy is the bedrock of empowerment, self-actualization, and economic progress—that is often presented to students rather than Mary Louise Pratt's notion of a complex transculturation whereby marginalized groups "select and invent from materials transmitted" by a dominant culture (17). Ryden ends with a word of caution about overstating the claims about the power of the literacy narrative to produce critical awareness in writing students.

276   Salas, Spencer. "Steep Houses in Basic Writing: Advocating for Latino Immigrants in a North Georgia Two-Year College." *Journal of Basic Writing* 31.1 (2012): 80–98. Print.

This article is an ethnographic narrative account of the controversy surrounding a town hall meeting on "illegal" immigration held at a two-year college in Georgia. The meeting was spearheaded by the ESL Learning Support program coordinator who was advocating for Generation 1.5 students in the wake of Georgia SB-529, a proposal that would deny public education to undocumented Latino immigrants. Because of the stance taken by the coordinator, the coordinator's job was in jeopardy, the two-year college was almost denied state funding, and a death threat was anonymously left on an answering machine at the Dean's office. The article makes the point that basic writing scholarship and scholars do not address how contemporary legislation has attempted to deny Latino immigrants' access to public education. It argues that basic writing scholarship should engage more explicitly with state legislation, and basic writing scholars should advocate on behalf of Generation 1.5 students.

277   Shepard, Alan, John McMillan, and Gary Tate, eds. *Coming to Class: Pedagogy and the Social Class of Teachers*. Portsmouth: Boynton, 1998. Print.

In this collection of twenty-one original essays by working-class academics, the common goal was to uncover unspoken class suppositions and strictures at play in the culture of academe. The authors offer a book that focuses on how social class shapes the ways teachers work in their classrooms, while the individual essays approach this topic from differing theoretical positions, subject positions, and socioeconomic realities. Essays address issues connected with the role of working-class affiliation in academe, the inattention to class in course content, and the ways that composition is seen in some English departments as "second class" or "service."

278   Sullivan, Patrick, and David Nielsen. "'Ability to Benefit': Making Forward-Looking Decisions about Our Most Underprepared Students." *College English* 75.3 (2013): 319–43. Print.

Sullivan and Nielsen discuss the detriment that "ability to benefit" will have on community colleges, students, and the economy. Ability to benefit seeks to admit only individuals who measure within a range of capabilities, essentially disregarding underprepared students and ending the democratic right of open admissions. Angered by the dismissiveness toward underprepared individuals, calling it a "radically impoverished understanding of developmental students" (230), Sullivan and Nielsen provide data that supports their argument: developmental education is not only vital for the lives of those who are underprepared, but it is a benefit to our communities and economy. Their research demonstrates that standardized tests have notoriously failed to be accurate indicators of skills. According to their data, one-quarter of underprepared students successfully complete first-year composition within a three-year span. With ability to benefit, these students would never receive the opportunity. The authors offer a more comprehensive understanding about the lives of community college students and discuss the influence of race, class, and childhood poverty. The authors conclude with seven suggestions that revise practices in developmental education.

279   Tassoni, John Paul, Richard Lee Walts, and Sara Webb-Sunderhaus. "Deep Shit: A Dialogue about Rhetoric, Pedagogy, and the Working Class." *Open Words: Access and English Studies* 1.2 (2007): 24–47. Print.

The authors share their after-class e-mail list conversations from a graduate seminar in the Histories and Theories of Rhetoric and Composition. For all three members of the class, one instructor and two students, identified as "working class academics," the term *shit* became a dialectical and rhetorical term as they considered how they took or did not take any shit, but gave shit, stepped into deep shit, and questioned shitty cultural ideologies. The dialogue frequently returned to discussion of one of Webb-Sunderhaus's students, a working-class woman who became pregnant and was struggling with the first-year writing course. To what extent should instructors get involved in the "deep shit" of students' personal lives? At what point do attempts to help a student cross over into a hero narrative or a banking model in which the instructor has all the answers and fixes the student's problems? The term *shit* opened intersections between class and gender and became a third space for discussing working-class voices in academia.

280   Thurston, Kay. "Mitigating Barriers to Navajo Students' Success in English Courses." *Teaching Developmental Writing: Background Readings.* 3rd ed. Ed. Susan Naomi Bernstein. Boston: Bedford, 2007. Print.

Reflecting on her experiences teaching at a two-year Native American tribal college, Thurston argues that teachers of writing should look at how "global factors" influence student success rates (356). She identifies five major obstacles that students face: financial difficulties, family obligations, attitudes toward Standard American English (SAE), instructor/faculty ethnocentrism, and ambivalence toward Western education (356). Thurston explains how poverty affects learning in myriad ways, including lack of access to technology and the inability to purchase textbooks. Second, family obligations can easily require a student to miss classes or assignment deadlines more frequently than is acceptable. Additionally, what Thurston calls a "prescriptive attitude" toward Standard American English on the part of instructors makes it such that many Navajo students are not as familiar with SAE as is presumed, and, in turn, instructors are not aware of Navajo English conventions (359). Instructors are encouraged to see Navajo English and SAE as different dialects as opposed to competing discourses. Fourth, often-unconscious instructor ethnocentrism disadvantages Navajo students by alienating them and by failing to validate different rhetorical styles. Finally, a sense of ambivalence toward Western education on the part of Navajo students can be misinterpreted as low motivation or ability, but in fact, Thurston argues, students can themselves interpret the teaching of SAE as negating or oppressing their tribal language and culture. Thus instructors should focus on helping students see how SAE can serve their families and communities. Thurston concludes that instructors need to do more to overcome these obstacles because failing to pass composition often means failing to earn a degree.

281   Troyka, Lynn Quitman. "Perspectives on Legacies and Literacy in the 1980s." *A Sourcebook for Basic Writing Teachers.* Ed. Theresa Enos. New York: Random, 1987. 16–26. Print.

Troyka argues for support for the challenges that nontraditional students in college writing classes face. She describes the challenges in terms of positive legacies: students' gregarious and social natures, their comfort with and enthusiasm for oral communication, their holistic thinking patterns, and their ambivalence about learning (particularly that they want to learn but do not know how they feel about the changes that learning will bring to their lives). Troyka reminds readers that these strengths and talents can lead to good self-directed writing. Her strategies and perspectives fit all levels of writing courses; she provides excellent evidence for a constructionist classroom philosophy.

282   Zamel, Vivian, and Ruth Spack, eds. *Negotiating Academic Literacies: Teaching and Learning across Languages and Cultures.* Mahwah: Erlbaum, 1998. Print.

In response to the growing diversity in higher education, instructors need to reconceptualize academic discourse and acknowledge multiple types of literacy and approaches to learning. Students' backgrounds and previous knowledge are important resources. In classrooms where students and teachers of various languages and cultures connect, there is the potential for growth and transformation of the academy. Zamel and Spack advocate for an expanded, pluralistic definition of literacy and challenge assumptions regarding academic discourse. They point to the need for "a dynamic process of negotiation, involving both adaptation and resistance" (xii) between teachers and students. The book includes twenty-two previously published readings that address these issues from various fields—such as composition, English as a second language, anthropology, literature, and education—presented in chronological order, beginning with Mina P. Shaughnessy's "Diving In: An Introduction to Basic Writing" [89] and Mike Rose's "The Language of Exclusion: Writing Instruction at the University" [34]. The included essays discuss the process of writing and constructing an identity in more than one culture, explore issues of language and power, examine definitions of literacy, critique academic discourse, and challenge exclusionary notions of what academic literacy and discourse are.

Second-Language Learners/Special Populations

283   Barber-Fendley, Kimber, and Chris Hamel. "A New Visibility: An Argument for Alternative Assistance Writing Programs for Students with Learning Disabilities." *College Composition and Communication* 55.3 (2004): 504–35. Print.

As educators become involved with teaching students with learning disabilities, the issue of what is "fair" treatment has become more troublesome. Generally, students with learning disabilities have been expected to accomplish exactly what students without them can accomplish and in the same ways. The authors shed light on the injustice of rules for accommodations and other approaches to learning disabilities that often prevent LD students from demonstrating their skills through alternative means. As Susan Ohanian noted years ago, the one-size-fits-all approach rarely fits anyone adequately, and this is

Barber-Fendley and Hamel's main issue. They argue against traditional forms of learning-disability accommodation and in favor of the creation of an alternative approach to assisting LD students in first-year composition programs. Their approach is a useful one for anyone dealing with the challenges of diversity across a much broader spectrum than learning disabilities alone. There are many disabilities that would benefit from approaching students as unique, and there are many students who come to us without physical or psychological disabilities but who would nonetheless benefit from unique attention in their first-year composition courses, such as students with family problems, homesickness, or financial stresses. We are in a unique position to help our students to become acclimated to college, while increasing the likelihood of their success and retention. The focus of this article on providing a unique experience for individual learners also fits the research done on teaching students with disabilities, as well as the research conducted on access and retention at the University of Minnesota's Center for Research in Development Education and Urban Literacy.

284   Becket, Diana. "Uses of Background Experience in a Preparatory Reading and Writing Class: An Analysis of Native and Non-native Speakers of English." *Journal of Basic Writing* 24.2 (2005): 53–71. Print.

Becket critiques the placement of "so-called Generation 1.5 students," who "moved with their parents to the U.S. when they were young children or adolescents" (54), into ESL settings alongside international students. She cites the ways their placement in these courses often works against their current literacy and social and educational needs. She then studies a group of six students in a developmental reading/ writing sequence at an open-admissions college at a large university in the Midwest. Three participants are native speakers. The other three are "Generation 1.5" ESL students. Although the study shows significant differences in the ways these two groups of students perceived their literacy and efficacy as writers and communicators, their experience of education at the university and high school level, and their approach to writing tasks, the study also concludes that the ESL-labeled writers are often better at idea development, grammatical fluency, and meeting paper length than their native-speaking peers and that their inclusion in a non-ESL setting is more appropriate than placement with international students in a traditional ESL context. Becket concludes that other factors shared with native-speaker developmental reading/writing students, including motivation, attitude, time management, and willingness to revise, are more significant contributors to success than ESL status and that Generation 1.5 students are most appropriately placed in non-ESL developmental reading/writing settings.

285   Belcher, Diane, and George Braine, eds. *Academic Writing in a Second Language: Essays on Research and Pedagogy*. Norwood: Ablex, 1995. Print.

This collection of sixteen essays explores the problems inherent in empowering college ESL students by allowing them access to the skills necessary to participate in the academic community. From the outset, this project is defined in the broadest sense, using the discipline of composition studies as a springboard into suggestions of various transformative, participatory, and resistant strategies within academic discourse. To help the ESL student feel more welcomed than threatened by the academic discourse community, the overarching aim of this collection is familiarization—on the part of the ESL student and teacher alike. The text is divided into three parts: Issues, Research, and Pedagogy.

286   Blanton, Linda Lonon, and Barbara Kroll, eds. *ESL Composition Tales: Reflections on Teaching.* Ann Arbor: U of Michigan P, 2002. Print.

Inspired by a panel at the 1996 TESOL Colloquium on Writing, several veteran educators of ESL students, including Alister Cumming, Ilona Leki, and Tony Silva, ruminate on their teaching careers, obstacles they have faced, and successes they have achieved. The introduction by Barbara Kroll, "What I Certainly Didn't Know When I Started," combines her personal teaching stories with a history of the panel and the creation of the essays into a text. She notes that framing the text with her introduction and Paul Kei Matsuda's epilogue places these stories into different contexts; the introduction and the epilogue help create a discourse that does not exclude younger generations of ESL educators. Each section of the book focuses on a theme, such as instruction, course creation, or theories of ESL education, culminating with advice for educators in the field. Many of the contributors discuss how research has affected their teaching choices. For example, in "The Best of Intentions," Melinda Erickson develops the idea of the "pendulum swings" that teachers experience throughout their careers, particularly at the beginning when it is easy to lose confidence. Erickson describes a failed classroom assignment that makes her overreact, or "swing," in the opposite pedagogical direction. Leki's "Not the End of History" and Cumming's "If I Had Known Twelve Things . . ." reflect on previous teaching pedagogy and how to improve, and possibly change, what appear to be fixed ideas of instruction methods. In his epilogue, "Reinventing Giants," Matsuda reiterates the importance of ESL education, describes the changes that ESL instruction has gone through institutionally, and reflects on the changes that the writers have experienced in their teaching careers. Matsuda reinforces the idea of growth that the writers attest to in their stories: through reflection and by learning from others, one can become a more effective teacher.

287   Brueggemann, Brenda Jo, et al. "Becoming Visible: Lessons in Disability." *College Composition and Communication* 52.3 (2001): 368–98. Print.

Brueggemann and colleagues focus on legitimizing students with learning disabilities as possessing valid disabilities, different from mental retardation, and needing different responses. Along with Kimber Barber-Fendley and Chris Hamel's "A New Visibility" [283], this article reflects the problems of substantiating the very real disabilities of students with various learning challenges, of working with existing standards that demand educational conformities that often further handicap LD students, and of making disability visible in an academic world that privileges those people considered able-bodied. The authors look at the place of disabilities in composition, whether it is teaching disability issues, reading texts in which disability is the primary thematic material, working to help LD students write, or claiming a space for teachers and students with varying disabilities in higher education classrooms. For the issue of disability to be adequately addressed in the twenty-first century, we need to transform how we approach the issue of diversity, as these authors note, by creating a more inclusive definition of "normal" such that people who have disabilities are defined as normal, fully human, whole and capable individuals, regardless of whether they are learning disabled or have some other type of disability.

See: Kimber Barber-Fendley and Chris Hamel, "A New Visibility" [283].

288   Casanave, Christine Pearson. *Controversies in Second Language Writing: Dilemmas and Decisions in Research and Instruction*. Ann Arbor: U of Michigan P, 2004. Print.

Casanave succinctly synthesizes historical studies and arguments in second-language (L2) writing. She discusses issues and arguments concerning decision making in L2 writing classrooms, contrastive rhetoric, controversies about fluency versus accuracy in students' writing, the process-product argument, and the issue of explicit versus implicit responses to students' assignments. The assessment dilemma is also raised. The interactions of students' writing to audience (with readers) and to plagiarism (with texts) are asserted as controversies in L2 writing. Casanave also discusses the political issue of whether assigned writings in class reflect the teacher's or the students' needs or help students in being more critical in their thinking and writing. The debate over the use of the Internet is also mentioned.

289   CCCC Committee on Second Language Writing. "CCCC Statement on Second Language Writing and Writers." *College Composition and Communication* 52.4 (2001): 669–74. Print.

Produced by the Conference on College Composition and Communication (CCCC) of the National Council of Teachers of English (NCTE), this policy statement consists of three parts: a general statement, guidelines for writing programs, and a selected bibliography. The general statement describes various types of second-language writers in North American universities. It urges writing instructors and program administrators to recognize the growing number of second-language learners in writing classes, to understand their linguistic and cultural needs, and to develop instructional and administrative practices that are sensitive to these special needs. The statement also urges graduate programs to prepare writing teachers and scholars for working with college writers who are increasingly diverse, both linguistically and culturally, and it stresses the need to include second-language perspective in developing writing theories and studies. The guidelines for writing programs provide recommendations regarding the placement and assessment of second-language writers and discuss issues of class size, academic credit, teacher preparation, and teacher support.

290   Center, Carole. "Representing Race in Basic Writing Scholarship." *Journal of Basic Writing* 26.1 (2007): 20–42. Print.

Center notes that Susanmarie Harrington's detailed examination of essays in the *Journal of Basic Writing* found that most essays focused on pedagogical approaches or basic writing programs, instead of focusing on students. Center examines the journal's essays for evidence of "visibility or invisibility" of race in those essays that do focus on students and argues that "[m]aking race visible in scholarly writing . . . can help basic writing teachers to reflect on the implications of difference." She suggests that "student identities and voices should be seen and heard in all their complexity" and that they cannot be if race is invisible in our scholarship.

291   Connor, Ulla. *Contrastive Rhetoric: Cross-Cultural Aspects of Second-Language Writing*. New York: Cambridge UP, 1996. Print.

Connor provides a comprehensive discussion of how contrastive rhetoric relates to the theories of applied linguistics, linguistic relativity, rhetoric, text linguistics, discourse types and genres, literacy (cultural and cross-cultural), and translation (structural analyses and literal translation). Connor acknowledges the value of syntactical concerns, such as those advocated in Chomskyan-like models, and expands on the theory that "linguistic and rhetorical conventions of the first language interfere with writing in the second language" (5). Detailed student examples, instructors' comments, tables, and specific language comparisons illustrate her argument. The extended table of contents, subject index, and author index render this book easily navigable. An exhaustive reference list creates an invaluable source for those interested in contrastive rhetoric as it relates to process rather than product.

292   Dong, Yu Ren. "The Need to Understand ESL Students' Native Language Writing Experiences." *Teaching Developmental Writing: Background Readings*. Ed. Susan Naomi Bernstein. Boston: Bedford, 2001. 288–98. Print.

Dong uses her own ESL students' voices to highlight cross-cultural writing differences. She argues that teachers need to understand the diverse native literacy backgrounds of their ESL students if they are to build on that knowledge and help students develop strategies to improve their proficiency in English reading and writing. She invited twenty-six first-year college students to compose autobiographies describing their native-language writing instruction, the writing assignments they were given in their home countries, and the differences between writing in English and writing in their native language. Dong presents the students' stories in their own words, and they illustrate a wide variety of experiences and perceptions. From them, Dong concludes that teachers who ask students to reflect on and share their native-language backgrounds can use this information to expand the ways they identify and address each student's unique needs. Students also become more aware of how their previous experiences affect their expectations and approach to learning English.

293   Ewert, Doreen E. "ESL Curriculum Revision: Shifting Paradigms for Success." *Journal of Basic Writing* 30.1 (2011): 5–33. Print.

This article reviews the background, context, and initial data from an ESL language development curriculum at a large Midwestern university. The ESL program at the university constructs a curriculum that privileges fluency over linguistic accuracy and places emphasis on helping second-language students develop a rhetorical awareness of the variety of academic literacies required for college-level writing. It notes that the rise in international student acceptance rates coupled with a desire to more accurately measure the growth and matriculation of these students through the university creates a context for rethinking old assumptions about ESL literacy instruction. The author details the different ways that fluency is promoted and developed through a three-course sequence that ESL students must test into before moving on to the next sequence in their graduation schemes. Using data from placement and holistic exams, grade distribution lists, and student interviews, the curriculum is evaluated providing intriguing data on an ESL program that challenges the overemphasis sometimes placed on grammar instruction in ESL student training.

294   Ferris, Dana. "One Size Does Not Fit All: Response and Revision Issues for Immigrant Students." *Teaching Developmental Writing: Background Readings*. 3rd ed. Ed. Susan Naomi Bernstein. Boston: Bedford, 2007. 83–97. Print.

Ferris challenges the practice of treating all ESL students in the same way when it comes to giving feedback on their writing. She recommends, instead, differentiating between international students and immigrant students (what some today may refer to as Generation 1.5 students); international students have learned English as a foreign language (EFL), and immigrant students have already spent some time in the US academic system. The response to teacher commentary within each of the two populations indicates a difference in motivation and ability to respond to feedback. International students, unfamiliar with the notion of revising and having multiple drafts, may actually become confused by comments that extend beyond the grammar and vocabulary lessons that were the focus of their EFL studies in their native countries. Ferris observes that this confusion can lead to inaction. Immigrant students, on the other hand, take teacher feedback "very seriously" (88), using "a variety of resources to deal with teacher commentary" (89). Ferris goes on to discuss the void in research that compares and distinguishes the L2 writing of the two populations and how teacher feedback in various forms and under various scenarios can lead to revision. She does, however, discuss findings from the research conducted to date, which have significant bearing on pedagogy. She notes, for example, that one form of commentary that leads to improved writing for international students is that which discusses *patterns* of error, with examples highlighted within the student's text and offers suggestions for remedying those types of errors. Immigrant students, though, do better with an indication of where the errors are; they do not necessarily need suggestions on how to correct them.

295   Ferris, Dana. "Preparing Teachers to Respond to Student Writing." *Journal of Second Language Writing* 16.3 (2007): 165–93. Print.

Because responding to student writing is one of the most challenging and time-consuming aspects of a writing instructor's job, it is an important component of preservice teacher training courses. In her paper, Ferris describes the "approach/response/follow-up" training sequence that the author uses with preservice writing instructors. The "approach" section presents various issues, questions, and options available in responding to student writing based on previous L1 and L2 research on teacher feedback. In the "response" section of the sequence, teachers discuss principles and techniques of responding to L2 writing and participate in hands-on practice activities. The last section of the sequence, "follow-up," includes three components: (1) discussions about helping students utilize commentary effectively and holding them accountable, (2) conversations about qualitative and quantitative ways to evaluate teacher commentary and its effectiveness, and (3) a required project with an L2 student writer. The article concludes with special considerations for language-based feedback and ideas for working with inservice instructors.

296   Ferris, Dana R., and John Hedgcock. *Response to Student Writing: Implications for Second Language Students*. Mahwah: Erlbaum, 2003. Print.

In this book, Ferris and Hedgcock comprehensively survey research on the response to student writing and link the research to detailed descriptions of sound response practices. The book is divided into two main parts: five chapters on research and three chapters on practice. Each part features chapters on teacher response, error correction, and peer response. The research section has additional chapters on the relationship between first-language (L1) writing research and second-language (L2) writing research. Throughout the first five chapters, Ferris and Hedgcock summarize major research studies on the response to writing, noting the type of study (from empirical studies to surveys to case studies, from studies with hundreds of participants to those with only a handful), research questions, and major findings, as well as research limitations. Their use of charts and lists throughout these chapters makes it easy to grasp the major trends at a glance. The final three chapters build on the research to focus on practice. In each of these chapters, Ferris and Hedgcock emphasize the links between sound practices and the research discussed in the earlier chapters. Each chapter offers guiding principles, specific suggestions, and clear examples.

The authors use charts and lists effectively and include many examples of assignments, student texts, feedback forms, and teacher responses both in the chapters and in useful appendices.

297   Ferris, Dana, and John S. Hedgcock. *Teaching ESL Composition: Purpose, Process, and Practice.* Mahwah: Erlbaum, 1998. Print.

This comprehensive resource is designed to help prospective and current English as a second language composition teachers to design and implement syllabi and lesson plans, choose textbooks, and confront most of the pedagogical obstacles that such courses present. Charts, samples of ESL student writing, and suggested classroom activities fill each chapter. In addition, the application activities that conclude the chapters provide direct practice in such tasks as developing lesson plans and writing commentary on student papers. Ferris and Hedgcock argue that the ESL teacher really must ascertain the needs of each particular ESL class separately. No two are quite alike in terms of ethnic profile and language capacity, so teachers are at pains to adapt curricula carefully once the term has started. The book then outlines how to do that in terms of text selection, instructor feedback, class activities, and so forth. Included are chapters that focus on theoretical and practical issues in ESL writing, the reading-writing relationship in ESL composition, syllabus design, text selection, instructor feedback, editing, assessment issues (including the use of portfolios), and the uses of technology. Ferris and Hedgcock also examine important research on the relationship between reading proficiency and writing ability for both first-language and second-language students, finding that among both, good readers are good writers.

298   Fredericksen, Elaine, and Isabel Baca. "Bilingual Students in the Composition Classroom: Paving the Way to Biliteracy." *Open Words: Access and English Studies* 2.2 (2008): 24–40. Print.

Bilingual students grow up learning two languages simultaneously: the languages or dialects spoken at home and at school, either of which can be their dominant language, "the one they feel most comfortable in" (24). However, many bilingual students face challenges in the writing classroom because they "fear writing in English and lack confidence to succeed" in these situations. In freshman composition, these fears can hinder the bilingual student from developing critical thinking skills and the ability to generate ideas. And while instructors aid these students in developing the writing process, from freewriting to drafting to proofreading and so on, they often force the students to complete each of these steps in English. Focusing on students whose dominant language is not English, Fredericksen and Baca suggest a method that "fosters biliteracy—fluency in reading and writing two languages" (24). Looking at the writing experiences of their students and sharing examples of their writing processes, the authors encourage students to generate ideas, prewrite, freewrite, and write journal entries in their dominant language, allowing for improvement in their writing processes and encouraging biliteracy and success in writing.

299   Friedrich, Patricia. "Assessing the Needs of Linguistically Diverse First-Year Students: Bringing Together and Telling Apart International ESL, Resident ESL, and Monolingual Basic Writers." *Writing Program Administration Journal* 30.1/2 (2006): 15–36. Print.

Friedrich acknowledges the presence of three kinds of students in composition programs: international ESL writers, monolingual basic writers, and resident ESL writers (Generation 1.5 students). Friedrich distinguishes between the three groups of student writers based on twelve "attributes": register, strategies, awareness of linguistic background, language acquisition, oral and written language, level of acculturation, educational history, attitudes-placement, grammatical knowledge, attitudes-errors, learning style, and language and emotions. By separating the three groups of first-year composition students on these twelve counts, the article highlights their differences and then focuses on resident ESL writers. The charted distinctions represent where resident ESL learners stand vis-à-vis the other two groups and suggest their expectations from a writing class. Friedrich deliberates on what can be done to mitigate the lapses in the traditionally set disciplinary practices of first-year composition classes. Among her many suggestions, Friedrich seems to reiterate a call for action on the part of instructors and the institution. Developing need-based teaching and curriculum, improving communication between mainstream and ESL programs, deliberating on the usefulness of maintaining separate sections for mainstream and ESL students, increasing the availability of tutoring centers, and rethinking feedback practices are some of the suggestions that Friedrich offers for customizing and even revamping current ineffective practices, which tend to overlook the needs of resident ESL students.

300   Grandin, Temple. *Thinking in Pictures: My Life with Autism.* New York: Random, 2006. Print.

In Grandin's first book, *Emergence,* we learn about autism as a child or an adolescent might describe it. In this book, the focus shifts to a more scientific and medical explanation of the challenges of working with an autistic student. As the title suggests, students with autism have brains that work somewhat differently than the brains of students who don't have autism. The scientific evidence has yet to fully reveal why this is; however, the very real differences in brain structures and function cause equally real differences in student responses in our classes. Grandin's books remind us that the differences autistic people have do not necessarily mean a lack of intelligence. Many people labeled as autistic can become educated and contribute to the world from their own perspectives, which adds to our insights. In this book, Grandin talks about professors who agreed to work with her on her animal handling research in graduate school. One characteristic shared by her professors, and by her previous teachers, is the willingness to ask how her abilities might aid her education, rather than demanding other abilities more foreign to her. While she thinks in pictures, some less successful professors demanded that she think in words like they do. More successful professors acknowledged her ability to think in pictures and supported her skills in that area, which, she testifies, allowed her to continue to grow and develop as an academic.

301   Grandin, Temple, and Sean Barron. *Unwritten Rules of Social Relationships: Decoding Social Mysteries through the Unique Perspectives of Autism.* Arlington: Future Horizons, 2005. Print.

The boundaries of teaching for many writing instructors can often constrain our understanding of what a child or an adult with autism needs to be taught. Grandin and Barron begin by demonstrating that their path to being well-socialized adults was sometimes fairly smooth and sometimes quite rocky, depending on the situation. For children with autism who may not be as quick to pick up social cues, the path is often difficult, and this can affect overall classroom performance. The authors have created the following rules to help children with autism function with less stress for themselves and for the other people near them: (1) Rules are situation- and person-based. (2) Things have different levels of importance. (3) We all make mistakes, and that's OK. (4) Honesty is different from diplomacy. (5) Politeness is always appropriate. (6) Nice people aren't always our friends. (7) There are differences between public and private behavior. (8) You must learn to recognize when you are turning other people off. (9) It is possible to learn how to fit in. (10) People are responsible only for their own behaviors. In the epilogue, the authors acknowledge that learning to be socially accepted by others remains challenging into adulthood for people with autism, but also that learning does continue to help them to improve how they relate to and work with others. When teachers understand how to help that growth, they can make a real difference in the lives of students who have autism by making clear both the academic and the social expectations for all students, not just those with autism. Today, some students who don't have autism have an equivalent need for classroom rules and clear social expectations.

302   Grandin, Temple, and Kate Duffy. *Developing Talents: Careers for Individuals with Asperger Syndrome and High-Functioning Autism.* Shawnee Mission: Autism Asperger, 2004. Print.

For many academics, this book can evoke a startlingly significant awakening of their awareness of just how often and how powerfully we have set up the processes of higher education to focus solely on the kinds of skills we have, while refusing to educate students who are in some ways different. Grandin and Duffy remind us that we too often focus on what students cannot do, while ignoring what they are able to do. In the foreword, Tony Atwood notes that we must understand that many successful adults with autism achieved their success not by learning to be more like nonautistic learners, although improving people skills did help, but by being themselves. This book contains many examples of adults with autism and Asperger syndrome who haven't become "wordies," and the overall message it sends is that we need to take students as they are instead of using a scalpel to shape them as we might like them to be. The final chapter looks at the kinds of careers in which adults with autism have succeeded, demonstrating that students with autism can perform many kinds of work if they receive adequate guidance in their choices of majors and courses along with some moderate on-the-job support.

303   Grandin, Temple, and Margaret Scariano. *Emergence: Labeled Autistic*. New York: Warner, 2005. Print.

In stunning fashion, Grandin tells the story of her early years as an autistic child whose mother fought to keep her in a regular school, despite her father's insistence that she go "to a school for the retarded" (90) and despite her outbursts, her fears, and her inability to explain to others why she was behaving in such strange ways. Through her eyes, ears, and voice, readers slowly begin to understand autism from the inside, instead of as outsiders criticizing what they do not understand. Teachers, Grandin tells readers, influenced her profoundly because she encountered some teachers who believed she had much to say and an intellect that would grow to help her say it. Most important, she tells us what those teachers did that was effective in helping her to develop her talents. They believed in her potential to do well. They were patient with her awkward stages of growth and development, which were unlike those of many other children but were equally able to propel her into a rewarding career and eventually a PhD in animal science from the University of Illinois. Her final chapter helps us to further refine our understanding, detailing which classroom activities are helpful to autistic children, and other children too, and which are not as useful or are even harmful.

304   Harklau, Linda, Kay M. Losey, and Meryl Siegal, eds. *Generation 1.5 Meets College Composition: Issues in the Teaching of Writing to U.S.-Educated Learners of ESL*. Mahwah: Erlbaum, 1999. Print.

The editors discuss "equitable and appropriate" ways to identify and serve the classroom needs of immigrant, refugee, and permanent-resident populations that do not speak English as a native language. They argue that existing ways of categorizing nonnative or bilingual English speakers do not sufficiently address the range of student backgrounds, experiences, and needs. Institutional curricula and program design need to reconsider the automatic designation of such students as "remedial" or unfamiliar with US language and culture. Chapters explore specific needs of various nonnative English-speaking populations, including social construction of writing, language, identity, and ownership; the preparation of teachers and institutional programs to work with specific cultural and linguistic groups; and strategies for program reform and assessment with a view to incorporating these groups.

305   Hillenbrand, Lisa. "Assessment of ESL Students in Mainstream College Composition." *Teaching English in the Two-Year College* 21.2 (1994): 125–30. Print.

Hillenbrand uses responses from an informal survey of teachers of ESL students on her college campus to identify areas of frustration in the assessment of ESL writing and to offer suggestions for meeting the challenges that ESL writers face. She emphasizes the importance of understanding differences in rhetorical patterns between cultures and explains the difficulty of adapting to the common rhetorical patterns of English. To assist ESL students, she suggests providing writing models or encouraging the use of writing strategies like outlining. In addition, she suggests that teachers respond to ESL student writing as a whole, avoiding the temptation to focus just on grammatical and mechanical errors. She suggests that both holistic and analytical scoring can benefit ESL students as well as one-on-one conferences with the teacher, and she especially encourages writing teachers who work with ESL students to be aware of the unique linguistic challenges that their students face.

306   Hyland, Fiona. "The Impact of Teacher Written Feedback on Individual Writers." *Journal of Second Language Writing* 7.3 (1998): 255–86. Print.

Hyland investigates ESL writers' reactions to and uses of written feedback. Using a case study approach and a variety of data sources, including questionnaires, observation notes, interview transcripts, and written texts, Hyland discusses overall findings on six students' use of written feedback in an English proficiency program course at a New Zealand university. She then focuses on two student writers who showed contrasting patterns of feedback use and who both became much less positive about their writing during the course. The student revisions after receiving teacher written feedback are analyzed and contextual data is used to gain a deeper understanding of the students' motivations and responses to the feedback. The data show that use of teacher written feedback varies due to individual differences in needs and student approaches to writing. It also appears to be affected by the different experiences students bring with them to the classroom setting. Some implications for teachers giving feedback are also presented. Because the data suggest that the feedback situation has great potential for miscommunication and misunderstanding, there must be a more open teacher-student dialogue on feedback.

307   Hyland, Ken. "Genre Pedagogy: Language, Literacy, and L2 Writing Instruction." *Journal of Second Language Writing* 16.3 (2007): 148–64. Print.

Hyland examines the emerging field of second-language (L2) writing instruction through the pedagogical lens of focusing on genre. Hyland outlines the two leading schools of thought in genre pedagogy, SFL (Systemic Functional Linguistics) and ESP (English for Specific Purposes), and demonstrates how a teacher would implement the theory into actual practice. According to Hyland, teachers employing genre pedagogy assess the needs of their students and incorporate only real-world genres into the class, therefore narrowing the scope of the course to what students will encounter in their given field of interest. Hyland also stresses the importance of teaching students how pieces of text work as a means of communication, and what rhetorical moves authors are employing to make the reader understand their message. He says, "Teachers of *writing* clearly need to be teachers of *language*, as it is an ability to exercise appropriate linguistic choices in the ways they treat and organize their topics for particular readers which helps students to give their ideas authority" (151).

308   Jurecic, Ann. "Neurodiversity." *College English* 69.5 (2007): 421–42. Print.

Citing the increasing prevalence of autism spectrum disorders and a personal experience teaching a student on the autism spectrum, Jurecic argues that students with neurological differences—and autism spectrum disorders in particular—are likely to begin appearing more frequently in college writing classrooms, creating new pedagogical challenges for writing teachers. Responses to these challenges, she argues, can be informed by both social constructivist theories and cognitive science: that is, while writing teachers must continue to be wary of stereotyping students based on a medical diagnosis, cognitive science can provide useful insight into the way characteristics of autism—such as impairments with empathy and social awareness—make writing and writing classrooms difficult for many students on the autism spectrum. Ultimately, Jurecic calls for writing teachers to seek greater understanding of "neurodiverse" students, finding a middle ground where both scientific knowledge and social constructions of difference and normality can mutually inform their pedagogical approaches.

309   Kasper, Loretta F. "ESL Writing and the Principle of Nonjudgmental Awareness: Rationale and Implementation." *Teaching Developmental Writing: Background Readings.* Ed. Susan Naomi Bernstein. Boston: Bedford, 2001. 277–86. Print.

Kasper argues that a more student-centered, process-oriented approach to writing can demonstrably increase intermediate English as a second language students' (TOEFL score of approximately 350) confidence, motivation, and ability to write well. Noting that both basic writing research and ESL writing research suggest that instructor feedback dramatically affects students' development as writers, Kasper describes how she adapted W. Timothy Gallwey's principle of nonjudgmental awareness—originally developed to train tennis players—to her teaching. Kasper describes how to incorporate Gallwey's principle into writing instruction and feedback by using a series of task-oriented questions that encourage students to reflect on their communicative goals and strengths. After conducting an informal three-semester study, Kasper found that incorporating Gallwey's principle to her method of instruction produced much better results than her earlier product- and error-driven methods did: students' confidence and awareness became more noticeable, and they improved their ability to identify and revise essays for content and grammar.

310   Kroll, Barbara. *Exploring the Dynamics of Second Language Writing*. New York: Cambridge UP, 2003. Print.

Including the works of numerous scholars such as Paul Kei Matsuda, Alister Cumming, Tony Silva, Liz Hamp-Lyons, William Grabe, and Ilona Leki, this collection contains fourteen readings in five sections: "Exploring the Field of Second Language Writing," "Exploring the Voices of Key Stakeholders: Teachers and Students," "Exploring Writers' Finished Texts," "Exploring Contextualities of Texts," and "Exploring Technology." The readings provide an orientation to the field of second-language (L2) writing and represent a collection of scholarly insights about a range of L2 writing issues, including conducting writing research, curriculum design, assessment and feedback, reading and writing relations, and the impact of computers in L2 writing. Each of the five sections begins with a brief introduction to contextualize specific areas of L2 writing. The book ends with an epilogue that challenges L2 writing professionals to thoughtfully consider the importance and relevance of this field.

311   Leki, Ilona. "Reciprocal Themes in ESL Reading and Writing." *Landmark Essays on ESL Writing*. Ed. Tony Silva and Paul Kei Matsuda. Mahwah: Erlbaum, 2001. 173–90. Print.

Leki describes the many parallels between second-language reading and writing research since the 1970s but notes that they are often kept separate from each other. This, she suggests, is a by-product of institutional pressures and the need for disciplinary legitimacy. According to Leki, this unnatural segregation limits instruction, especially in reading. She argues that writing research emphasizes the recursive and reciprocal processes of constructing meaning but that this understanding is distorted in many second-language reading courses through text selection and pedagogical practices that ultimately make reading much harder. The bigger questions about why the text is being read or how it adds to or complicates students' knowledge are downplayed so that reading becomes more about learning skills than creating and negotiating meaning. Leki explains that bringing the fundamentally integral processes of reading and writing together enables students to work with texts in more realistic and holistic ways. She offers strategies to create a more reciprocal, socially transactional model of instruction that incorporates research findings in both reading and writing.

312   Leki, Ilona. *Undergraduates in a Second Language: Challenges and Complexities of Academic Literacy Development*. New York: Erlbaum, 2007. Print.

Leki demonstrates the complexity of ESL literacy development in this qualitative study, which traces the undergraduate careers of four ESL students, each in a different major: nursing, social work, business, and engineering. Based on a rich collection of data, Leki claims that focusing on academic literacy alone does not allow us to understand student experiences, and she stresses the importance of understanding the social and ideological contexts for developing literacy. Leki finds that the students did not represent academic literacy as a priority in their academic lives; she questions the relevance of first-year writing courses in relation to the "lived experiences" of the students she interviewed. Based on her findings, Leki suggests that we question the rationale behind first-year writing instruction when composition genres may not connect with the genres that students encounter after the first year.

313   Leki, Ilona. *Understanding ESL Writers: A Guide for Teachers*. Portsmouth: Boynton, 1992. Print.

Leki argues that although teaching writing to English as a second language writers is similar in many ways to teaching native speakers of English, ESL writers also bring many unique experiences and characteristics to the classroom. For this reason, writing teachers without much experience or preparation working with ESL writers may find it difficult to imagine the characteristics, needs, and backgrounds of those writers. Leki explains that we cannot conflate the motivational, cultural, and linguistic needs of L2 writers with those of L1 writers, including basic writers. Leki offers a practical introduction to the teaching of ESL writing—especially the teaching of international visa students—for future ESL writing teachers and for practicing writing teachers who are not familiar with second-language issues. The first section of the book provides an overview of historical and theoretical background. The second section explores the characteristics of ESL students, beginning with a comparison of ESL and basic writers. The third and final section focuses on writing issues. While each of the chapters can stand easily on its own (e.g., "Classroom Expectations and Behavior," "Contrastive Rhetoric," "L2 Composing," and "Sentence-Level Errors"), they are better understood within the context of the framing chapters, which synthesize perspectives on the history of L2 writing instruction, L2 acquisition research, and a comparison of ESL and basic writers. In "ESL and Basic Writers," she explains how various student groups bring uniquely different histories into the academic writing classroom. Leki's book predates the research on Generation 1.5 writers, but it is still relevant and still the best choice for a one-stop text for new and developing teachers aiming to better understand their ESL students.

314   Leki, Ilona, Alister Cumming, and Tony Silva. *A Synthesis of Research on Second Language Writing in English*. New York: Routledge, 2008. Print.

For many ESL instructors and researchers, issues related to research teaching in second-language writing have remained an unknown area. To meet the needs of both teachers and researchers, this book synthesizes research in the area of L2 writing in English. Focusing on three main areas—contexts for L2 writing, instruction and assessment, and basic research in L2 writing—it aims to uncover a range of issues, some that have been well researched and others that require additional attention. Section 1 offers a wide range of research in various contexts, including different levels of school (e.g., secondary school, undergraduate level, and graduate level) as well as settings outside school (e.g., professional environments). The last chapter of this section also touches on different dimensions in these settings, such as ideological and political issues. Section 2 uncovers different dimensions of teaching and assessing writing in English. It includes an analysis of curricular issues, such as conceptual foundations and theoretical orientations of L2 writing curricula. It further explores various issues in L2 writing assessment, including different types of assessment and responding to L2 students' writing. The final section explores basic research in L2 writing. Prior work summarized in this section is grouped into four main categories: writer characteristics, composing processes, textual issues of written texts, and grammatical issues of written texts. This section also includes an annotated bibliography presented in both alphabetical and chronological order. This outstanding synthesis of research serves as a reference book for anyone interested in understanding prior work in L2 writing and for those wanting to investigate both pedagogical and future research implications in this area.

315   Mason, Katherine. "Cooperative Learning and Second Language Acquisition in First-Year Composition: Opportunities for Authentic Communication among English Language Learners." *Teaching English in the Two-Year College* 34.1 (2006): 52–58. Print.

Mason asserts that using cooperative learning activities with English language learners (ELLs) in a first-year composition course helps students improve writing and speaking proficiency and allows the instructor to respond "effectively, professionally, and compassionately" (53) to students' linguistic needs. The author advocates using collaborative learning activities with an awareness of Spencer Kagan's four principles of cooperative learning, to help students build confidence, naturally integrate the four modes of literacy, and facilitate "a sense of positive interdependence among classmates, thus reducing the affective filter that hinders language acquisition" (57). Mason discusses a few specific collaborative strategies that she has found effective and notes that teacher feedback is often used to complement or supplement peer feedback during collaborative activities. Overall, collaborative activities are represented as an effective supplement to traditional classroom activities since they encourage ELLs to take linguistic risks while "simultaneously engaging in their composing processes" (58).

316   Matsuda, Paul Kei. "Basic Writing and Second Language Writers: Toward an Inclusive Definition." *Journal of Basic Writing* 22.2 (2003): 67–89. Print.

Matsuda questions the generalized notion of basic writers often appropriated by academe. With a diverse body of students coming into basic writing classrooms, it is practically impossible to define basic writers in set terms. Studies have shown that linguistic identity labels like "basic writer" do not give a complete picture of a student's identity. As a result, the student could be placed in a mainstream section of basic writing by one institution and categorized as an ESL learner by another. Matsuda gives a historical overview of the field of basic writing by relating how the literature from the 1960s has classified basic writers. He then focuses on the presence of ESL writers, especially resident nonnative (Generation 1.5) students. Given the broad array of incoming first-year composition students, he suggests that institutional practices should take into consideration the requirements of ESL students while rethinking discussions and decisions on basic writers and how to improve their writing skills. While considering how ESL learners have fared in the conventional "disciplinary practices of basic writing," Matsuda suggests changes in the conceptualization of the field itself. The need for awareness among instructors, coupled with professional help to prepare them for ESL-specific teaching skills, is severely felt in this changing frame of basic writing classrooms. Furthermore, it is essential to encourage channels of communication between basic writing teachers and ESL specialists to devise thoughtful pedagogical skills.

317   Matsuda, Paul Kei. "Composition Studies and ESL Writing: A Disciplinary Division of Labor." *College Composition and Communication* 50.4 (1999): 699–721. Print.

English as a second language writing has not been considered part of composition studies since it began to move toward the status of a legitimate profession during the 1960s. Matsuda recovers the histories of teaching English as a second language and composition studies and recounts how the formation of professional identities led to a disciplinary division of labor. He states that the absence of second-language writing discussions is reflected in the way composition studies has been constructed in this historical context, as evidenced in the works of influential historians of composition studies, such as James Berlin, Robert Connors, Susan Miller, and David Russell. He provides possibilities for a cultivated relationship between composition and ESL instructors. For example, composition specialists need to learn about ESL writing and writers by reading relevant literature and by attending presentations, workshops, and special-interest group meetings on ESL-related topics at professional conferences; compositionists need to consider second-language perspectives in their work (empirical research); graduate programs in composition studies should incorporate second-language writing into their curricula; and writing program administrators should provide an ESL-friendly environment.

318   Matsuda, Paul Kei. "Contrastive Rhetoric in Context: A Dynamic Model of L2 Writing." *Journal of Second Language Writing* 6.1 (1997): 45–60. Print.

Although research in contrastive rhetoric (CR) has grown significantly in recent times, the pedagogical implications of CR have not been successfully translated into practice. One of the reasons behind this is an outgrowth of a static theory that implicates limiting views of second-language writing. For example, an underlying assumption of this static theory is that an L2 writer is like a programmed machine, devoid of any agency, that produces L2 texts. Furthermore, the explanation of the production of L2 texts solely based on a writer's linguistic, cultural, and educational background is quite simplistic and inaccurate. A dynamic model of L2 writing, on the other hand, views L2 writing as a product of the interrelationship between various elements, such as the background of both reader and writer, their shared discourse community, and the bidirectional interactions between them. The proposed dynamic model attempts to provide a heuristic about the dynamics of L2 writing and points at the complex processes involved in the construction of L2 texts. Keeping the importance of context in mind, as proposed by the model, both teachers and students can gain a better understanding about L2 writing.

319   Matsuda, Paul Kei. "The Myth of Linguistic Homogeneity in U.S. College Composition." *College English* 68.6 (2006): 637–51. Print.

The curricular "containment" of second-language students is as old as US college composition itself. Matsuda demonstrates that decades of curricular strategies to "contain" language difference (e.g., preadmission filtering, segregated composition tracks, postmatriculation remediation, etc.) have "kept language differences in the composition classroom from reaching a critical mass, thus creating the false impression that all language differences could and should be addressed elsewhere" (648). Not only has the institutional assumption that all postsecondary students are by default native speakers never been true; it is moreover increasingly out of step with demographic reality. Countering the possibility—even the desirability—that the college classroom can be a "monolingual space," Matsuda asks composition teachers to imagine their classrooms as places where "the presence of language differences is the default" (649).

320   Matsuda, Paul Kei. "Process and Post-Process: A Discursive History." *Journal of Second Language Writing* 12.1 (2003): 65–83. Print.

Matsuda sets out to show how the discursive constructions of composition have contributed significantly to the historical constructions of the field. He begins by tracing a brief history of the process movement, based on the centrality of student writing to the course and the empirically driven studies of the composing process, as a deliberative break from the "product model" of composing. Matsuda argues, however, that the process movement was just one in a long series of attempted reforms and that the discursive constructions of the process movement as unified in opposition to current-traditionalism was little more than a convenient way of "creating a daemon for the sake of expelling it" (70). Matsuda then outlines some major tenets of the postprocess movement designed to critique the "grand narrative" of process. Finally, he illustrates how the discursive formations of composition have affected, contributed to, and in many cases been anticipated by developments in the field of second-language writing. Through his historical outlines he argues that broad discursive constructions like "process" and "post-process" have the tendency to ignore the complexities of pedagogical and theoretical movements, and that "postprocess" thinkers need to be careful not to reject process thinking outright, for doing so risks casting off the beneficial developments that the process movement stimulated.

321 Matsuda, Paul Kei. "Situating ESL Writing in a Cross-Disciplinary Context." *Written Communication* 15.1 (2008): 99–121. Print.

Matsuda deplores the lack of attention paid to the writing needs of the increasing number of ESL students in US higher education. One of the reasons for the unsatisfactory situation lies in the lack of qualified ESL writing teachers (i.e., composition teachers with training in ESL or ESL teachers with specific training in writing). Matsuda attributes this deficiency in teacher preparation to how ESL writing has been constructed in relation to two interrelated disciplines: teaching English as a second language (TESL) and composition studies. He examines two existing models, the division-of-labor model and the intersection model, and identifies the two models' negative effects on the development of the ESL writing field. The division-of-labor model "separates TESL and composition studies completely, positioning ESL writing as part of TESL but not of composition studies" (104). The intersection model brings the two disciplines together and fosters communication and cooperation between the two. However, Matsuda points out the rather restricted space for ESL writing within composition studies in the intersection model. He argues for the symbiotic model where ESL writing is given a more autonomous status and does not belong exclusively to either TESL or composition studies. In the symbiotic model, ESL writing, concerned with both writing and second language, has a metadisciplinary discourse of its own that transcends the two related disciplines. Matsuda argues that only the symbiotic model can be conducive to the field of ESL and truly respond to the writing needs of ESL students.

322 Matsuda, Paul Kei, et al. "Changing Currents in Second Language Writing Research: A Colloquium." *Journal of Second Language Writing* 12 (2003): 151–79. Print.

This article, based on a colloquium at the 2002 meeting of the American Association for Applied Linguistics, discusses how second-language writing has evolved into "an interdisciplinary field of inquiry with its own disciplinary infrastructure" (151). The authors provide insight into the changing current of L2 writing, focusing on the emergence of the field, the research that is being conducted, and potential directions for future research. Linda Harklau begins by examining the research on Generation 1.5 writers and the issues associated with these writers in North American high schools and colleges. She suggests that the current perspectives on Generation 1.5 writers need to be transformed to build on students' multilingual talents. Suresh Canagarajah considers the notion of multiliteracies and how it pervades the traditions of writing. He contends that writing is largely influenced by our beliefs, values, and subject positions, and therefore we need to extend how we view multiliteracy. Mark Warschauer discusses the influence of technology on writing and how it has changed the way we interact and communicate. He argues that alternative research, other than short-term classroom-based studies, needs to be conducted, and he points to the potential of ethnographies, longitudinal studies, and corpus studies for future research. Ken Hyland emphasizes the importance of discourse analysis for understanding second-language writing. He suggests that an understanding of discourse would familiarize writers with how the writer-audience relationship changes as the context and purpose for writing changes. Finally, Matsuda explains that the field of L2 writing has begun to develop its own identity and has developed a metadisciplinary inquiry of its own, indicating that L2 writing now has its own status, scope, and characteristics.

323 Matsuda, Paul Kei, et al. *Second-Language Writing in the Composition Classroom: A Critical Sourcebook*. Boston: Bedford, 2006. Print.

This collection of articles by well-known second-language scholars is intended primarily for L2 composition professionals. It brings together some of the most significant, and some of the most current, research involving L2 writers and writing. Divided into five major sections, the book covers areas as diverse as the current position of L2 writing within the broader field of composition studies, the language needs of international students as well as resident US writers, ESL writers and academic writing, the role of students' home language in L2 writing, effective classroom writing assignments for L2 learners, the role of computers in L2 writing, and responding to L2 writing, including error feedback. The essays included are both theoretical and practical in nature, and their wide scope indicates the complexities involved in L2 writing. There is also a very useful list of additional readings at the back that L2 scholars and those interested in multicultural composition issues will find to be a very valuable resource.

324 Matsuda, Paul Kei, Christina Ortmeier-Hooper, and Aya Matsuda. "The Expansion of Second Language Writing." *The SAGE Handbook of Writing Development*. Ed. R. Beard. Thousand Oaks: Sage, 2009. 457–71. Print.

Matsuda and colleagues offer an overview of the field of second-language writing in higher education from its early, marginalized beginnings in the 1960s to its current, widely relevant position in the twenty-first century. The expansion of L2 writing correlates with the shifting population in higher education to include more international students, the prevalence of English as the lingua franca, and the emergence of modern linguistics. In the 1960s, discussion addressed the placement of

L2 writers in writing courses. The decade also debated fluency or accuracy in L2 writing. At the close of the 1960s and into the 1970s, the
work of Jerome Bruner shifted the conversation to focus "more on the
production and organization of meaningful text" (6) and ushered in a
process movement in L2 writing. By the late 1970s and in the 1980s,
the research matured as the field generated its own "communities of
practice" and posed questions from the classroom and other studies.
Throughout the 1980s, advanced literacy became a central concern,
and by the decade's close, the field came of age: the term *second-
language writing* emerged, and the *Journal of Second Language Writing*
began. The 1990s brought the creation of yet another research outlet:
the Symposium on Second Language Writing. And the twenty-first
century has also offered its share of "comprehensive overviews of the
field" (8). Beyond this decade-by-decade overview, the article considers
traits of L2 writers, noting that the research shows that the writing processes of L2 writers differ significantly from those of first-language writers. Further, most L2 writers have had little practice or instruction with
writing longer compositions. Then the article discusses the research
that has considered the curricular implications, such as the question
of whether to separate or integrate second- and first-language writers,
writing beyond the writing classroom, the supporting roles of writing
centers, and supporting faculty development. In addition to the curricular implications, this article notes the research on pedagogy as it relates
to four areas: developing "effective writing assignments and curriculum,
teacher and peer response, the treatment of error, and assessment" (15).
Finally, a section on new areas of research—early L2 writing, who owns
English, World Englishes, English studies in non-English cultures, and
teaching writing in other languages—closes the article.

325   Matsuda, Paul Kei, Christina Ortmeier-Hooper, and Xiaoye You, eds.
       The Politics of Second Language Writing: In Search of the Promised Land.
       West Lafayette: Parlor, 2006. Print.

       This collection grew out of the 2004 Symposium on Second Language
       Writing. The editors use Barbara Kroll's metaphor of the "promised
       lands" for nonnative English-speaking (NNES) students as an over-
       arching frame for this volume. To envision the "promised lands" of
       excellence in academic English, the editors bring together a collection
       of sixteen articles that analyze classroom practices within the frame-
       work of institutional policies and politics "because instruction is always
       shaped by larger institutional contexts" (vii). This volume is designed
       to help educators, researchers, administrators, and members of second-
       language writing programs and departments make connections between
       their individual practices and the institutional policies and politics
       that influence their practices. Moreover, this collection may foster
       discussion of the politics of L2 writing in geopolitical areas around the
       globe, as Xiaoye You suggests. You analyzes an educational decree on
       college English and its effects in two Chinese universities while urging
       English educators to participate in the institutional imagination of new

literacies in China. This volume is organized in five sections: K–12 education; language support programs in higher education, featuring a study on the role of writing centers; English for academic and professional purposes, including a study on the preparation of international teaching assistants; assessment, featuring arguments on online directed self-placement and positive washback; and the politics of the profession. The editors conclude this volume with Kroll's assertion to address the obstacles that prevent NNES students from reaching the "promised lands." According to Kroll, the obstacles include a lack of identification of NNES students, noneffective placement tests, English courses that do not cater to students' needs, lack of English requirements in other departments and colleges, and higher tuition for NNES students. This collection illustrates how to confront some of these obstacles to get closer to the "promised land."

326   Matsuda, Paul Kei, and Tony Silva. "Cross-cultural Composition: Mediated Integration of U.S. and International Students." *Composition Studies* 27.1 (1999): 15–30. Print.

Matsuda and Silva argue that a cross-cultural composition course of first-year writing should be offered as a placement option to prevent the binaries associated with ESL-only sections or mainstreamed sections of First-Year Writing. Matsuda offers an exemplary course that he taught at Purdue University in 1997 and outlines writing projects that focus on cross-cultural experiences as the subject for inquiry in the first-year classroom, such as reflective journal entries on cross-cultural experiences, a profile of a linguistic or cultural group that focuses on dissonance and productive conflict, primary investigation of nonverbal communication within and among groups, a primary survey of a linguistic or cultural group, the translation of insights from writing projects into a forum outside the classroom, and the development of a portfolio that highlights the cross-cultural writing done over the course of the semester. Matsuda's students reported that the cross-cultural course provided an ESL-friendly environment and opportunities for cross-cultural learning. The authors note that writing courses that focus on cross-cultural experiences should be staffed by instructors with experience working with both ESL and native English-speaking (NES) students, that the placement of these students in this course should be an option, and that the class itself should be equally comprised of both ESL and NES students. This course can be especially valuable at institutions where there is little linguistic or cultural diversity.

327   Matsuda, Paul Kei, and Tony Silva, eds. *Second Language Writing Research: Perspectives on the Process of Knowledge Construction.* Mahwah: Erlbaum, 2005. Print.

This volume, consisting of eighteen scholars' self-reflections about their research on writing in English as a second or foreign language, explores the complexities of researchers' thought processes and research decisions, which often are not transparent to readers of their published work. Matsuda and Silva organize the sixteen chapters into four sections that focus on different aspects and issues of second-language writing: research as situated knowledge construction, conceptualizing research programs, collecting and analyzing data, and practical issues of conducting research. Through its inclusion of chapters that bring to bear various aspects of L2 writing research, such as philosophical, historical, and narrative modes of inquiry, multimodal and cross-modal research processes, and discourse analytic methods, this unique, highly informative volume provides both novice and experienced researchers with valuable insights into the decision-making processes behind various research projects; issues in the process of conceptualizing, conducting, and crafting L2 writing research; and the ways in which different methodologies might be applied to address specific research questions.

328   McAlexander, Patricia J. "Using Principles of Universal Design in College Composition Courses." *Basic Writing e-Journal* 5.1 (2004): n. pag. Web. 21 May 2014.

The increasing diversity of college student populations calls for acknowledgment that no single teaching approach will be appropriate for students with wide variations in individual learning strengths and sources of motivation. The Americans with Disabilities Act requires that students with documented disabilities receive accommodations that often include modifying instructional procedures. McAlexander believes that Universal Design for Learning (UDL) theory calls for instructors to do whatever possible to adjust their teaching approaches to meet the diverse learning styles, interests, and abilities of all students. She focuses on three UDL principles: (1) provide material that is personally relevant to students, (2) offer a flexible curriculum with appropriate challenges for each student, and (3) give students individualized feedback. She outlines specific strategies for applying these three principles in the college composition classroom while following a mandated curriculum, maintaining standards, and engaging students in common classroom activities.

329   Mlynarczyk, Rebecca Williams, and Marcia Babbitt. "The Power of Academic Learning Communities." *Journal of Basic Writing* 21.1 (2002): 71–89. Print.

Mlynarczyk and Babbitt describe the Intensive English as a Second Language program developed at Kingsborough Community College to help ESL students complete their English courses before depleting their financial aid. Complementing this objective were three additional goals: helping students to succeed in credit courses during their first semester in college, improving the retention and graduation rates of ESL students, and integrating ESL students into the social and academic life of the college. In the program, students acquired proficiency in "academic English" by taking credit-bearing courses while receiving language support in ESL and speech courses. Mlynarczyk and Babbitt report that the program helped facilitate high pass rates, good grades, and a collegial classroom atmosphere. The authors posit that collaborative, interdisciplinary approaches to learning; student-centered pedagogy emphasizing reading and writing to learn; and enhanced student perceptions of self-efficacy are central to the program's continued success.

330   Mohamad, Mutiara, and Janet Boyd. "Realizing Distributed Gains: How Collaboration with Support Services Transformed a Basic Writing Program for International Students." *Journal of Basic Writing* 29.1 (2010): 78–98. Print.

This essay describes how unexpected "thirdspace" collaborations gradually transformed two newly established writing programs supporting international basic writers: a credit-bearing remedial ESP program (with a noncredit EAP component) and a writing center "studio" offering basic tutoring and specialized workshops for L2 English learners. Benchmarking from UNC–Chapel Hill's "distributed resources model" (Kubota & Able, 2006), the program directors describe innovations they made that accelerated the acquisition progress for low-scoring international students by encouraging (then mandating) participation in the studio and other support services. Vital to this model was the development of a template for tracking individual's accomplishments across programs. As collaborations became more deliberate, this distributed capacity to mentor students increased. Grounded in intensely focused, credit-bearing, discipline-specific ESP classes, these increasingly diverse, noncredit components afforded international students maximal exposure to relevant academic resources without sacrificing tactical support structures. The emergent network presents a cohesive yet flexible model for basic writing capable of meeting L2 English learners' needs. Decentralized yet trackable, it affords both students and staff the freedom needed to stimulate, create, nurture, and mutually evaluate their evolving relationships.

331   Murie, Robin, Molly Rojas Collins, and Daniel F. Detzner. "Building Academic Literacy from Student Strength: An Interdisciplinary Life History Project." *Journal of Basic Writing* 23.2 (2004): 70–92. Print.

Recognizing a need for projects structured to encourage the writing of Generation 1.5 students, the authors present a life history project that focuses on a "real" purpose. Generation 1.5 students have experienced a disrupted education transitioning between their native country and an American school. The disruption in education that the misnomer *Generation 1.5* denotes may also include a less developed native language literacy and English learned more through exposure than instruction. Recognizing that the traditional model of ESL courses is not very effective and that many teachers are unprepared to teach a student with these specific issues, the authors developed the Life History Project at the University of Minnesota "to engage multilingual students in extensive writing for real purposes" (71). This project allows students to write to a real audience with a clear purpose; to complete extensive, repetitive data collection contextualized by their understanding of their interviewee's life and culture; to demonstrate a consistent con-nection between the student's writing and literature with the same themes and situations; to emphasize the creative process of writing; to develop fluency through extensive drafting and reader response; and to demonstrate to students where they fit in the university's curriculum. These personal connections and the positioning of the student writers as bilingual, bicultural experts further strengthen students' develop-ment of personal voice and sense of self in their writing. The Life His-tory Project allowed students to build academic literacy by creating a tangible product. Furthermore, the project rejected the "deficit model of 'remediation'" (85), thereby allowing students to see themselves as valuable members of the university community while simultaneously learning "a great deal about writing" (86).

332   Ortmeier-Hooper, Christina. "English May Be My Second Language, but I'm Not 'ESL.'" *College Composition and Communication* 59.3 (2008): 389–419. Print.

Making a case for what she argues are the "problematic" terms *ESL* and *Generation 1.5*, Ortmeier-Hooper presents three case studies of im-migrant first-year composition students. She focuses on the concept of identity—in particular, how students negotiate the multiple identities that evolve out of their cultural, personal, and academic experiences. She argues that as instructors, we often oversimplify our students' per-formances and forget about the myriad factors that affect their writing and learning. She asserts that our field's current categorizations and labels for second-language learners and writers too fully dictate how we see a student. Ortmeier-Hooper is careful to point out that she is not advocating we abandon our attempts at encouraging openness and diversity in our classrooms. To avoid further essentializing them as we unintentionally do with terms like *ESL*, we need to proceed carefully with the label *Generation 1.5* and instead remember that students do not always want their personal backgrounds and differences becoming their primary attribute. The key to addressing all students' needs is to build stronger rapport with all students. Instructors can also, Ortmeier-Hooper asserts, gain a better understanding of the world circumstances that predate our students' presence in our classrooms. By continuing to support instructor training programs and studies on identity construc-tion, we can move away from a false concept of singular identity and learn to accept that writers' and learners' identities are often multiple and even "messy" (414–15).

333   Phillips, Talinn, Candace Stewart, and Robert D. Stewart. "Geography Lessons, Bridge Building, and Second Language Writers." *Writing Pro-gram Administration* 30.1/2 (2006): 83–100. Print.

The authors use a bridge metaphor to discuss the divide at their institu-tion, and a number of other institutions, in which native English speak-ers (NESs) are taught writing in the English department, while second-language writers receive their first-year writing instruction through the

TESOL department. Using Paul Kei Matsuda's explanation of a "disciplinary division of labor," the authors illustrate how these disciplinary divisions often persist because those who desire to bridge the disciplines lack institutional power to make that change. The authors describe the university writing center, which at their institution is housed in the university's Writing across the Curriculum program, as a "third site which . . . is *already* cross-disciplinary—for discussions and experimentation in second language writing" (89). In this case, the writing center serves as a resource for L2 writing for the campus community by providing tutoring to L2 writers, workshops for cross-disciplinary faculty, materials for interested instructors, and a space for graduate students from multiple disciplines to develop and experiment with strategies for working with L2 writers. The authors conclude by encouraging readers to view these sites as "places of convergence at which the networks and collaborations we have developed individually can come together to generate larger networks and collaborations" (99).

See: Paul Kei Matsuda, "Composition Studies and ESL Writing" [317].

334   Price, Margaret. "Accessing Disability: A Nondisabled Student Works the Hyphen." *College Composition and Communication* 59.1 (2007): 53–76. Print.

Arguing that the subject of disability is in danger of becoming another "add-and-stir policy" in multiculturalism, Price suggests that teachers of writing move beyond disability to *disability studies* in critical pedagogies. Price describes a student, Tara, who struggled to navigate her nondisabled perspective while she researched and wrote about issues of access for people with disabilities. Based on the texts and interviews gathered in this case study, Price questions the common perception that students' critical thinking can be assessed solely from written texts. She concludes by noting that critical pedagogy at its best calls for change on behalf of the teacher as well as the student, that "no one is excluded, and no one is exempt" (72).

335   Reid, Joy, ed. *Writing Myths: Applying Second Language Research to Classroom Teaching.* Ann Arbor: U of Michigan P, 2008. Print.

This collection of essays addresses common pedagogical "myths" or issues that revolve around ESL education and course instruction, with personal reflections of educators in the field and with research and applications of this research in the classroom, as inspired by Keith Folse's *Vocabulary Myths: Applying Second Language Research to Classroom Teaching.* In her introduction, Reid discusses the need for addressing these common pedagogical assertions, which appear in common misconceptions about fundamental concerns, or "myths," such as regimented teaching of grammar in the classroom. The "myths" in this collection revolve around how to address common beliefs or concerns about ESL education, as Folse addresses in the first essay "Teaching Vocabulary Is Not the Writing Teacher's Job." To develop this argument, Folse uses rubrics and test scores to attend to this issue in the classroom. Other myths addressed are Pat Byrd's "Where Grammar Is Concerned One Size Fits All" and Paul Kei Matsuda's "International and U.S. Resident ESL Writers Cannot Be Taught in the Same Class." Both of these essays utilize personalized teaching strategies and examine how they are implemented, or ignored, in the classroom. The deliberations about each myth are followed by Reid's overview in "Myth(s) 9: Student Myths about Academic Writing and Teaching," which shows how ESL teaching and resources have changed since Reid began teaching in 1966. This last section addresses how students respond to these myths, with an analysis of versions of their own myths, such as "I have to wait until the idea hits me." Reid's approach to these student conceptions offers a more open dialogue with the students, in particular letting them know that writing can be a difficult process, even for educators. In the end, the essays point toward the importance of opening this dialogue between educators and students to address the common "myths" that continually emerge inside and outside the classroom.

336   Shapiro, Shawna. "Stuck in the Remedial Rut: Confronting Resistance to ESL Curriculum Reform." *Journal of Basic Writing* 30.2 (2011): 24–52. Print.

Shapiro describes the process of transforming the Academic ESL Program at Northern Green University. Using surveys, interview data, and participant observations, she illustrates why institutions are stuck in a "remedial rut," despite progress to reform curriculum from remediation to institutional mediation. Her five-year case study reveals how a remediation model served a deficient orientation, which negatively impacted student writers. Shapiro's findings indicate that institutions must revise their purposes from basic skills to rhetorical effectiveness, while acknowledging the diversity—rather than the deficiency—of students' language. She further contends that the process of reform involves partnerships with entities invested in student support and institutional mediation, and she exposes the value of dialogue and collaboration across the university.

337   Shuck, Gail. "Combating Monolingualism: A Novice Administrator's Challenge." *WPA: Writing Program Administration* 30.1/2 (2006): 59–82. Print.

Focusing on the pervasive idea of monolingualism in composition instruction, Shuck critiques the ways second-language students are positioned within both composition studies and the pedagogy and administration of her own institution. She critically assesses the ESL sequence at Boise State University, which reaffirms the "myth of transience," an idea that holds that ESL students "simply need a few more courses before they can participate in 'real' academic courses" (62). She shows how this idea and course sequence, inadvertently aided by her positioning within an English department, reaffirms the idea that ESL issues can be considered the sole responsibility of a single person or department, rather than part of the entire university's mission. Describing the steps she has taken within her current university, she offers suggestions to challenge "exclusionary practices based on a fallacious view of the world as essentially monolingual" (68), while considering implications for other writing program administrators and teachers. Shuck concludes with two major suggestions. The first is the development of cross-cultural environments for writing. While not explicitly ESL, these course sections offer greater support for ESL students without labeling them as the "other" within the university. Her second strategy involves educating faculty, finding ways to "help our colleagues understand in more depth the strengths and struggles that multicultural students bring to our classroom" (72), and advocating for programs including faculty liaisons, advisory committees, and public events featuring ESL student voices.

338   Silva, Tony, and Paul Kei Matsuda, eds. *Landmark Essays on ESL Writing*. Mahwah: Erlbaum, 2001. Print.

One in a series of volumes presenting influential essays in various fields, this collection of sixteen previously published articles traces the development of scholarship in English as a second language writing across the last four decades of the twentieth century. The writers represented include some of the most familiar names in second-language writing. In addition, the essays, chosen for their significance in the field, continue to generate numerous further commentaries, rebuttals, and revisions. Perhaps the best example of such a text is Robert B. Kaplan's "Cultural Thought Patterns in Inter-Cultural Education" (the so-called doodles article), in which the author speculated as to the effects of cultural backgrounds on the success or failure of second-language writers. In another example, John Hinds's "Reader-Writer Responsibility: A New Typology" also presented an exploration of the influence of culture on L2 writing, using the difference between Japanese and English writers to explain a distinction between reader-responsible and writer-responsible languages. Possibly indicating the recent explosion of interest in writing skills within ESL research, more than half of the articles included here were originally published in the 1990s. Among the articles from that decade are Joan G. Carson's "Becoming Biliterate: First Language Influences," which added to Kaplan's work by focusing on the effect of culture on L2 acquisition, and Tony Silva's "Toward an Understanding of the Distinct Nature of L2 Writing: The ESL Research and Its Implications," a survey of studies on L2 writers in which he proposed using new methods in the L2 writing classroom that focus on the unique characteristics of students who have to write in a second language. The collection is introduced with a useful historical overview by Silva and Matsuda, cofounders and chairs of the Second Language Symposium, both of whom also contributed to this volume.

339   Silva, Tony, and Paul Kei Matsuda, eds. *On Second-Language Writing*. Mahwah: Erlbaum, 2001. Print.

This collection contains fifteen original articles by the scholars who presented papers at the historic first Symposium on Second Language

Writing held at Purdue University in 1998. The symposium has remained an important event in the field, and the contributors and their work have continued to be prominent as well. In the preface, the editors outline a guide both to the volume and to the second-language writing field itself, starting with Barbara Kroll's autobiographical essay and ending with Alister Cumming's study of the problems inherent in applying educational standards to L2 writing. In between, the articles focus on topics that remain a concern to the L2 writing community: the student writers themselves, L2 writing theory, research on L2 writing, assessment, working with university-level ESL students, politics and L2 writing, and the interface between L2 writing and other disciplines, such as second-language acquisition (SLA) and rhetoric. Other contributors include Ilona Leki, Pat Currie, William Grabe, Diane Belcher, Lynn Goldstein, Charlene Polio, Liz Hamp-Lyons, Trudy Smoke, Joy Reid, Sarah Benesch, Terry Santos, Joan Carson, and Carol Severino.

340   Smoke, Trudy. "Mainstreaming Writing: What Does This Mean for ESL Students?" *Mainstreaming Basic Writers: Politics and Pedagogies of Access.* Ed. Gerri McNenny. Mahwah: Erlbaum, 2001. 193–214. Print.

Smoke complicates the notion of mainstreaming as an option for English as a second language students. Smoke questions the new definitions of the ESL student that have emerged as part of recently legislated educational policies limiting college remedial and ESL programs. She then looks closely at the overall sociopolitical context of ESL at the City University of New York and specifically at her own campus, Hunter College. The author also examines a variety of pedagogical approaches developed to meet the needs of ESL students in colleges in Alabama, Arizona, California, Indiana, and other states. After describing stand-alone ESL classes, mainstream classes, and out-of-class workshops, she discusses how teachers perceive the effectiveness of the various models. Smoke advocates offering options to students, and if mainstreaming is chosen, questions the best ratio for native speaker to nonnative speaker students. Smoke recognizes the limitations that today's political environment presents to writing directors and stresses the need to maintain the best program with as many options as are viable while keeping in mind program survivability in an uncertain future.

341   Williams, Jessica. "Undergraduate Second-Language Writers in the Writing Center." *Journal of Basic Writing* 21.2 (2002): 73–91. Print.

Second-language writers are increasingly using writing centers and are often sent there by instructors who are unsure how to deal with L2 problems. Since L2 writers come from diverse social, linguistic, cultural, and educational backgrounds, they are not a monolithic group, but their writing shows many characteristic difficulties. Their limited vocabulary also makes academic reading and hence academic writing challenging for them. Unfortunately, writing center tutors are often unprepared to assist L2 writers. To be effective, tutors should understand English grammar rules, L2 learning processes, and the ways that those processes affect learner production. Two second-language acquisition theories—the interaction hypothesis, which stresses negotiation of meaning in language acquisition, and sociocultural theory, which sees interaction as a social process leading to the creation of new knowledge—can enable tutors to provide guidance at a level appropriate for each learner without editing or appropriating student texts.

342   Zamel, Vivian. "Engaging Students in Writing-to-Learn: Promoting Language and Literacy across the Curriculum." *Journal of Basic Writing* 19.2 (2000): 3–21. Print.

Zamel's article resulted from an invitation by the journal editors to revisit a keynote speech she gave at a faculty development meeting at the City University of New York. Zamel establishes the terrain by using student writing in response to English as a second language classroom activities and also in conjunction with academic work in other disciplines. Analyzing these samples, Zamel demonstrates the efficacy of integrating writing as a learning tool. In her discussion, she indicates how this process—using reading journals, ungraded mini-papers, and in-class summaries of class activities—allows for more open communication between faculty and students. This in turn increases the students' ability to acquire the language and meanings of various disciplines and provides faculty with a better understanding of their students' learning processes. While the article uses examples of ESL student writing, the argument applies to native English-speaking students as well. Zamel concludes that faculty need to attend to meanings and issues in "correcting" student writing. Error correction alone, she notes, leads away from language proficiency and actually may increase student frustrations.

343   Zamel, Vivian, and Ruth Spack, eds. *Enriching ESOL Pedagogy: Readings and Activities for Engagement, Reflection, and Inquiry*. Mahwah: Erlbaum, 2002. Print.

Including the works of such scholars as Mike Rose, Sarah Hudelson, Amy Tan, Stephen Krashen, H. G. Widdowson, Vivian Zamel, Judith Wells Lindfors, and Simon Ortiz, this collection contains twenty-two readings in five sections: Questioning the Nature of Methods, Seeing in the Classroom, Theories into Practice: Promoting Language Acquisition, Theories into Practice: Keeping Language Meaningful, and Questioning Assumptions about Language Identity. The readings represent a range of genres, including theoretical explorations, ethnographies, personal essays, and research reports. Each unit begins with open-ended questions about the readings and ends with questions and prompts that help readers make connections between the readings and their own experiences in the academic and personal arenas of life. Each unit also includes a list of recommended readings and possible projects for inquiry.

344   Zamel, Vivian, and Ruth Spack. "Teaching Multilingual Learners across the Curriculum: Beyond the ESOL Classroom and Back Again." *Journal of Basic Writing* 25.2 (2006): 126–52. Print.

Zamel and Spack challenge the deficit model of language and learning that views ESOL students as deficient and less competent, a view that permeates the thinking of faculty across the curriculum. They call for all faculty members to facilitate ESOL students' acquisition of language and literacy by assigning meaningful writing tasks, providing supportive feedback, and, most important, acknowledging and valuing ESOL students' unique historical and cultural perspectives. This article draws on many firsthand experiences of both ESOL students and faculty in undergraduate courses across the curriculum and comes to the conclusion that ESOL students are as fully capable of succeeding in content courses as their English-speaking counterparts are. The ESOL students' successful experience is directly attributable to a variety of pedagogical strategies enacted by some faculty—strategies that benefit English-speaking students as well. The article also provides some pedagogical implications for ESOL composition classes as well as any other ESOL courses, where writing should play a central role because it can provide a chance for students to take risks, generate ideas, engage in intellectual thinking, and promote language and literacy acquisition.

An Administrative Focus

Placement and Assessment

345 Adams, Peter Dow. "Basic Writing Reconsidered." *Journal of Basic Writing* 21.1 (1993): 22–35. Print.

Studying data from students placed into basic writing classes at the community college where he teaches, Adams was curious to learn about the effect of the classes. He found that students who were placed into basic writing courses but enrolled in first-year composition performed better than those who were placed into and took basic writing courses. Adams uses these findings to argue for the mainstreaming of basic writers.

346 Adler-Kassner, Linda, and Susanmarie Harrington. "In the Here and Now: Public Policy and Basic Writing." *Journal of Basic Writing* 25.2 (2006): 27–48. Print.

Adler-Kassner and Harrington discuss how public policy documents, such as those by the American Diploma Project and the Spellings Commission on the Future of Higher Education, offer the public and policy makers conflicting insights and frame education crisis discussions as institutional problems rather than individual learning concerns. As an institutional problem, the education crisis can be seen as requiring reform through national standards and standardized testing. The authors show how a three-part public policy narrative construction can justify the education crisis and the exclusion of educators from reform efforts: secondary schools do not prepare students for college or work, which costs higher education institutions, businesses, and taxpayers; to avoid the consequential extra burden on taxpayers and institutions, agents outside the secondary school system need to solve the school-based problem of underpreparing or not preparing students and workers. Surfacing this fallacious narrative, the authors remind readers of previous basic writing public policy efforts by Lynn Troyka, Stanford Goto, and Deborah Mutnick, and they review insights offered by basic writing professionals' cultural studies efforts, including the authors' own. The authors also exemplify how to reframe public policy arguments that can meaningfully communicate the knowledge of writing studies professionals to the public and to policy makers. In addition, they call on writing studies professionals to research issues, collect data, and determine useful strategies and program information to share in public policy texts addressed to readers beyond our programs and institutions.

347   Barlow, Aaron. "Leading Writers, Teaching Tests." *Basic Writing e-Journal* 5.1 (2004): n. pag. Web. 21 May 2014.

Barlow, an adjunct lecturer at the New York City College of Technology, tackles a tough dilemma facing many teachers of composition; that is, how to live up to their own pedagogical standards while also fulfilling the immediate needs of their institutions—in this case, the need to prepare students for success on the CUNY/ACT exam. He discusses his strategies for maintaining a process-centered approach while still addressing the form and style demanded by the exam. Rather than letting his "frustration reign" by falling into current traditional pedagogy that arbitrarily focuses on form, Barlow works on combining the skills that connect both the ACT exam and preparation for Composition I; these skills include the ability to focus on a clear point, to elaborate, and to edit one's own work. Additionally, he makes use of refined prompts for practice (which focus on school and community issues), diagnostic tests, peer review, and portfolio assessment. Anchoring his discussion in work by scholars such as Peter Elbow and Pat Belanoff, Hans-Georg Gadamer, and David Bartholomae and Anthony Petrosky, Barlow also includes practical elements to depict his daily classroom practices. For example, he provides a sample syllabus from his 2002 Developmental Writing II course, which showcases his focus on both pedagogy and exam preparation. Barlow's essay is largely exploratory, offering a kind of snapshot of his current pedagogy and a meta-analysis of his thought process in bridging the gap between teaching to the test and preparing students for success in future, real-world writing.

348   Bedore, Pamela, and Deborah F. Rossen-Knill. "Informed Self-Placement: Is a Choice Offered a Choice Received?" *Writing Program Administration Journal* 28.1/2 (2004): 55–78. Print.

This article draws on communication theories and on assessment research (surveys, focus groups, interviews, and program material review) conducted by the authors in their composition program to discuss whether helping students make informed decisions about their first-year composition course placement (informed self-placement, or ISP) offers students more authentic participation in their own educational choices than does directed self-placement (DSP), to which ISP's origins can be traced. Offering both a review of DSP successes and a nuanced critique, Bedore and Rossen-Knill suggest that communication complications, such as the need for first-year students to learn how to hold critical discussions about their college writing, can hinder students' abilities to engage fully in real and valid placement choices for themselves as they enter college. Thus while the authors embraced ISP, they also engaged in an organic assessment process that added assessment phases based on insights revealed in the process. The authors acknowledge the role of resource reallocation and the value of careful consideration of assessment results in helping to create a dialogic program that educates students about their composition placement and course choices and results in students' enhanced ability to make valid and real choices within the program that the authors facilitate.

349   Belfield, Clive, and Peter M. Crosta. "Predicting Success in College: The Importance of Placement Tests and High School Transcripts." *Community College Research Center*. Teachers College, Columbia University. Feb. 2012. Web. 21 May 2014.

Belfield and Crosta study data from a statewide community college system to analyze the validity of ACCUPLACER and COMPASS tests for placing students in developmental English and math courses. They claim that their data show that three out of every ten students are severely misplaced in English courses when using placement test cutoff scores, and that using high school GPA instead reduces the severe error rates by half. They argue that the validity of placement tests is strongly dependent on how the tests are used, and that lack of consistency and compliance in that usage creates invalid data. They conclude that high school GPA is the best predictor of college performance in both developmental and college-level courses, and that for students whose GPA indicates success in college-level courses, it might be justifiable to waive college placement tests and developmental education.

350   Bernstein, Susan Naomi. "Teaching and Learning in Texas: Accountability Testing, Language, Race, and Place." *Journal of Basic Writing* 23.1 (2004): 4–24. Print.

Basic writing instructors and students can benefit from tackling the implications of federally mandated standardized testing in public education. Bernstein examines Texas's use of high-stakes accountability testing of public school students—the model for the No Child Left Behind Act—to determine grade promotion and "college readiness" (6). In a basic writing course at an open-admissions urban public university, Bernstein focuses on "education as a systemic process" (10) to help her students examine how their subject positions as English language learners are shaped by and through the language education they experienced at secondary public schools that are controlled by state-mandated accountability testing. Focusing on the writing of one student, Noah, Bernstein argues that critical reflection on the chasm between secondary education determined by high-stakes testing and college writing instruction framed by critical thinking can be used to encourage students to occupy a position of advocacy that works toward changing the inequalities of the educational system.

351   Bernstein, Susan Naomi. "Writing and White Privilege: Beyond Basic Skills." *Pedagogy: Critical Approaches to Teaching Literature, Language, Composition, and Culture* 4.1 (2004): 128–31. Print.

Examining the implications of labeling students as "basic writers," Bernstein uses her own experiences of teaching basic writing to argue that standardized tests undermine students' ability to become imaginative thinkers and writers. In her classes, her students explore their personal public school experiences through literacy narratives and analysis, and as a result Bernstein becomes more aware of what she calls the "marker of educated middle class" (130)—being able to write in and recognize standard English. Bernstein argues that the "basic writer" label only widens the education gap between whites and minorities, pointing out that standardized tests are biased toward students from a higher socio-economic background. The tests are particularly challenging for students whose first language is not English. Consequently, when students are unable to demonstrate their fluency in "standard" English, they are labeled as "remedial," resulting in minority or nonnative speakers being marked as "other" or "outsider" (130). Using examples of student writing, Bernstein argues that imaginative writing creates a space for students not only to develop analytical skills but to find a forum to speak about and resist the "remedial" label. She issues a call to teachers who occupy the "privilege of educators" (130) to become aware of these issues and challenges.

352   Bruna, Liza, et al. "Assessing Our Assessments: A Collective Questioning of What Students Need—and Get." *Journal of Basic Writing* 17.1 (1998): 73–95. Print.

This article is an edited transcript of an online discussion among six City University of New York graduate students who covered theoretical and political issues behind the teaching of basic writing. Much of the discussion centers on students' desire for Standard English as access to power and the political and cultural repercussions of that desire. The graduate students also discuss the insufficiency of assessment, the activist role of the composition class and the composition teacher, the disjuncture between instruction in literature and composition, and the appropriate place of code switching and transculturation in composition pedagogy.

353   Gleason, Barbara. "Evaluating Writing Programs in Real Time: The Politics of Remediation." *College Composition and Communication* 51.4 (2000): 560–88. Print.

Gleason argues that program evaluation is political and requires examination of social context. At the City College of New York, Gleason supervised a pilot program of thirty-seven sections of composition that included basic writing students. To evaluate the program, Gleason examined formative evaluations written by teachers and students, statistical analysis of student success (grades being the main variable), and the expert judgment of an outside observer. Policy at the college dictated that no basic writer could take core curriculum classes until he or she passed basic writing, but the college waived that policy for basic writers in the pilot sections that included first-year and mainstreamed basic writing students. Gleason found that students who first took basic writing and then took the core curriculum classes passed the core courses at higher rates than both pilot students and the general population. After three years of mainstreaming basic writers into standard composition classes, college administrators largely ignored the data that came from the pilot study. Instead, the institutional research office wanted to control distribution of the data and pushed Gleason to use more experimental methodologies. Hostility developed as the faculty council voted to require the passing of both basic writing *and* standard composition before students could enroll in core classes. In the future, various agents should be involved more directly in the execution and evaluation of projects such as this, and researchers should pay closer attention to context.

354   Haswell, Richard H. "Dark Shadows: The Fate of Writers at the Bottom." *College Composition and Communication* 39.3 (1988): 303–14. Print.

Using holistic grading scales of student essays as his database, Haswell discusses the consistency of judgment of bad papers. One criterion he often used was the work done by workplace writers, who presumably had been chosen to write material for their companies because they were considered competent writers in their workplaces. Because such writers have a lean style both in classrooms and in the workplace, their abilities and disabilities are much easier to diagnose. Among the disabilities are causes that teachers often regard as behavioral (lack of confidence or motivation, confusion of context), but Haswell suggests that simplicity and wit can often be the better framework for building up a student's writing rather than tearing it down.

355   Hilgers, Thomas. "Basic Writing Curricula and Good Assessment Practices: Whene'er Shall the Twain Meet?" *Journal of Basic Writing* 14.2 (1995): 68–74. Print.

Hilgers argues that students become basic writers through assessment, most often through their scores on inappropriate tests like the SAT, ACT, or Nelson-Denny. Furthermore, these bad assessments drive the curriculum and the evaluation procedures in many basic writing classes. Viable assessment methods, such as those employed by Mina Shaughnessy, can be used to discover students' needs, but these are not as cheap and easy as standardized, multiple-choice instruments. The Conference on College Composition and Communication Position Statement on Assessment can ensure that better assessments are used to identify basic writers at the college level and to certify them as ready for "regular" composition. The reauthorization of Chapter I funds of the Elementary and Secondary Education Act, which supports educational remediation, offers additional hope that assessment will focus more on helping identify students' needs so that all students can achieve high standards.

356   Hodara, Michelle, Shanna Smith Jaggars, and Melinda Mechur Karp. "Improving Developmental Education Assessment and Placement: Lessons from Community Colleges across the Country." *Community College Research Center*. Teachers College, Columbia University. Nov. 2012. Web. 21 May 2014.

The authors focus on current approaches and placement processes for matching incoming students to community colleges, arguing that traditional processes are limited by poor course placement accuracy and inconsistent standards of college readiness. By interviewing 183 respondents at thirty-eight institutions in seven states, the authors conclude that states, systems, and colleges were mainly incorporating one approach—a measured approach—to address a single limitation. Only two colleges utilized a comprehensive approach, which attends to multiple limitations of the process and requires a larger effort to improve developmental education. The authors favor this approach for transforming the long-term academic success of students. Based on their findings, the authors recommend that colleges should implement systematic pretest preparation, consider a more comprehensive approach to course placement accuracy, and develop a greater need for experimentation regarding incorporating noncognitive measures in the placement process. The authors also advocate for colleges to focus on creating consistent standards by collaborating across colleges and educational sectors, committing to evaluate these policies, and maintaining standards across a state or system.

357   Miraglia, Eric. "A Self-Diagnostic Assessment in the Basic Writing Course." *Journal of Basic Writing* 14.2 (1995): 48–67. Print.

Miraglia puts the traditional basic writing diagnostic essay into context, suggesting that the genre helps to situate writers in their own lived experience and to evaluate the student's writing characteristics. However, the prompts on which the diagnostic essay usually depends may elicit misleading data and results because they make three questionable assumptions: masked intentions, in which the prompt's question is poorly designed; magical thinking, in which (after Janet Emig) it is assumed that the teacher can both diagnose and address the range of writing problems in a writing class; and assumptions of expertise, in which rhetorical expertise is assumed to rest with the teacher, not the student. Miraglia describes a new diagnostic essay model that emphasizes students' assessment of their own needs, which results in a rubric of attributes, concerns, and desired skills, as articulated by the incoming basic writing student. Because the model is based on attention to rhetorical levels of content and form, with less emphasis on intimate personal revelation, the result is a more reliable map of discourse characteristics to help guide a student throughout the course.

358   Scott-Clayton, Judith. "Do High-Stakes Placement Exams Predict College Success?" *Community College Research Center.* Teachers College, Columbia University. Feb. 2012. Web. 21 May 2014.

Scott-Clayton's study examines the predictive validity of a widely used placement exam at a large urban community college system. The author analyzed data from four groups representing about seventy thousand students who enrolled between 2004 and 2007. The results demonstrate that math outcomes are more accurate than English outcomes as predictors of student success, and that such exams predict who will do well more easily than who will not succeed. The study concludes that the combination of placement exams and high school achievement measures raises the proportion of variation. Therefore, the use of multiple measurements to inform placement could lower serious misplacements by approximately 15 percent with no effect on remediation or reduce the remediation rate by 8 to 12 percent and simultaneously maintain or raise success rates in college-level courses.

359   Shor, Ira. "Illegal Literacy." *Journal of Basic Writing* 19.1 (2000): 100–12. Print.

Shor argues that the City University of New York burdens students with excessive assessments of their reading and writing proficiencies. Basic writers must pass the remedial composition course and a timed impromptu writing test before they are permitted to register for regular composition. In some cases, students who fail the timed writing test violate policy and register for regular composition anyway. Such students, Shor writes, are "guilty of illegal literacy and unauthorized progress" (102) and are examples of resistance to the bureaucratic and oppressive nature of testing and remediation. This process is part of a conservative attempt to discourage success among the minority and working-class populations that are heavily represented in basic writing classes. A more democratic alternative, Shor writes, would involve mainstreaming basic writers and transforming first-year writing into Critical Literacy across the Community. This new curriculum would consist of community service, field research, and ethnographic writing instead of drills in usage and mechanics and allegiance to academic discourse.

360   Singer, Marti. "Moving the Margins." *Mainstreaming Basic Writers: Politics and Pedagogies of Access.* Ed. Gerri McNenny. Mahwah: Erlbaum, 2001. 101–18. Print.

Stories shared among basic writing professionals seem to carry common themes: student access and success in the academic community, teachers' experiences, and the training of writing instructors. Singer argues that we need to revisit and to listen to our stories, whether they exhibit successes or generate questions or propose new programs, if we are to understand the political and cultural impact of decisions made about basic writing. The article focuses on the story of one faculty member's reflections on marginalization. It describes a course created to bridge the isolated remedial courses to the freshman composition program without entirely mainstreaming the students. Singer explores multiple perceptions of language use, audience, collaboration, and belonging in the academic community; her twenty years' experience of teaching, research, and service in a basic writing program at a large urban university; and the constant moving of the margins during that time.

361   Sweigart, William. "Assessing Achievement in a Developmental Writing Sequence." *Research and Teaching in Developmental Education* 12 (1996): 5–15. Print.

Emphasizing that writing program administrators should respond to both local needs and increasing demands from administrators (and legislatures) for sensible assessment procedures, Sweigart reports on an evaluation of the developmental writing program at a midsize public university. A two-year study within the writing program generated an assessment model whereby essays written for placement were compared to essays the same students wrote at the end of the semester. Using the model, the author demonstrates that statistically significant gain scores ($p < .01$) are achieved for the writing program based on the writing scores at these two times. The study provides one method for establishing a baseline measure in a writing program, and it supports a systematic assessment of writing that can be used to link developmental writing courses to the regular, first-year English classes. The author notes that "while campuses obviously differ, the model may prove useful for assessment in a variety of settings" (6).

362   White, Edward M. "The Importance of Placement and Basic Studies: Helping Students Succeed under the New Elitism." *Journal of Basic Writing* 14.2 (1995): 75–84. Print.

White argues that the movement in the 1990s to abolish the first-year composition requirement masks a dangerous elitism that is trying to prevent opportunities for the poor, for racial minorities, and for students who come to the university underprepared for its writing requirements. This elitism stems from budget cuts that have led to raised tuition and restricted enrollments, turning writing into a gate-keeping "wing of the admissions office" (76). To counter what he sees as an elitist abolitionist movement, White uses data from two sets of studies — one of "1978 First-Time Freshmen" in the California State University system and one from New Jersey postsecondary institutions conducted in 1988, 1991, and 1992 — to suggest that effective placement programs and supportive basic writing programs will help to retain minority and underprepared students who might otherwise leave the university. While there are various reasons for students to leave school at various points in their studies, White argues that well-supported placement and basic writing programs will keep basic writers in school. At the very least, he hopes such studies will shed some light on the social biases he sees behind the abolitionist movement of the last decade.

See: Sharon Crowley, "Response to Edward M. White's 'The Importance of Placement and Basic Studies'" [376].

See: Edward M. White, "Revisiting the Importance of Placement and Basic Studies: Evidence of Success" [364].

363   White, Edward M. "Process vs. Product: Assessing Skills in Writing." *AAHE Bulletin* (October 1988): 10–13. Print.

White examines fundamental issues behind different methods of writing assessment, dividing his discussion into two parts. In the first part, White explores the two paradigms of writing instruction, product and process, by teasing out the pedagogical and political implications behind each. He concludes that the product approach and its concomitant means of assessment disrupt the development of writers' attitudes toward writing as discovery and as a valuable exercise. The second, much briefer section lists the advantages and disadvantages of the three basic writing assessment methods—multiple-choice usage tests, essay tests, and portfolios—concluding that portfolios best measure writing as process. The discussion of portfolio assessment is admittedly limited, given the date of the article. Nonetheless, White provides a lucid summary of the principles that underlie writing assessment methodology.

364   White, Edward M. "Revisiting the Importance of Placement and Basic Studies: Evidence of Success." *Mainstreaming Basic Writers: Politics and Pedagogies of Access.* Ed. Gerri McNenny. Mahwah: Erlbaum, 2001. 19–28. Print.

A new elitism and its (however unintended) theorists, the new abolitionists, seek to abandon the required freshman composition course and the placement tests that help students succeed in the course and in college. This essay is a follow-up to White's "The Importance of Placement and Basic Studies: Helping Students Succeed under the New Elitism" [362]. As the data show, a placement program, followed by a careful instructional program, allows many students who would otherwise leave school to continue successfully in the university.

365   Wiener, Harvey S. "Evaluating Assessment Programs in Basic Skills." *Journal of Developmental Education* 13.2 (1989): 24–26. Print.

In 1983, three professors at the City University of New York conducted a national survey in which they discovered that 97 percent of the 1,269 responding institutions assess entering students. The assessments were often used to determine admission, program acceptance, and placement, and students' persistence often was affected by the assessments. Wiener wondered how educators know if assessment tests measure what they are supposed to measure and if basic writing assessment programs are working. Thus Wiener and two colleagues, in association with the National Testing Program in Writing, followed up on this study with another designed to find out what types of instruments were being employed. Their study revealed resistance by many postsecondary institutions to using nationally developed standardized tests; instead, many institutions employ instruments that are not evaluated for reliability, validity, or even relationship to current curricula. Furthermore, those institutions that do employ nationally developed tests are using the SAT or ACT incorrectly since these tests are designed to measure potential college success and create stratification among students; they are not intended to evaluate skill levels. In response to the ongoing institutional desire for assessment, Wiener and his colleagues developed the College Assessment Program Evaluation (CAPE), a self-assessment program, and trained facilitators to use it. CAPE allows institutions to engage in self-evaluation and to design instruments that relate to their particular curricula.

366   Wolcott, Willa. "Evaluating a Basic Writing Program." *Journal of Basic Writing* 15.1 (1996): 57–69. Print.

Instructors do not like writing assessment because it is often not an indicator of student writing ability. Based on a program she developed with a colleague, Wolcott advocates a more accurate picture of student assessment that includes before and after impromptu essays, a multiple-choice editing test, and portfolio assessment. After evaluating this program, Wolcott found that "multiple sources of data [are] preferable to a single data source" (67). Balancing writing assessments with port-folio assessment gave a more comprehensive picture of student writing ability. Through multifaceted program evaluation, instructors are more accountable to themselves, the program, and basic writers.

367   Yancey, Kathleen Blake. "Outcomes Assessment and Basic Writing: What, Why, and How?" *Basic Writing e-Journal* 1.1 (1999): n. pag. Web. 21 May 2014.

Yancey briefly outlines possibilities for what program assessment might look like within a basic writing program and discusses what needs to be addressed before assessment begins. The practical considerations outlined include considering the purpose of the assessment, identifying stakeholders, identifying materials already in place and available, and determining the time frame during which the assessment must take place. A variety of scenarios for assessment are outlined, with links included to either Web sites or e-mail addresses so that readers can con-tact others who have used these methods (portfolio assessment, faculty surveys, and follow-up studies done with graduating seniors).

368   Young, Sandra. "Academic Legerdemain: When Literacy Standards Become a Sleight of Hand." *Open Words: Access and English Studies* 1.1 (2006): 37–53. Print.

Young describes the impact of a FIPSE grant designed to help Native Alaskan students at a university acclimate themselves to academic life through the creation of a living situation similar to their home com-munities and through recruitment of local Native Alaskans to serve as mentors. Examining what happens when "assessment, standards, and culture collide" (38), Young responds to factors that curtail the project's effectiveness: difficulties involved in locating mentors and ap-proximating students' home lives within such a short amount of time and increased pressure to retain students through relaxed standards and assessment. Ultimately, Young argues, the grant isolates students from their peers and generates an environment where maintenance of the grant outweighs its educational aims. Taking these contextual elements into account, she reflects on her own struggles as the students' writing instructor and on their inconsistent attendance, underpreparedness, and resistance to western culture. Borrowing from Kathleen Cotton, Young recommends a restructured grant that would involve culturally heterogeneous cooperative learning teams rather than exclusionary enclaves.

Writing Program Administration

369   Adler-Kassner, Linda. "Digging a Groundwork for Writing: Underprepared Students and Community Service Courses." *College Composition
and Communication* 46.4 (1995): 552–55. Print.

For underprepared students, community-service courses emphasizing
academic writing may serve students better than traditional writing
classes, because of the service-learning aspect. When students combine
community service with their writing assignments, the "sum" of what
they get out of the classes is often greater than its component parts.
Adler-Kassner shows how a service-learning model got students to consider how to write most effectively for their college courses.

370   Adler-Kassner, Linda. "Service Learning in the Basic Writing Classroom: Mapping the Conceptual Landscape." *Basic Writing e-Journal* 1.1
(1999): n. pag. Web. 21 May 2014.

This article, based on a presentation at an all-day workshop at the
Conference on College Composition and Communication in Atlanta,
discusses how service-learning activities can be included in the basic
writing classroom without interfering with the intended goals of the
composition course. With careful planning, Adler-Kassner suggests,
teachers can facilitate an integration of service-learning goals and
writing goals. The article includes a detailed matrix that describes the
goals, sites, literacies, relationships, and means of assessment for socially
and academically motivated writing. It also includes brief summaries of
comments, suggestions from participants in the workshop, and several
definitions of service learning.

371   Berger, Mary Jo. "Funding and Support for Basic Writing: Why Is There
So Little?" *Journal of Basic Writing* 12.1 (1993): 81–89. Print.

Acknowledging the history of limited support for basic writing in higher
education, Berger analyzes the positive role basic writing teachers can
play in gaining budgetary support for their programs. She discusses
characteristics of higher education that have budgetary implications
and that stress the importance of individual participation. She recommends becoming a member of decision-making committees, attending
meetings, seeking political allies across the disciplines, staying in touch
with former students and their parents, organizing for action in favor of
basic writing programs, and informing administrators and other teachers about "how much more challenging and how much more fulfilling it
is to teach the underprepared than the already prepared" (88).

372   Boylan, Hunter R., and Barbara S. Bonham. "The Impact of Developmental Education Programs." *Research in Developmental Education* 9.5
(1992): 1–3. Print.

Boylan, director of the National Center for Developmental Education
(NCDE), and Bonham, a senior researcher at NCDE, report some of
the results of a comprehensive national study of the effectiveness of

developmental education, specifically focusing on the effects of developmental programs on cumulative grade point average (GPA), long-term retention, and subsequent performance in regular college courses. These programs appear to succeed since developmental students have cumulative GPAs above the minimum 2.00, pass initial courses, and are likely to graduate. This study could serve as a model for collecting empirical data at any college or university.

373   Collins, Terence, and Melissa Blum. "Meanness and Failure: Sanctioning Basic Writers." *Journal of Basic Writing* 19.1 (2000): 13–21. Print.

Collins and Blum focus on the state of meaningful access to higher education among disenfranchised students, particularly low-income single-parent women, in the wake of national and state welfare reform and the 1998 election. They describe the previously successful Higher Education for Low-Income People program in the General College at the University of Minnesota; the potential of the Minnesota Family Investment Program (MFIP), the pilot program that followed it; and the change in the political climate that caused the sanctioning of basic writers. Using the writing of two women enrolled in the MFIP, the authors attempt to put a face on the issue to illustrate the real economic and social possibilities traditional baccalaureate education once offered to disenfranchised students and their children.

374   Collins, Terence, and Kim Lynch. "Mainstreaming? Eddy, Rivulet, Backwater, Site Specificity." *Mainstreaming Basic Writers: Politics and Pedagogies of Access.* Ed. Gerri McNenny. Mahwah: Erlbaum, 2001. 73–84. Print.

Collins and Lynch argue for restraint in the conversation about mainstreaming because dialogues about it often ignore the fact that basic writing programs operate in specific institutional settings under local constraints. Collins and Lynch note that the case for mainstreaming often has been built on theoretical narratives that posit an overly—sometimes conveniently—homogenized basic writing status quo against which mainstreaming is placed as a universally desirable fix. They also illustrate that competing research bases are relevant to the discussion of mainstreaming and that these databases need to play a more significant role in the discussion than they have to date. They note that basic writing, specifically, and developmental education at large are varied as a function of the local situation.

375   Crouch, Mary Kay, and Gerri McNenny. "Looking Back, Looking Forward: California Grapples with 'Remediation.'" *Journal of Basic Writing* 19.2 (2000): 44–71. Print.

This study examines documents issued by legislative bodies and public responses from the press and writing programs as they grapple with the changing scenario of remediation in California's higher education system. More conflicts seem to arise about the needs of nontraditional students as defined by legislators, scholars, and program administrators at times when the social and academic profiles of students entering the college system undergo rapid changes. Crouch and McNenny argue that these conflicts can best be addressed if needs assessment relies on collaboration between community leaders, college and high school instructors, and writing professionals. They also argue for collaborative outreach programs at the high school level that can address the needs of basic writers.

376   Crowley, Sharon. "Response to Edward M. White's 'The Importance of Placement and Basic Studies.'" *Journal of Basic Writing* 15.1 (1996): 88–91. Print.

Crowley agrees with Edward White that elitist forces are threatening open admissions and other initiatives to increase campus diversity. However, she refutes White's suggestion that abolishing composition as a requirement might further the same elitist ends. The abolition argument, made most vocally by Crowley herself, is a response to composition's historic role as an "instrument of exclusion" (89). White's attempt to situate the abolition argument as complicit with exclusion is misguided, Crowley writes, since conservative groups like the National Association of Scholars are threatening diversity initiatives and are also calling for higher standards and more requirements in subjects like composition. Further, when White paints abolitionists as "conservative," he appeals to the "liberal" nature of compositionists. A more viable position, Crowley writes, is "radical" ideology that critiques elitist movements and makes progressive suggestions (like abolishing required composition) for more ethical and diverse institutions.

See: Edward M. White, "The Importance of Placement and Basic Studies: Helping Students Succeed under the New Elitism" [362].

377   Fitzgerald, Sallyanne. "Basic Writing in One California Community College." *Basic Writing e-Journal* 1.2 (1999): n. pag. Web. 21 May 2014.

Since basic writers are unique to each community and situation, programs need to develop comprehensive approaches that enable students to meet the goal of successful college-level writing. Fitzgerald details the evolution of Throughline, a comprehensive program philosophy at Chabot College. This philosophy does not approach basic writing as a separate entity. It allows basic writing courses to flow smoothly into other courses by integrating reading, writing, thinking, speaking, and listening at all levels. The program at Chabot serves as a model for those who advocate mainstreaming basic writers, especially since it addresses the needs of students to establish college-level writing skills within a specific context.

378   Fitzgerald, Sallyanne H. "Serving Basic Writers: One Community College's Mission Statements." *Journal of Basic Writing* 22.1 (2003): 5–12. Print.

Fitzgerald chronicles her experience at Chabot College to illustrate how revising a community college's mission statement can be a legitimizing force in re-envisioning the role that basic writing plays in that mission. Previously, basic writing courses were taught with a concentration on a "hierarchal model of English where skills proceed from words to sentences to paragraphs to essays" (10). The new, refashioned mission statement and "throughline"—a semester-by-semester sequence of courses and expected outcomes for those courses—replaced this "skills" model with "a basic writing curriculum that mirrors the demands of the transferable freshman composition courses" (11). These guidelines better articulated the assumptions that would form the basis for basic writing pedagogy at Chabot, including a clear statement of what students who completed these basic writing courses should be able to do. By fashioning a "throughline" for all English courses, this particular community college was able to include a strong commitment to basic writing as more than just "a legal mandate" (5).

379   Glau, Gregory R. "Hard Work and Hard Data: Getting Our Message Out." *The Writing Program Administrator's Resource: A Guide to Reflective Institutional Practice.* Ed. Stuart C. Brown and Theresa Enos. Mahwah: Erlbaum, 2002. 291–302. Print.

The bane of most newly minted writing program administrators is the level of hard data that university administrators require. Early in their careers, most writing program administrators do not have the training or expertise to undertake high-level quantitative program-assessment projects. Glau believes that even the busiest, most inexperienced administrator can mine for "nuggets" of statistical data. He suggests looking at the percentage of students who pass first-semester composition and move directly into second semester and how that number has changed, how enrollments have varied with funding changes over the past few years, and what the grade distribution in first-year writing is. Glau states that thinking about the situation rhetorically is key: ask who wants the data and for what purpose, find out if the data are already being collected, and—if they are not—design surveys or other data-gathering tools to do so. Glau suggests designing invention heuristics for determining what data to track, what information is already available, and how to process it.

380   Glau, Gregory R. "*Stretch* at 10: A Progress Report on Arizona State University's *Stretch Program*." *Journal of Basic Writing* 26.2 (2007): 30–48. Print.

Glau chronicles the inception of the Stretch Program at Arizona State University (ASU), the changes that have marked the program, and its successes and struggles. In 1992, Director of Composition David Schwalm and John Ramage (then director of the Writing across the Curriculum program at ASU) designed two pilot programs to better aid students recognized as "high risk" in terms of university success. The first program, named Jumbo, was a six-semester-hour basic writing class. The second program, called Stretch, was "a two-semester sequence designed to stretch ENG 101 over two semesters" (31). The Stretch Program was markedly more successful and is still in use at ASU today. Glau describes the Stretch Program in detail, focusing on results as seen through long-term statistics. The Stretch Program utilizes the same texts, the same assignments, and the same teachers as the more traditional first-year composition curriculum at ASU. This "stretching" of the content to a two-semester sequence allows a more guided writing experience and ideally allows students to build a stronger writing community. Statistics from the last ten years show this two-semester sequence not only increased students' pass rates for their entire first-year composition sequence (English 101 and 102) but also increased overall college retention. Taking into account the profile of a Stretch student, Glau contends that the long-term benefit to the student is worthwhile. He acknowledges that this program may not be the perfect model for every institution but notes that as students' needs change, the Stretch Program can be adapted accordingly.

381   Goen-Salter, Sugie. "Critiquing the Need to Eliminate Remediation: Lessons from San Francisco State." *Journal of Basic Writing* 27.2 (2008): 81–105. Print.

For more than two decades, the California State University (CSU) system has been trying unsuccessfully to "reduce the need for remediation" on its campuses, primarily through initiatives aimed at high schools. This article examines a basic writing reform project, San Francisco State's Integrated Reading/Writing Program, in the context of CSU's history of remediation. The success of this project, in light of CSU's remedial past, provides the grounds to advocate for higher education as the appropriate location for basic writing and reading and to advocate, in turn, for the resources necessary to theorize, develop, and sustain a rich variety of approaches to basic writing instruction. Goen-Salter's analysis also suggests the need for more graduate programs and faculty development initiatives to help prepare a new generation of basic writing teachers and scholars to meet the needs of the next generation of basic writing students.

382   Goggin, Peter, et al. "The Universal Requirement in First-Year Composition: A Forum." *Basic Writing e-Journal* 1.2 (1999): n. pag. Web. 21 May 2014.

In a special event at the Western States Composition Conference in October 1999, Sharon Crowley and John Ramage debated the politically charged first-year writing requirement. This article provides a transcript of the debate as well as a succinct introduction written by Peter Goggin and a transcript of the discussion following the debate compiled by Kohl Glau. During her opening remarks, Crowley provides an overview of her well-known arguments for the abolishment of the first-year writing requirement. Ramage responds by noting that, while he usually argues against the "status quo," doing away with the requirement entirely is not the answer. As Goggin notes in the introduction, there was no clear "winner" of the debate, but the presentations of Crowley and Ramage and the discussion that followed provide a helpful overview of this complex issue, which is of the utmost importance to writing instructors. In fact, Goggin suggests that the lack of a clear winner of the debate simply underscores the fact that the field is "far from resolving the pedagogical and political conflicts that mark the requirement" (par. 5).

383 Kraemer, Don J. "The Economy of Explicit Instruction." *Journal of Basic Writing* 26.2 (2007): 93–112. Print.

Kraemer highlights the economic metaphors guiding some discussions about explicit instruction and suggests that explicit instruction does not have to position students as passive consumers of knowledge. Rather, explicit instruction that takes account of both the practical and human elements of writing instruction can position students as apprentices to the academic community. Kraemer discusses a curriculum he developed that emphasizes economics. It is based on the explicit teaching of Steven Levitt and Stephen Dubner's *Freakonomics*, a book that challenges conventional wisdom through a rhetorically savvy presentation of data and facts. He found that asking students to read and challenge the ideas and rhetoric in the book in their writing gave them an opportunity to practice the knowledge-making rituals and intellectual practices of the academic community they hoped to enter.

384 Kraemer, Don J. "Servant Class: Basic Writers and Service Learning." *Journal of Basic Writing* 24.2 (2005): 92–109. Print.

Kraemer describes three rhetorical situations for writing in service-learning projects: writing *with* the community, writing *about* the community, and writing *for* the community. But Kraemer notes that because of the lack of university funding for oversight of their work with service-learning projects, students often are left writing *for* the community. Even though service learning is supposed to blur the lines of hierarchy inside and outside the classroom by empowering students through the collaborative production of a document, students often have little to say regarding the content or design of the final written text, and thus are relegated to the "servant class." Kraemer points out that John Dewey's aim for "perplexity, confusion, and doubt" in the classroom was reduced to easy work within clearly prescribed or heavily guided parameters in service-learning projects; academic writing, on the other hand, challenged students and allowed them room for interpretation and agency. With some service-learning projects, time constraints denied the students an opportunity to do reflective writing about the implications of a document's complexity, their claim on it, or their roles in persuading an audience with it. However, academic writing allowed students to have a thoughtful "role in public deliberations." Thus the realities of service-learning projects should be measured against the pedagogical claims some scholars purport.

385 Lalicker, William B. "A Basic Introduction to Basic Writing Program Structures: A Baseline and Five Alternatives." *Basic Writing e-Journal* 1.2 (1999): n. pag. Web. 21 May 2014.

Lalicker describes a brief survey that was conducted via the Writing Program Administrators' e-mail list. The survey asked respondents to identify their basic writing program as approximating one of five models: the prerequisite model, in which basic writing students take a course before the standard first-year composition course; the stretch model, in which basic writers take the standard first-year course over two semesters rather than one; the studio model, in which the standard course is augmented by additional hours of small-group work; the directed self-placement model, in which students are guided in making their own choice about which writing course in a sequence they would like to take; and the intensive model, in which the basic writing course mirrors the standard course but with "additional instructional time or writing activities tailored for basic writers" (par. 8). Respondents also provided insight into the advantages and disadvantages of each model. No pattern was discovered between type of program and institution size, demographics, or mission. Specific institutional needs and the "theoretical or epistemological assumptions driving the writing program" (par. 2) seemed to exert greater influence on program design.

386   Lamos, Steve. "Basic Writing, CUNY, and 'Mainstreaming': (De)Racialization Reconsidered." *Journal of Basic Writing* 19.2 (2000): 22–43. Print.

Lamos argues that the current movement toward eliminating open admissions, mainstreaming basic writers, and ending first-year composition programs exists in the context of an institutionalized racism that continues to reinforce racialized thinking in both students and institutions. Lamos describes the overt racism with which open admissions was greeted in New York in the early 1970s.

387   Laurence, Patricia. "The Vanishing Site of Mina Shaughnessy's *Errors and Expectations*." *Journal of Basic Writing* 12.2 (1993): 18–28. Print.

In this article, first presented as a talk at the Fourth National Basic Writing Conference in 1992, Laurence asks all practitioners in the field of basic writing to consider the factors that influence basic writing at particular times and institutions. Min-Zhan Lu's "Redefining the Legacy of Mina Shaughnessy: A Critique of the Politics of Linguistic Innocence" [107] and Stephen North's *The Making of Composition: Portrait of an Emerging Field*, both reassessments of Shaughnessy's 1977 landmark *Errors and Expectations* [126], are critiqued for what they fail to consider—the complexities, multiplicities, histories, and differences present in any educational movement. Laurence's defense of Shaughnessy and her colleagues' work at the City College of New York (CCNY) points to the lack of historical understanding in Lu's and North's critiques. Each situation has its political needs, and the 1970s was a time that called for subtlety in expression regarding open-admissions students at CCNY. These students' abilities were questioned, as was their credibility and potential as students. Laurence contends that Shaughnessy should be praised for her understanding of the political situation.

388   Lewiecki-Wilson, Cynthia, and Jeff Sommers. "Professing at the Fault
       Lines: Composition at Open Admissions Institutions." *College Composi-
       tion and Communication* 50.3 (1999): 438–62. Print.

       Open-admissions work largely remains invisible to the general public
       and even to the profession of rhetoric and composition. Intellectual
       work can and does take place in open-admissions settings, such as the
       basic writing classroom and various domains within two-year colleges.
       Through qualitative interviews and thick description, Lewiecki-Wilson
       and Sommers outline what constitutes this particular academic life-
       style. Critical pedagogy, process-based teaching, and teacher research
       all thrive in open-admissions environments, so the field should stop
       devaluing knowledge construction there. Also, practitioners at open-
       admissions institutions get the chance to be agents of institutional,
       curricular, and social change because teaching various sections over a
       longitudinal period of time is conducive to reflective, developmental
       teaching and sustained research. Therefore professionals in the field
       should work on placing open-admissions practice at the center of our
       disciplinary identity.

389   McAlexander, Patricia J. "Mina Shaughnessy and K. Patricia Cross:
       The Forgotten Debate over Postsecondary Remediation." *Rhetoric Re-
       view* 19.1/2 (2000): 28–41. Print.

       McAlexander reconstructs the dialogue between Mina Shaughnessy
       and K. Patricia Cross on open admissions and remediation for "new
       college students" in the 1960s and 1970s. Both educators favored doing
       away with elitist admissions policies and replacing them with open
       admissions to accept the low-achieving students. Shaughnessy saw the
       problems in racial terms; students at the City College of New York were
       minorities who had previously attended racially prejudiced schools.
       Cross believed her students at the University of California at Berkeley
       were different; because of California's three-tiered system, only the top
       12 percent of high school graduates appeared at Berkeley; the others
       were enrolled at either state colleges or in two-year programs. Cross's
       "new college students" were different from Shaughnessy's in that they
       were "mostly [not] socially disadvantaged minorities" (33). They were
       not motivated and lacked the proper effort for success. Cross recom-
       mended alternative curriculum routes (vocational and business train-
       ing) for the "new college students." Shaughnessy favored strengthening
       the remedial methods. Today, most agree that Cross's conclusions were
       correct: that remedial classes do not help the students and may, in fact,
       harm them.

390   Pine, Nancy. "Service Learning in a Basic Writing Class: A Best Case
       Scenario." *Journal of Basic Writing* 27.2 (2008): 29–55. Print.

       Pine explores the particular challenges and possibilities of service-
       learning pedagogy for basic writers. Because a number of scholars of
       service learning and basic writing (such as Linda Adler-Kassner and
       Don Kraemer) are concerned primarily with developing underprepared

students' academic literacies, Pine investigated how the students in a service-learning basic writing class situated their service experience—represented that "text" rhetorically—in their major academic research essay for the course. The article draws on one student's experience of making connections among the "rich mix" of course texts, including personal experience, as a best case. From this example, Pine argues for strategies of service-learning pedagogy that could better help basic writers achieve their goals for academic writing.

See: Linda Adler-Kassner, "Service Learning in the Basic Writing Classroom: Mapping the Conceptual Landscape" [370].

See: Don J. Kraemer, "Servant Class: Basic Writers and Service Learning" [384].

391   Preto-Bay, Ana Maria, and Kristine Hansen. "Preparing for the Tipping Point: Designing Writing Programs to Meet the Needs of the Changing Population." WPA: Writing Program Administration 30.1/2 (2006): 37–58. Print.

The "tipping point" that lies ahead for writing programs is the demographic shift that brings increasing numbers of immigrants and refugees into college composition classrooms. The needs of these "crossover" or "Generation 1.5" populations are different from those of other international and multicultural students and must be equally considered and represented in curriculum design. Training programs for graduate students and adjunct faculty, as well as books and materials for preparing teachers of composition, still largely assume a homogeneous, English-speaking, American-acculturated student population. A rhetorical or socioliterate approach to composition curriculum design will better serve the needs of crossover groups than formalist, critical-cultural, or expressivist approaches. Greater collaboration between mainstream and second-language fields, including the hiring of L2 professionals in writing programs, is also a vital part of the adjustment.

392   Reynolds, Thomas. "Training Basic Writing Teachers: Institutional Considerations." Journal of Basic Writing 20.2 (2001): 38–52. Print.

Reynolds notes that the training of basic writing teachers has not received sufficient attention by researchers. This problem can and should be addressed within the sponsorship and care of institutional structures. Teacher training can also be seen as a space to study and make critical decisions about whether and how to perpetuate institutional histories. Linking teacher training to the interests and concerns of an administration produces an effective situation, he argues, because the training can serve as an instrument for connecting basic writing programs to an influential administrative structure. In addition, practitioners should be willing to meet across institutions to establish ties and examine common issues concerning training. Reynolds concludes with a set of useful questions for discussion regarding the training of basic writing teachers.

393   Reynolds, Tom, and Patty Fillipi. "Refocus through Involvement: (Re)Writing the Curricular Documents of the University of Minnesota–

General College Basic Writing Program." *Journal of Basic Writing* 22.1 (2003): 13–21. Print.

Reynolds and Fillipi briefly describe the challenges and rewards that they and their colleagues experienced while collaboratively rewriting the curricular documents for the basic writing program at their school. The process of collaborative revision was sometimes challenging because not everyone's vision prevailed. The authors point to several positive outcomes: considering connections between the writing program and the university's mission, creating space for the needs of a diverse writing faculty, and including faculty in the curriculum's design. All of these reduced the sense of faculty isolation and created a greater sense of mission and purpose within the program. Reynolds and Fillipi include the opening statement of the resultant document, "Toward a Deepened Notion of Access: The Writing Program at the University of Minnesota General College."

394   Rigolino, Rachel, and Penny Freel. "Re-Modeling Basic Writing." *Journal of Basic Writing* 26.2 (2007): 51–74. Print.

Rigolino and Freel describe the SUNY–New Paltz basic writing program as a model of supplemental writing workshops (SWWs) and seamless support, where basic writing students attend a for-credit Composition I class, meet with their instructors in workshop one hour per week, and meet with a writing center tutor one hour per week. This model places students directly into the first-year composition sequence without a semester's detour in a noncredit writing course. The idea of seamlessness is central to providing three spaces of instruction that are separate yet holistically bound to one another. Assessment measures after ten years suggest that SWW students approach the levels of achievement and retention of non-SWW students.

395   Rodby, Judith. "What's It Worth and What's It For? Revisions to Basic Writing Revisited." *College Composition and Communication* 47.1 (1996): 107–11. Print.

Rodby focuses on the efforts and complications involved in the reconfiguration of instruction of basic writers at California State University, Chico. Because of the stigmas and limitations attached to the "basic writing" category, administrators and teachers decided to mainstream basic writing students. Rodby discusses two predominant issues that arose against this effort that suggest that the slotting of basic writers is largely political in nature. First, she describes the administration's circular arguments against giving credit for the course: that the noncredit course was necessary for the students to take the work seriously and that it was also important for the retention of minority students. Foundational to the resistance to change, Rodby argues next, is the issue of nostalgia as an ideological state that shapes everything from attitudes toward basic writing students to curricular and institutional choices. Rodby concludes by suggesting steps to break nostalgia's grasp and urges increased and constant communication and learning among others in the field as a shield against the assault by those who would eliminate these programs altogether.

396   Rodby, Judith, and Tom Fox. "Basic Work and Material Acts: The Ironies, Discrepancies, and Disjunctures of Basic Writing and Mainstreaming." *Journal of Basic Writing* 19.1 (2000): 84–99. Print.

Rodby and Fox outline how and why they dismantled the noncredit basic writing curriculum at California State University, Chico. Working from the belief that designating students entering their institution as "basic" did not describe students' writing abilities but merely created a population for basic writing courses, they mainstreamed all students into first-semester composition courses and provided additional adjunct workshops for students with low test scores. Consequently, first-year writing has come to be seen as more meaningful by students. Additionally, instructors of first-year writing and adjunct workshops have a more complex context for discussions of student writing.

397   Rogers, Laura. "Finding Our Way from Within: Critical Pedagogy in a Prison Writing Class." *Open Words: Access and English Studies* 2.1 (2008): 22–48. Print.

Rogers presents a narrative analysis of her attempt to implement Freirean pedagogy as a teacher of college writing in a correctional facility. She discusses ways this institutional context complicates principles of trust, ethics, and power. Even though the pedagogy helps generate interesting student papers and class discussions, issues of surveillance and facility control compromise the degree to which her students can critique larger institutional forces that shape their lives. These factors restrict the extent to which they can share knowledge of this institutional life with their teacher, let alone make public their compositions or realize desired changes in their circumstances. In the end, Rogers uses her example to point to ways all teachers and students work within some institutional limitations, and she suggests acknowledging that these conditions of living "can help both students and teachers, as they listen to each other, become more fully human" (44).

398   Rose, Mike. "Remedial Writing Courses: A Critique and a Proposal." *College English* 45.2 (1983): 109–28. Print.

Rose argues that basic writing classes need to offer students challenging, engaging work that will enable them to participate more fully in the discourse of the university. In particular, five common practices tend to limit students' experience of writing and need to be examined and changed. First, basic writing courses need to move from being self-contained to fitting into the intellectual context of the university. Second, topics for writing need to be substantial rather than simplistic. Third, students need opportunities to experience the composing process as complex and expansive rather than as narrow and rule-bound. Fourth, the writing course needs to integrate reading and thinking into the composing process rather than focusing exclusively on skills. Finally, teachers should reimagine ways of using academic discursive strategies to enable, rather than restrict, students' writing.

399   Royer, Dan, and Roger Gilles. "Basic Writing and Directed Self-Placement." *Basic Writing e-Journal* 2.2 (2000): n. pag. Web. 21 May 2014.

Directed self-placement "fosters student agency, particularly for basic writers who have historically been given very little control over the shape and focus of their early college careers." Royer and Gilles cite scholars specializing in education, learning, thinking, and psychology as providing the philosophical and pedagogical justification for directed self-placement. Readers are referred to an earlier article titled "Directed Self-Placement: An Attitude of Orientation" for a detailed explanation of the system. Royer and Gilles also believe this system creates an important initial educative moment for college students through a re-articulation of the following elements involved in placement decisions: agency (both student knowledge and faculty expertise matter), articulation (students clarify their experiences and skills through thought and discussion with parents, teachers, and counselors), and assessment (students are assessed when they have completed a course instead of at the beginning with an unreliable, one-shot instrument).

400   Segall, Mary. "The Triple Helix: Program, Faculty, and Text." *Basic Writing e-Journal* 2.1 (2000): n. pag. Web. 21 May 2014.

At Segall's college, basic writers enroll in a jumbo composition course in which they meet with instructors for five hours per week. Developmental reading, basic English, and first-year composition are rolled into one for this program. Arguing that most developmental textbooks are simplistic and "convey a powerful message to developmental students about their place in the academy" (par. 7), Segall and her colleagues decided that they needed a textbook that provided readings with a range of levels of difficulty and that offered interrelated reading and writing activities. They used the same text for the regular and jumbo sections of composition, a decision that allowed them to justify granting the same credit in the end to students enrolled in the jumbo sections. Citing a plethora of compositionists who argue that the teaching of basic writing is still essentially conservative, Segall claims that writing program administrators can effect gradual change in their programs by bringing attention to textbook selection for basic writing classes.

401   Soliday, Mary. "From the Margins to the Mainstream: Reconceiving Remediation." *College Composition and Communication* 47.1 (1996): 85–100. Print.

Soliday describes the development of a basic writing student, Derek, who participated in a pilot project designed to promote a progressive version of mainstreaming while supporting the goals of open admissions. Derek was enrolled in a writing course at the City College of New York. The Enrichment Approach project, sponsored by the Fund for the Improvement of Postsecondary Education, bypasses test scores that place students in remedial courses and instead places college students in a six-credit, two-semester writing course. The course's curriculum is responsive to the experiences and histories of nontraditional students with diverse language and cultural backgrounds and encourages students to describe, interpret, and analyze aspects of everyday language use and familiar cultural experience in the unfamiliar language of the academy. The mainstreamed curriculum enabled Derek to use the forms of academic discourse to more deeply explore complex, personal topics, such as Black English and rap music, in ways that helped him negotiate two "codes," his own and academic discourse, positioning himself as both an insider and a cultural critic. A mainstreamed curriculum that emphasizes such linguistic and cultural self-consciousness offers a progressive alternative to traditional remediation.

402   Soliday, Mary, and Barbara Gleason. "From Remediation to Enrichment: Evaluating a Mainstreaming Project." *Journal of Basic Writing* 16.1 (1997): 64–78.

Soliday and Gleason describe the pilot of a three-year enrichment project that substituted a two-semester writing course in place of the traditional sequence of two remedial courses and one college-level course. The two-semester course, in contrast to the traditional sequence, carried full college credit, mainstreamed students who placed into remedial writing with students who placed into college-level writing, and allowed teachers rather than exit tests to decide whether students should pass their courses. The two-semester course was designed to build a stronger community of peers, class tutors, and teachers and to utilize students' cultural diversity. Assessments of student writing indicated that most students in the two-semester course improved their ability to produce good essays, evaluate their own writing, and conduct research. The writing assessments also indicated that students who would have been placed into remedial courses were competitive with students who would have been placed into college-level courses. Student self-assessments and teacher assessments of the same students generally indicated that students in the two-semester course were satisfied with their learning and could concretely describe what they had learned. Soliday and Gleason recommend giving students the option of taking either the traditional or the mainstreamed course sequence.

403   Strickland, Donna. "Errors and Interpretations: Toward an Archaeology of Basic Writing." *Composition Studies* 26.1 (1998): 21–35. Print.

Strickland addresses basic writing scholarship that claims composition studies should abolish basic writing programs because such programs often fail to mainstream basic writers and position basic writing students as "other." Strickland contends that the decision to terminate or sustain basic writing programs will not be made by scholars but rather by deans and legislators. What scholars can do, however, is interrogate the discourse of basic writing, which works to convince teachers and university administrators to conceive of basic writers as educable and to understand the ways in which this discourse competes for the power to interpret and thereby construct basic writing. To view discourse in this way, Strickland suggests that scholars examine the history of basic writing scholarship, reflect on their positions as "knowers" in relation to students' positions as "known," and listen to students' words, reading students' texts as "living acts of communication from other human beings" (33).

404   Tabachnikov, Ann. "The Mommification of Writing Instruction: A Tale of Two Students." *Journal of Basic Writing* 20.1 (2001): 27–36. Print.

Tabachnikov examines the dynamic of "teacherhood as motherhood" that is at work in composition classrooms, especially when student writing becomes intensely personal. Tabachnikov uses two of her own students to illustrate opposite ends of the motherhood spectrum. The first student, Cindy, was repeatedly ill and expected to be treated as a sick child might be. Tabachnikov responded to Cindy as a guilt-inducing mother might. Unable to endure this treatment, Cindy quit coming to class, and Tabachnikov dropped her from the class roster. This behavior led Tabachnikov to question and then embrace her "mommyness"—her parental role in teaching. The second student, Pete, was a middle-aged man who was eager to learn. His openness, candor, and eagerness to succeed led Tabachnikov to respond to him with a friendship that had an appropriate amount of distance but was reminiscent of the adult-child relationship where power and role differences are omnipresent. Despite being protective of Pete, a behavior she identifies as maternal, Tabachnikov maintained that her dynamic regarding him was parental rather than simply motherly. This parental role is one that Tabachnikov believes needs further consideration.

405   Tassoni, John Paul. "(Re)membering Basic Writing at a Public Ivy: History for Institutional Redesign." *Journal of Basic Writing* 25.1 (2006): 96–124. Print.

Tassoni recalls the evolution of the Miami University basic writing program and its studio counterpart. For Tassoni, the supplemental writing studio workshop is concerned with "reinforc[ing] for us the importance of students' understanding the rhetorical contexts within which they write, as well as the ways these contexts affect how and what students write" (102). Additionally, he demonstrates how many basic writing programs are implemented as reactionary retrofits as opposed to curricular redesigns that accommodate the changing literacy patterns of at-risk students. Thus, Tassoni perceives the basic writing course, along with a studio workshop, as a way of making the university more accessible to students who have been traditionally excluded from the Public Ivy university.

406   Tassoni, John Paul, and Cynthia Lewiecki-Wilson. "Not Just Anywhere, Anywhen: Mapping Change through Studio Work." *Journal of Basic Writing* 24.1 (2005): 68–92. Print.

In this "autoethnographic, institutional narrative," the authors draw on cultural geography and postcolonial theory to think through their efforts to reform basic writing at their university. Through Tassoni and Lewiecki-Wilson's account of their struggle to implement a version of Rhonda Grego and Nancy Thompson's "Studio" alternative to remedial coursework, they illustrate how curricular transformation necessarily takes place in spaces already "densely populated by overlapping and knotted social, cultural, and institutional contexts and constraints" (81). Yet the authors find this transformation worthwhile, for "colonizing" sites of composition instruction for students from multiple classrooms creates opportunities both to provide a broader context to specific pedagogies "tucked away within individual writing classrooms" as well as to incrementally "intervene in our campus's writing culture" through strategic outreach to instructors about the work going on in their students' writing studios (83–84).

407   Uehling, Karen S. "Creating a Statement of Guidelines and Goals for Boise State University's Basic Writing Course: Content and Development." *Journal of Basic Writing* 22.1 (2003): 22–34. Print.

Uehling describes the development of the statement of goals and guidelines for Boise State University's basic writing course. She also considers the statement's effects, emphasizing that its goal was to transform attitudes and that it structured the required first-year writing sequence. She also analyzes the conditions that produced the document—the urban, commuter nature of the institution; its fulfillment of various community college functions; the placement of the course in the English department; and the noncredit, one-semester status of the course. In addition, she shares her thoughts about the student competencies that the document supports, including building confidence; viewing writing as a multifaceted process; using multiple strategies for viewing written texts over time; producing coherent drafts with introductions, body paragraphs, and conclusions; employing format in appropriate ways; reading actively and critically; and editing assignments so that surface features do not interfere with communication.

408   Warnick, Chris, et al. "Beyond the Budget: Sustainability and Writing Studios." *Journal of Basic Writing* 29.2 (2010): 74–96. Print.

Although sustainability is a central concern in the scholarship on Writing Studios, there has been little thorough research on the issue. The authors take as their task, then, to "fill this gap in the scholarship by discussing, from different perspectives" (75), the demise of a Writing Studio at the College of Charleston. Working from two perspectives, an assistant professor and two MA students, the article reviews the formation of the Studio, describes its ten-year run, and, finally, proposes ways of sustaining a Writing Studio—ways that were unavailable or unforeseeable to the authors. Based on their experiences, the authors argue that first-year writing programs must be established prior to the creation of a Writing Studio and that both programs must have different directors; that an embedded Writing Studio—embedded in a required composition course—offers a permanent pool of students to enroll in the Studio and provides coordination and communication between instructors of both courses; and that instructors of the composition course must be required to contribute to and participate in the Writing Studio.

409   Wiley, Mark. "Mainstreaming and Other Experiments in a Learning Community." *Mainstreaming Basic Writing: Politics and Pedagogies of Access.* Ed. Gerri McNenny. Mahwah: Erlbaum, 2001. 173–91. Print.

Debates over mainstreaming basic writers often settle into either-or positions and fail to consider local institutional factors. Before deciding whether to mainstream basic writing students, writing program administrators need to examine the basic writing courses offered at their respective institutions, the type of literacy promoted, and any extracurricular factors that might affect the long-term success of these students. Knowing that the merits of mainstreaming basic writing students are open to debate, Wiley reports on the generally successful results of several experiments that he and his colleagues conducted with their institution's learning community, the Learning Alliance. The experiments include trying to mainstream a contingent of basic writing students and combining two semesters of basic writing into one. The results of these experiments have been instructive for all parties involved, and several program changes followed. The lower-level basic writing course was dropped; the upper-level course was increased from three to four instructional hours per week; the English placement test cutoff score for eligibility for the university-level writing course was lowered three points; and more mainstreaming experiments were planned. Most important is the change in thinking about how the campus perceives and works with basic writers as students in transition.

410   Ybarra, Raul. "Cultural Dissonance in Basic Writing Courses." *Journal of Basic Writing* 20.1 (2001): 37–52. Print.

Ybarra seeks to understand the cultural implications of basic writing as a mainstream educational framework imposed on Latino students through placement procedures, retention methods, and pedagogical assumptions. This qualitative study of one Latino student and a basic writing instructor argues that theories of resistance alone do not address the specific problems presented by Latino dropout rates within the university system. Ybarra suggests that placement in basic writing courses sends Latino students the message that they are not good enough to communicate within the mainstream culture. This misunderstanding is then compounded when writing instructors do not understand patterns of Latino discourse, resulting in a general dismissal of students. Ybarra suggests that instructors might actively seek out and motivate those students who do not participate in class discussions, who are regularly absent, or who might otherwise disappear from the class.

Cross-Institutional Connections

411   English, Hugh, and Lydia Nagle. "Ways of Taking Meaning from Texts: Reading in High School and College." *Journal of Basic Writing* 21.1 (2002): 37–51. Print.

English and Nagle describe a collaborative, qualitative study of reading practices that grew out of their participation in a seminar on "Looking

Both Ways," a project that brings together faculty from City University of New York universities and colleges and New York public school teachers to share and reflect on their literacy education practices. As part of their work, the authors visited each other's classrooms at Queens College–CUNY (English) and Flushing High School (Nagle). Borrowing from Shirley Brice Heath's "What No Bedtime Story Means: Narrative Skills at Home and School," English and Nagle were interested in learning about students' expectations about reading practices in each other's classrooms. They found fewer differences between students' reading practices in high school and college than they expected. In both places, they found similarities between students' reasons and purposes for reading when compared to the motivations ascribed to reading by high school and college instructors.

412   Gabor, Catherine. "Writing Partners: Service Learning as a Route to Authority for Basic Writers." *Journal of Basic Writing* 28.1 (2009): 50–70. Print.

Though some might assume basic writers are not ready to "go public" with their writing via service-learning projects, Gabor demonstrates otherwise. Writing Partners is a service-learning project wherein basic writers exchange letters with grade school children. These college students write from a position of expertise, introducing their elementary partners to college life and answering their questions. Basic writers gain confidence and write from a position of authority that allows them to "relax and express themselves clearly" (66). They gain audience awareness and learn to negotiate between academic discourse and their home literacies as they spend the semester writing alternatively for their teacher and their grade school partners. As an appendix, Gabor includes a reflective essay assignment asking students to analyze the choices they make as they write in different discourse communities.

413   McNenny, Gerri. "Collaborations between Basic Writing Professionals and High School Instructors: The Shape of Things to Come." *Basic Writing e-Journal* 4.1 (2002): n. pag. Web. 21 May 2014.

For successful collaborations between high school instructors and basic writing professionals, McNenny argues, power relations must be acknowledged, and roles reconsidered. In response to mandated state standards and in an effort to cut costs, the California State University system issued a call for proposals for aligning students' writing competence at high school graduation with college entry-level requirements. This alignment would preempt the need for remediation in college. The CSU initiative tied the success of the collaboration directly to the English Placement Test, a timed exam that includes writing. Under these conditions, McNenny's university team and high school partners designed and proposed a partnership that reflected Freirean principles of learning. The resulting project emphasized high school teachers' roles in identifying site-specific issues and solutions, stressed the role of basic writing professionals as facilitators to help bridge the gap between experience and scholarship, and used teacher-researcher projects and reflective writing to help high school writing instructors create real-world rhetorical situations that engage students.

414   Otte, George. "High Schools as Crucibles of College Prep: What More Do We Need to Know?" *Journal of Basic Writing* 21.2 (2002): 106–20. Print.

Otte outlines the growing pressure on high schools to prepare an increasing number of college-bound students, noting that some 50 percent of beginning college students require remedial classes. While high schools are blamed for these students' need for remedial attention, Otte notes that about one-third of underprepared students did not take requisite classes and that nearly 50 percent of them are at least twenty-two years old—long out of high school. These pressures—often in the form of state-mandated tests—are turning high schools into "crucibles of college prep," rendering high schools and colleges the "most essential learning communities we have" (112–13). Otte suggests that creating high school and college collaborative partnerships is a better solution than state mandates and quick fixes. (He is involved with Looking Both Ways, a collaborative effort to resolve mutual problematic issues.)

See: Hugh English and Lydia Nagle, "Ways of Taking Meaning from Texts: Reading in High School and College" [411].

Developmental Books from Bedford/St. Martin's

Below, you'll find a list of some of Bedford/St. Martin's titles that are of interest to developmental and basic writing instructors. We publish a complete line of handbooks, rhetorics, readers, research guides, and professional resources. Please visit **macmillanhighered.com** for a complete listing, full descriptions, and ordering information, or contact your local sales representative.

Developmental Writing Texts

Susan Anker, *Real Reading and Writing: Paragraphs and Essays*, 2015.
———, *Real Essays with Readings: Writing for Success in College, Work, and Everyday Life*, Fifth Edition, 2015.
———, *Real Essays Interactive*, 2014.
———, *Real Skills Interactive*, 2014.
———, *Real Writing Interactive*, 2014.
Larry Beason and Mark Lester, *A Commonsense Guide to Grammar and Usage*, Seventh Edition, 2015.
Dana Ferris, *Language Power: Tutorials for Writers*, 2014.
Chris Juzwiak, *Stepping Stones: A Guided Approach to Sentences and Paragraphs*, Second Edition, 2012.
———, *Touchstones: A Guided Approach to Writing Paragraphs and Essays*, 2013.
Laurie G. Kirszner and Stephen R. Mandell, *Foundations First with Readings: Sentences and Paragraphs*, Fifth Edition, 2015.
———, *Writing First with Readings: Paragraphs and Essays*, Sixth Edition, 2015.

Developmental Writing Media

Cheryl E. Ball and Kristin L. Arola, *ix visualizing composition 2.0*, 2011.
LaunchPad Solo for Readers and Writers, 2015.
Make-a-paragraph Kit: A Tutorial, 2007.
SkillsClass, Online course space, 2014.
WritingClass Solo, Online course space, 2014.

Developmental Reading Texts

Laurie G. Kirszner and Stephen R. Mandell, *Focus on Reading and Writing: Essays*, 2015.

Amy Lawlor and Kathleen Green, *Read, Write, Connect: A Guide to College Reading and Writing*, 2014.

Kathleen T. McWhorter, *Reflections: Patterns for Reading and Writing*, 2014.

Ellen Kuhl Repetto, *The Bedford/St. Martin's Textbook Reader*, Second Edition, 2013.

Writing Workbooks

Sapna Gandhi-Rao, Maria McCormack, and Elizabeth Trelenberg, *Bedford/St. Martin's ESL Workbook*, Second Edition, 2009.

Diana Hacker and Wanda Van Goor, *Bedford Basics: A Workbook for Writers*, Third Edition, 1998.

Elliott L. Smith, *Contemporary Vocabulary*, Fourth Edition, 1995.

Handbooks

Diana Hacker and Nancy Sommers, *The Bedford Handbook*, Ninth Edition, 2014.

————, *A Pocket Style Manual*, Seventh Edition, 2015.

————, *A Writer's Reference*, Eighth Edition, 2015.

Diana Hacker, Stephen A. Bernhardt, and Nancy Sommers, *Writer's Help 2.0 for Hacker Handbooks*, Second Edition, 2015.

Diana Hacker, Marcy Carbajal Van Horn, John Cullick, and Sara McCurry, *Teaching with Hacker Handbooks*, Second Edition, 2014.

X. J. Kennedy, Dorothy M. Kennedy, and Marcia F. Muth, *The Bedford Guide for College Writers*, Tenth Edition, 2014.

Andrea A. Lunsford, *EasyWriter*, Fifth Edition, 2014.

————, *The Everyday Writer*, Fifth Edition, 2013.

————, *The St. Martin's Handbook*, Eighth Edition, 2015.

————, *Writing in Action*, 2014.

Andrea A. Lunsford, Alyssa O'Brien, and Lisa Dresdner, *Teaching with Lunsford Handbooks*, 2014.

Readers

Jane E. Aaron, *The Compact Reader: Short Essays by Method and Theme*, Ninth Edition, 2011.

Robert Atwan, *America Now: Short Readings from Recent Periodicals*, Tenth Edition, 2013.

Paul Eschholz and Alfred Rosa, *Models for Writers: Short Essays for Composition*, Eleventh Edition, 2012.

Joan T. Mims and Elizabeth M. Nollen, *Mirror on America: Short Essays and Images from Popular Culture*, Fifth Edition, 2012.

Instructors' Resources

Sonya Armstrong, Norman A. Stahl, and Hunter Boylan, *Teaching Developmental Reading: Historical, Theoretical, and Practical Background Readings*, Second Edition, 2014.

Susan Naomi Bernstein, *Teaching Developmental Writing: Background Readings*, Fourth Edition, 2013.

Hunter Boylan and Barbara S. Bonham, *Developmental Education: Readings on Its Past, Present, and Future*, 2014.

Barbara Gleason and Kimme Nuckles, *The Bedford Bibliography for Teachers of Adult Learners*, 2015.

Paul Kei Matsuda, Michelle Cox, Jay Jordan, and Christina Ortmeier-Hooper, *Second-Language Writing in the Composition Classroom: A Critical Sourcebook*, 2011.

Staci Perryman-Clark, David E. Kirkland, and Austin Jackson, *Students' Right to Their Own Language: A Critical Sourcebook*, 2015.

Nedra Reynolds and Elizabeth Davis, *Portfolio Teaching: A Guide for Instructors*, Third Edition, 2014.

Leigh Ryan and Lisa Zimmerelli, *The Bedford Guide for Writing Tutors*, Sixth Edition, 2016.

Index of Authors Cited